The Culture of Citizenship

SUNY Series in Social and Political Thought
Kenneth Baynes, editor

The

Culture of
Citizenship

Inventing Postmodern Civic Culture

THOMAS BRIDGES

State University of New York Press

I wish gratefully to acknowledge support for this project
received from Montclair State University: specifically, a
sabbatical leave during the fall semester, 1991, and summer
research grants provided by the College Research Committee in
1990, 1991, and 1992.

Published by
State University of New York Press, Albany

© 1994 State University of New York

Printed in the United States of America

For information, address the State University of New York Press,
State University Plaza, Albany, NY 12246

Production by Bernadine Dawes
Marketing by Fran Keneston

Library of Congress Cataloging-in-Publication Data
Bridges, Thomas, date
    The culture of citizenship: inventing postmodern civic culture
Thomas Bridges.
        p.   cm. — (SUNY series in social and political thought)
    Includes bibliographical references and index.
    ISBN 0-7914-2033-7 (hc.). — ISBN 0-7914-2034-5 (pbk.)
        1. Liberalism.   2. Democracy   3. Citizenship.   4. Political culture.
    5. Postmodernism   I. Title.   II. Series.
JC585.B647   1994
320.5'1—dc20   93-48374
                                                         CIP

1 2 3 4 5 6 7 8 9 10

For Tania, Ted and John

CONTENTS

vii

PREFACE

During the period in which Europe and America enjoyed global hegemony, the cultural vehicle of their economic and political power was the universalist and secularist world view of the Enlightenment. During this period, Enlightenment concepts of reason and knowledge spoke with the same authority as Western bombs and machines. Where Western technological and military superiority made itself felt, there spread also the influence of the Enlightenment concepts of nature, freedom, and truth that defined cultural modernity. During this period, economic and technological modernization often seemed, at least to Americans and Europeans, inseparable from cultural modernization. It seemed that mastery of the vocabulary of modernist Western rationalism and naturalism was one of the necessary conditions for economic and technological progress. It seemed, in short, that Western concepts of cultural modernity defined advanced human civilization, as such.

This period in which economic development seemed linked to cultural modernization is now over. Led by the Japanese, non-Western nations have proven that thoroughly

ix

modern strategies of economic and technological progress
can be adapted to and supported by ancient non-Western cultural traditions. For the time being, Western nations still enjoy
technological, military and economic superiority over most
non-Western nations. In the future, this superiority is bound
to diminish. But, however this balance of power changes, it
seems evident that the modernist cultural world view that
Europeans and Americans once viewed as the necessary cultural condition for economic development and technological
progress has now become irrelevant in the non-Western
world. Most of the world has learned that it is no longer necessary, if it ever was, to speak the cultural language of the
European Enlightenment in order to prosper in a global market economy.

It is time now for the West to make this discovery also. In
Europe and America, the world view of the Enlightenment
was never alien to native cultural traditions in the way that it
was in non-Western nations. It had its roots in traditional
European religious and political vocabularies. Yet Enlightenment concepts of reason and knowledge were no less hostile
to those native European cultural traditions from which they
sprung than they were to the native religious and political traditions of the non-Western world. The cultural vocabulary of
the Enlightenment was hostile to cultural particularism of all
kinds. Its claim was to provide a purely universal language for
a universal humanity, a language purged of all perspectives
grounded in particularistic religious belief and the accidents
of local history. Whatever may have been the advantages to
the West that the use of this universalist cultural language
once gained, today its continued use in Europe and America
increasingly places them at a disadvantage in global economic
and political competition.

Non-Western nations are now beginning to tap the vast
motivational resources of native cultural traditions to support
strategies of economic development and technological
progress. With this new assertion of cultural particularism—
movements of "Asianization," "Hinduization," "re-Islamiza-
tion," and so on—a world is emerging whose primary divisions
are increasingly cultural and civilizational. To understand, let

alone compete in such a world, Western nations must also
begin to recover and to cultivate the particularistic cultural
perspectives that make them uniquely Western, as opposed to
Hindu, Islamic, Japanese, or Confucian. The cultural posture
of Enlightenment universalism gave cultural particularism a
bad name. Enlightenment concepts of reason and knowledge
led many Europeans and Americans to believe that they could
and should adopt a universalistic, culture-neutral, value-free
standpoint on all cognitive, moral, and political matters. This
standpoint dictated a neutral, if not an actually hostile, posture toward native Western cultural traditions as well. Ironically, with the growing worldwide assertion of cultural particularism, it has become clear that this universalist cultural posture
is itself a form of Western cultural particularism. Even worse,
it is a form of Western cultural particularism that produces an
alienation from its own sources in specifically Western religious and political traditions.

In an emerging global order, in which cultural and civilizational particularism is viewed more and more as a positive
good and embraced with a good conscience, the West must
learn to embrace its own inevitably particularistic native cultural traditions in a positive way. The difficulty of such a project must not be underestimated. As a distinct cultural or civilizational division within an emerging global community of
civilizations, the West is currently defined above all by its commitment to liberal democracy as a form of political association
and as a way of life. Liberal democracy arose in the West in
the early modern period as a modification of classical republican forms of political association. In its conception and basic
values, liberal democracy was profoundly influenced by Christian moral ideals. Yet, from their first establishment, North
Atlantic liberal democracies were wedded to the vocabulary
and the world view of the Enlightenment. Liberal democracies were established in England, America, and France in the
name of universal and natural human rights. These rights
were claimed for all human beings, regardless of their religious beliefs, ethnicity, social class, or nationality. Such claims
were justified by modernist political theories that produced
demonstrations showing how liberal moral and political ideals

are deducible from universally valid metaphysical concepts of nature or reason.

This dependence of liberal democracy, in its very self-conception, on the vocabulary and world view of the Enlightenment is what accounts for the peculiar difficulty involved in recovering the particularistic cultural identity of the West. What gives the West its contemporary identity as a distinct civilization is its commitment to the political institutions and moral ideals of liberal democracy. Western culture is today, above all, a culture of liberal democratic citizenship. Yet, from its modern beginnings, this culture of citizenship has defined itself exclusively in terms of a universalist world view that rejects the cognitive and moral validity of culturally particularistic beliefs and moral ideals. Thus, the task involved in the project of recovering the particularistic cultural identity of the West will be to find some way break this link between liberal democracy and the world view of the Enlightenment—to arrive at a concept of the Western culture of citizenship capable of affirming both its moral validity and its culturally particularistic status.

The question facing us in the emerging post-Enlightenment period, then, is this:

> How can the Western culture of citizenship, after being interpreted for three hundred years in terms of the universalist metaphysical world view of the Enlightenment, be reinterpreted today as defining merely one particularistic cultural way of life among others, a way of life whose norms are valid only for citizens of contemporary North Atlantic liberal democracies?

This book outlines one possible strategy for answering this question.

Introduction:
Salvaging Liberalism
from the Wreck
of the Enlightenment

Role of civic culture

The form of political association known as liberal democracy makes extraordinary cultural demands on those who live under it. In a liberal democracy, the state is committed to treat all citizens as individuals and to treat all individuals equally. But, in a developmental sense, human beings are never free and equal individuals *first*. Free and equal individuals (i.e., human beings who effectively regard themselves as such, and behave accordingly) are made, rather than found. They are produced through the influence of a special kind of political culture. Human beings (in a developmental sense) first are members of families and communities distinguished by ethnic, class, and religious cultural perspectives. Ethnic, class, and religious communities shape human desire and self-understanding in accordance with some more or less coherent world view or concept of the good life. As such, they introduce values and standards of conduct that establish a system of "preferences"—differentials of rank, status, and relative worth. Human beings whose self-understanding is shaped by these standards identify themselves and one another in terms of particular community membership and local ranking systems. In short, the defining attribute of liberal citizenship—free and equal individuality—is alien to the perspectives that most immediately shape human life.

This fact defines the basic cultural and educational challenge faced by any liberal democracy. In a liberal democratic regime, the state rules in the name of free and equal citizens. The free and equal citizens who are ruled are ruled in their own name: they rule themselves. But the state itself must play a role in the cultural creation of the free and equal citizens in whose name it rules. It must establish means of public education and encourage forms of culture that can produce and sustain identities consistent with citizenship. In liberal democracies where citizens fail in sufficient numbers to achieve such identities, thereby remaining bound in their self-definitions to particularistic cultural world views, liberal democratic political institutions can eventually lose not only their legitimacy, but their very intelligibility as well. Thus the legitimacy and, at the extreme, the very existence of the liberal democratic state depends upon its success in creating the constituency it serves.

Liberal democratic regimes are unique in this way. Forms of government based on principles intrinsic to ethnic, class, and religious world views do not face precisely this sort of cultural and educational challenge. Such regimes face other problems, of course, particularly in the modern world, where the long-term viability and effectiveness of governments often depend on their success in establishing educational institutions capable of producing and reproducing a class of technical experts and a skilled labor force. But monarchies, aristocracies, and clerocracies—whose authority is based upon ethnic or religious homogeneity, or internalized class domination—can expect the immediate processes of cultural reproduction operating in family and community life to be sufficient to produce identities consistent with the authority of the regime. In such regimes, governments rule over the entire course of human life in the name of the ethnic, class or religious values that govern human desire. The differentials of rank, status, and relative worth that legitimate rule are consistent with, and flow from, the values that shape identities within the educational processes and forms of culture already operative in family and community life. In such regimes, public educational institutions do not bear the burden of first creating in those who are ruled the cultural self-understanding consistent with the principles underlying governmental authority. Nor are special, countervailing forms of political culture required to sustain that self-understanding.

In liberal democracies, however, special countervailing forms of education and political culture play an absolutely vital political role. A liberal democratic state defines its citizens as free individuals who are only incidentally members of particular ethnic, class, and religious communities. The hierarchies generated by such communities are irrelevant to the state in its treatment of citizens. Public education, then, must produce persons who in their own self-understanding, at least insofar as they act within the public sphere, see their membership in such communities as in some sense subordinate to their membership in the broader civic community. This means that public education in a liberal democracy must have the effect of relativizing the hierarchies and ranking systems generated by particularistic cultural communities, so that the identities of citizens are not wholly or exclusively governed by the principles or values underlying those hierarchies. Of course, public education in liberal democracies today also serves other ends—notably, the creation of technical experts and skilled workers needed in a modern industrial economy. But the basic political work of public education in a liberal democratic regime is the creation of citizens, the creation of persons who identify themselves and one another as free and equal individuals. We call this basic political work of public education *civic education.*

To achieve its goals, of course, civic education must draw upon cultural resources available in the larger society. Most of the cultural resources available in any liberal democracy are not necessarily supportive of the goal of civic education. The goal of civic education is the inculcation of the normative standpoint—the ideal attitudes, dispositions, and values—

proper to citizenship. The particularistic ethnic, class, and religious communities making up the larger society, however, seek to reproduce and advance their own particularistic life ideals and concepts of the good. These communities tend to generate global outlooks or totalizing world views that are supportive of their own particular ways of life. These world views find expression in all sorts of popular cultural media. Each such community offers, in principle, some more or less coherent way of addressing the general issues of human life— sex, friendship, work, suffering, sin, death, and salvation. These global visions of life, embodied in various cultural representations, communicate the ranking systems, virtue concepts, and standards of achievement that distinguish one particularistic cultural community from another.

Cultural representations of this sort make up the greatest part of the cultural resources available in a liberal democracy. However, such cultural representations are not necessarily supportive of the values proper to citizenship and, therefore, do not necessarily serve the ends of civic education. To create and sustain in its members the standpoint proper to citizenship, therefore, every liberal democracy needs a countervailing culture—a culture supportive of citizenship, a set of ideas that can be embodied effectively in cultural representations for the purpose of shaping civic identities. We call this sort of culture *civic culture.*

Civic culture provides the resources for civic education. Civic education reproduces and strengthens civic culture. When civic culture and civic education function effectively, large numbers of people who have the formal status of citizens in a liberal democracy actually develop the attitudes, dispositions, and values proper to citizenship. Liberal democracies can exist only if their numbers are sufficient to meet whatever political challenges that arise. Of course, the generation and reproduction of civic identities and values are supported by secondary cultural, social and economic forces that operate independently of the dominant form of civic culture operative in any particular liberal democracy. In America, for example, a market economy of small producers, geographical mobility, an individualistic form of Protestant Christianity—all contributed different degrees of support to the creation and maintenance of civic attitudes during the nineteenth century. But all such secondary social and economic factors can effectively promote civic attitudes only within the interpretive framework of a civic culture whose central ideas can be given clear and coherent public articulation. Such ideas necessarily have a limited life span. They have a genealogy and logic that ties them to specific historical circumstances and audiences. When the ideas central to any particular form of civic culture lose their currency or credibility, the civic culture based on them soon loses its capacity to form habits of citizenship. This sort of critical cultural situation faces the citizens of North Atlantic liberal democracies today.

Demise of modernist liberal civic culture

During the last three hundred years, the ideas central to the form of civic culture prevalent in most North Atlantic liberal democracies have been those of modernist liberal political philosophy. On the occasions when some kind of coherent account or explanation was called for of the moral and political norms proper to liberal democracy, the ideas most readily available and rhetorically effective were those drawn from the tradition of political thought identified with authors such as Locke, Rousseau, Bentham, Kant, and Mill. These ideas provided an interpretation of the basic liberal democratic ideals of individual freedom and equality, and were used to articulate the concept of political justice underlying liberal political institutions. In popular political discourse, rhetoric that appealed to notions of popular sovereignty, social contract, and natural human rights, as well as to related ideas of authentic individuality and autonomous personhood, seemed to have an immediate intelligibility and validity. The plausibility of these notions then served to reinforce adherence to the norms and ideals proper to civic life. However, during the last fifty years the intelligibility and plausibility of these notions have increasingly eroded.

This erosion is largely due to a growing skepticism about

the universalist and essentialist assumptions underlying modernist liberal political thought. Modernist liberal political
philosophers drew their vocabulary and arguments largely
from the intellectual and rhetorical resources produced by
the Enlightenment. The Enlightenment itself was a broader
cultural movement that arose out of the religious and class
warfare that engulfed sixteenth- and seventeenth-century
Europe. Faced with the prospect of seemingly endless ethnic,
class, and religious conflict, intellectuals sought to establish
some neutral cultural ground upon which adherents of
opposing cultural world views could meet and reach agreement. Following the lead of Descartes and Galileo, they
sought to clear this neutral ground through appeals to new
concepts of reason and knowledge. Central to these new concepts of reason and knowledge was a cognitive method—the
method that, much later, became popularly known as the "scientific method"—powerful enough to guarantee the culture-
neutrality or "objectivity" of the beliefs generated by its use.
The universalism and essentialism characteristic of the doctrinal claims of modernist liberalism were grounded in these
universalist concepts of reason and knowledge that originated
in the conflict-ridden world of seventeenth-century Europe.
Modernist liberal doctrine, from its beginnings, spoke the language of the Enlightenment. Its concepts of the norms of civic
life were presented as a body of propositions about Man and
History, a set of cognitive claims about the nature of things as
they exist in themselves, beyond the realm of conflicting cultural world views.

It is our growing skepticism about this universalistic and
essentialist standpoint of Enlightenment culture that accounts
for the erosion of the credibility of modernist liberal interpretations of the norms of civic life. This skepticism has several
sources.

• First, the universalism and essentialism of the Enlightenment all too often has served as a cultural license for Western imperialism. Modern European claims to the possession of a privileged cognitive standpoint and, therefore, a
  privileged insight into universally valid metaphysical truths

invited and legitimized disparagement of non-Western cultures, a disparagement entirely consistent with military conquest and economic exploitation.

• Second, the very notion that universally valid knowledge can be achieved by the mere application of a single cognitive method now seems to be a vast oversimplification. Needless to say, research enterprises are more important than ever. But their organization is now viewed by most observers as far more sociologically complex, their procedures and rhetoric as far more intellectually diverse, than Enlightenment concepts of truth and knowledge could ever fully grasp.

• Third, worldwide intercultural communication has become so routine and so economically important that any form of culture claiming a metaphysically privileged status for one particular model of political organization now seems hopelessly parochial, and even an obstacle to international cooperation. Modernist liberal doctrine was based upon ideas that gave such privileged ontological status to liberal political institutions.

• Fourth, in America during the last 100 years, programs of civic and technical education based upon Enlightenment concepts of scientific objectivity and modernist liberal doctrine have been implemented extensively. Today, however, it is apparent to many people that these programs are failing not only as civic education (i.e., failing to produce full cultural citizens), but also as forms of technical education.

Thus, the modernist liberal political ideas crucial to the effectiveness of modernist liberal civic culture have lost their plausibility and, I would say, are rapidly losing even their intelligibility. This fact is gaining recognition in many of the institutional spheres of our society that have been most influenced by modernist liberal thought and by Enlightenment culture— the universities in particular. The demise of forms of civic culture dependent on modernist liberal doctrine, however, does not diminish our need for effective forms of civic culture and civic education. The proper functioning of free institutions requires citizens who have actually developed the normative attitudes, dispositions and values proper to the standpoint of citizenship. To produce and reproduce such citizens, we must have the cultural means of representing the liberal democratic norms of freedom and equality in a coherent and persuasive way. Accordingly, the question of whether liberal democracy, as a form of political association, can survive the collapse of modernist Enlightenment culture is the question of whether we can succeed in inventing a new, postmodern form of civic culture—one that can render intelligible the norms of civic life in a way that no longer requires claiming for those norms universal and objective cognitive and moral validity.

Particularistic cultural presuppositions of liberal democracy

Can a new form of liberal civic culture arise out of the ruins of modernist liberal doctrine? Can the central normative doctrines defining the liberal political ideals of freedom and equality be rethought coherently, even as they are being stripped of their universalist and essentialist Enlightenment trappings? This is the question, then, that defines perhaps the most formidable intellectual and cultural challenge that we (i.e., the citizens of North Atlantic liberal democracies) now face. One of the most significant obstacles we must overcome is the lingering influence of modernist liberal political theory itself. For where the vocabulary of modernist liberal political theory is still in use, it continues to generate universalist discourses and perspectives that do not even allow the definition of our postmodern task. This is because modernist liberal political philosophy was built upon a denial of the particularistic character of the civic culture that liberal political institutions require for their support.

The form of civic culture based upon modernist liberal doctrine was a strange civic culture indeed. Essential to Enlightenment concepts of reason and knowledge was their claim to articulate a standpoint that transcends all culturally particularistic and historically conditioned belief. The universalism of Enlightenment culture appealed to seventeenth- and eighteenth-century proto-liberals because, in an age rife with religious and class warfare, the conflicts between particularistic local cultures seemed to them to be the central political problem. The idea of a political program whose basic ideas and agenda could claim derivation from absolutely universal, culture-neutral principles had an irresistible rhetorical appeal. But the universalism and essentialism that governed Enlightenment concepts of knowledge and truth, when applied politically, tended to conceal systematically the particularistic cultural requirements for the support of liberal political institutions.

Modernist liberalism appropriated Enlightenment concepts of knowledge and truth for use as rhetorical weapons against the remnants of feudalism. Modernist liberal political philosophy presented itself as a purely theoretical discourse, articulating discoveries about the essence of human political association. As such, it constituted the first modernist political ideology, the prototype of all those that were to follow in its wake. Modernist liberalism did not originally conceive of itself as an attempt to provide the conceptual foundations of a particularistic form of political culture. It used a purely culture-neutral vocabulary. As a result, it not only concealed its own political function, but also discouraged systematic reflection on the characteristics of the particularistic political culture required for the support of liberal democratic institutions. Yet, paradoxically, in spite of its posture of cultural neutrality, modernist liberalism provided the basis of the peculiar form of civic culture that became increasingly dominant in Western countries throughout the nineteenth century, and that became dominant in the twentieth.

This form of civic culture was characterized by a distinctive interpretation of the normative standpoint of liberal citizenship. Modernist liberalism took over the classical republican political ideals of freedom and equality, and gave them a radically non-classical twist. Liberal democracy, as an historically specific form of political association, begins with the assumption that a liberal democracy will be composed of a number of diverse ethnic, class, and religious communities and assumes, therefore, that the citizens of a liberal democracy will disagree in their answers to the most basic questions of human life. Liberal political institutions are designed to function in spite of such disagreement or, perhaps better, to function best when such disagreement exists. The liberal state—however differently its legislative, executive, and judicial mechanisms may be designed to meet local historical and political circumstances—is above all designed to rule over persons who are willing to associate with one another in spite of the fact that they, as members of different ethnic, class, and religious communities, pursue conflicting concepts of the good life.

To make such rule a practical possibility, the citizens of a liberal democracy must be shaped by a political culture that supports the exercise of civic virtues such as tolerance of difference, a disposition to resolve disputes rationally, and a personal acceptance and attribution to others of individual (as opposed to group or collective) responsibility for actions. In short, for liberal political institutions to work, citizens must undergo a very unusual and difficult process of individualization, a process by which they must come to identify themselves *both* as members of particularistic ethnic, class, and religious communities *and* as members of a civic community that regards them as free and equal individuals (i.e., that disregards the rankings, privileges, and responsibilities they hold within any particularistic cultural community).

Thus, the normative standpoint of liberal citizenship (i.e., the *ideal* standpoint of the *ideal* citizen of an *ideal* liberal democracy) requires persons to develop a capacity to define themselves and others effectively within two very different and often conflicting cultural and moral perspectives. Specifically, citizens whose identities have already been shaped by some particularistic cultural concept of the good must learn to view themselves and others apart from the ranking systems, the standards of excellence, or the concepts of virtue that normally determine their judgments as members of particularistic ethnic, class, or religious communities. Within the context of seventeenth- and eighteenth-century European ethnic and religious conflict, modernist liberal doctrine had to assign a name to this normative standpoint of liberal citizenship. Since the rhetorical imperative faced by modernist liberals was to avoid identification of their political program with established warring ethnic and religious factions, they naturally sought to identify this normative standpoint of liberal citizenship in the most universalistic and culture-neutral terms. As a result, the normative standpoint of free and equal civic individuality came to be conceived of as the standpoint proper to the natural pre-political condition of all human beings—or, alternatively, as the universal standpoint proper to the faculty of autonomous human reason. In this way, the modernist liberal concept of the normative standpoint of liberal citizenship became inextricably linked to Enlightenment concepts of reason and nature.

Today, we see this universalist concept of the idealized standpoint of liberal citizenship as a rhetorical strategy. Needless to say, that was not the way that the founders of modernist liberal political theory understood their doctrines. For them, all serious cognitive efforts specifically excluded rhetorical calculation and embellishment. Nevertheless, as a rhetorical strategy, it was successful because it provided a vocabulary in which a set of entirely novel political norms and structures could be described as "natural." Liberal political philosophers could show that the coercive and objective order of nature itself made all human beings, as such—in their natural or pre-political condition, at least—free and equal individuals. Liberal political norms, economic structures, and organizational principles could henceforth, in the language of the Enlightenment, claim derivation from the natural order of things. Feudal social and economic structures could then be identified as arbitrary arrangements in need of special explanation and justification. But feudal structures are invariably tied to local cultures and histories. They cannot be explained and justified by reference to the universal and coercive order of nature—an order that is always the same, everywhere. Thus, feudal economic and political structures could easily be shown to be subversions of the natural freedom and equality of individuals.

In this way, the rhetoric of modernist liberalism pretty much turned the "natural order of things" on its head. It doesn't require much anthropological or historical insight for us to realize, today, that if any type of economic and social organizational principles can be called "natural," then it would be the type of feudal organizational principles that modernist liberalism attacked as unnatural. Hierarchical structures grounded in local ethnic, class, and religious cultures do in fact represent the "natural order of things" in matters political (i.e., these are the sort of political structures that we find most frequently and spontaneously occurring in human groups). On the other hand, it is the sort of political norms and institutions that modernist liberalism claimed to be in conformity with nature that, if anything, are utterly unnatural in this sense. That is to say, such norms and institutions can find widespread acceptance and can flourish only rarely, and only under the most extraordinarily favorable economic and cultural conditions.

It is this fact that the political rhetoric of modernist liberalism was forced systematically to conceal. Classical republicanism understood all too well how rare and fragile was the flower of political liberty. Classical republicans, both ancient and modern, reflected incessantly about the cultural presuppositions of political liberty. They were almost obsessive in their awareness of the threats to liberty produced by class, ethnic, and religious factionalism. But modernist liberalism is another story. To the extent that modernist liberalism spoke the cognitive and moral language of the Enlightenment, liberal political institutions had to be presented as those that would in fact occur spontaneously everywhere, in the absence of obstacles created by arbitrary and oppressive regimes. Liberal political norms had to be presented as those that would in fact be affirmed spontaneously by all human beings, in the absence of superstition and priestly domination. Thus, the rhetoric of modernist liberalism was governed by a logic that systematically concealed, or at least de-emphasized, the unique cultural requirements for the flourishing of liberal political institutions.

This feature of modernist liberalism continued to produce, well into the twentieth century, a blindness to the vital role of the very peculiar sort of political culture that is required to support liberal democratic institutions. For example, what sort of perception of political reality allowed Americans at the end of the Second World War to impose upon the Japanese a liberal democratic constitution so alien to their national culture—and to impose it with the expectation that it would "take," and produce a nation of liberal democrats? What is it that has led American governments since then to repeat the same mistake again and again in innumerable peasant societies? Of course, such policies can easily be explained as pretexts, as elements of an economic strategy to open foreign markets, and a Cold War strategy to impose friendly liberal regimes everywhere in order to "stop the spread of communism." But such a strategy would make no sense even as a pretext in the absence of a belief that liberal democratic political regimes were somehow expressions of the natural order of things. During the Cold War, liberals continued to view liberal democracy as the political order that people everywhere would spontaneously choose if they were genuinely permitted to do so. Liberal democratic regimes were imposed in the name of universal and natural human rights. Where such regimes did not exist, liberals believed that it was because those universal human rights were not recognized by backward and oppressive governments.

Ironically, the war against fascism and the Cold War extended the influence of modernist liberal rhetoric well beyond the time that its intellectual credibility had effectively ceased. John Dewey's project of rethinking the conceptual foundations of liberalism early in this century could not possibly have been as influential as it was, had it not spoken to a widespread sense that the world view of the Enlightenment had lost its relevance. But, during their long struggles against various forms of fascism and Marxism, Western liberal democracies found themselves opposed by enemies that, in different ways, provided a set of purely political motives for adherence to the doctrines of modernist liberalism. Fascism, with its virulent and nihilistic cultural particularism that was itself produced by a reaction to universalist Enlightenment values, seemed to demonstrate the cataclysmic political consequences of any abandonment of modernist cultural universalism.

In Marxism, on the other hand, Western liberal democracies faced an enemy armed with a world view no less rooted in the universalist culture of the Enlightenment than was modernist liberalism itself. In the same way that modernist liberals spoke of universal human rights deriving from the natural human condition, Marxists spoke of universal history—the class struggle, the laws of capitalist accumulation, the stages of development toward socialism and so on. Both sides supported their political agendas by offering grand historical metanarratives that provided totalizing narrative representations of the march of human events. In advancing these totalizing visions, both sides appealed to the doctrine that, through the application of one or another cognitive method, human beings can successfully free themselves from the limiting perspectives imposed by historical conditions, and adopt the transcendent standpoint of universal human reason. In this way, both fascism and Marxism during the middle years of this century provoked a cultural reaction in the West that strengthened the political appeal of modernist liberal rhetoric, even as the intellectual credibility of its assumptions continued to erode.

With the end of the Cold War, this artificially extended life of modernist liberalism has now ended. The universalist and essentialist philosophical vocabulary of the Enlightenment, the language used by liberals to explain and advocate the establishment of liberal political institutions, is now irretrievably lost. Central to the cultural project of the Enlightenment was the doctrine of the autonomy of human reason. This doctrine expressed the belief that human reason on its own, using methods derived from an analysis of its own powers, could transcend the limits imposed by historical circumstances and attain universally valid knowledge. It is this doctrine that simply no longer makes sense in the world that has emerged in the course of the twentieth century. In this world, we are everywhere confronted with the inescapable reality of cultural difference and the power of historical circumstance to shape belief. In this world, the particularism of the cultural assumptions underlying liberal political doctrine is also impossible to deny. In this world, liberal political institutions can no longer be credibly explained and justified by appeal to self-evident truths, universal natural law, the principles of pure practical reason, or any other supposedly culture-neutral metaphysical or epistemological theory. If liberalism is to survive the collapse of Enlightenment culture, liberals must now attempt to de-universalize or contextualize their political language—and learn to explain and advocate liberal democratic moral ideals in a vocabulary that can express the particularism of liberal political norms without thereby invalidating them.

In undertaking this cultural project, the challenges we face are many and significant. Even though the conceptual underpinnings of modernist liberalism have lost their credibility, the essentialist and totalizing language of modernist liberalism continues to be virtually the only political language available to us. As a result, all postmodernist initiatives in the sphere of political discourse are easily subject to misunderstanding. As I noted earlier, in appropriating the universalist rhetoric of the Enlightenment, modernist liberalism systematically concealed the particularistic character of the political culture required for the support of liberal political institutions. A vocabulary that allows us to comprehend and speak of liberal political norms in their cultural particularism can easily be taken as one that embodies a rejection of the validity of those norms. Out of this misperception arises the usual accusations that postmodern political vocabularies support "relativistic" or nihilistic world views. Such accusations have the effect of identifying liberal democracy, once and for all, as a form of political association with the defunct cultural vocabulary and world view of the Enlightenment. Such an identification would prevent us from undertaking, in the manner of classical republicanism, the sort of reflection upon the cultural presuppositions of liberal democracy that alone can open the way to the creation of a post-Enlightenment civic culture capable of supporting liberal political institutions in the years ahead. This sort of final identification of liberal democracy with the vocabulary of modernist liberalism constitutes a failure of imagination of fateful proportions, and must be avoided at all costs.

Plan of the book

The most significant cultural task facing North Atlantic liberal democracies in the 21st century is the invention of a new liberal democratic political culture—one that can succeed in rendering intelligible to citizens the civic ideals of individual freedom and equality, in a language that can affirm unambiguously the particularistic nature of those ideals. This book is a contribution to that cultural project.

The first two chapters of the book prepare the way for a rethinking of the cultural presuppositions of citizenship. I follow the general lead of John Rawls, who, in his writings published since 1980, has sought to reformulate liberal doctrine in a way that frees it of the totalizing and metaphysical interpretations characteristic of modernist liberalism. In chapter 1, I suggest one way in which those modernist liberal interpretations can be redescribed so as to make clear their rhetorical intention and effect and, therefore, the cultural resources they offered for the creation of a specifically modernist form of liberal democratic civic culture. In chapter 2, I examine Rawls's own attempt since 1980 to reformulate liberal doctrine in rhetorical and particularistic teleological terms. There, I argue that the rhetorical and teleological turns in Rawls's recent work mark the path that postmodern reflection upon the cultural presuppositions of liberal democracy must follow.

Chapters 3 and 4 offer a non-metaphysical and non-totalizing concept of the normative standpoint of liberal democratic citizenship. In chapter 3, I seek to extend what I call the rhetorical turn in Rawls's reconstruction of liberal doctrine. This requires an examination of the partial character of liberal democratic moral ideals, distinguishing the moral norms proper to the liberal democratic public sphere from norms grounded in the totalizing concepts of the good that define particularistic cultural communities. In chapter 4, I seek to extend what I call the teleological turn in Rawls's reconstruction of liberal doctrine. This requires an examination of the sense in which the norms of civic justice, even though they apply only to the part rather than to the whole of life, nevertheless constitute a particularistic cultural concept of the good.

Finally, in chapter 5, I seek to extend Rawls's concept of the overlapping cultural consensus required for the support of liberal democratic political institutions. According to Rawls, liberal democratic moral ideals, because of their partiality or restricted scope, make them unable, on their own, to provide sufficient cultural resources to motivate citizens to develop the moral capacities proper to full cultural citizenship. An overlapping consensus on the part of particularistic cultural communities is necessary to provide that motivation. To produce that overlapping consensus, citizens, as adherents of particularistic cultural world views, must rethink their local cultural traditions in order to discover or invent resources supportive of the realization of civic moral ideals. In chapter 5, I attempt to provide a model for the sort of rethinking of particularistic cultural traditions required for the production of an overlapping consensus. I attempt to show how citizens who are members of one particularistic cultural community, the Christian community, might rethink the main components of Christian belief and practice in terms of a strong analogy with the pursuit of the civic good, thereby producing a certain congruence of the Christian life with a life spent in the pursuit of civic freedom and civic justice.

1 Modernist Liberalism and Its Consequences

Civic culture and the modernist rhetoric of pure theory

In a liberal democracy, the state is committed to treating all citizens as free individuals, and to treating all individuals as equals. For such a regime to be intelligible to the governed, the members of a liberal political community must, to some extent at least, come to see themselves and one another as free and equal individuals. This means that they must see themselves and others as not entirely defined and encompassed by family, ethnic, or religious identifications. This means that they must be able, at least for certain purposes and on certain occasions, to put aside measures of human worth based on those family, ethnic, and religious identifications and adopt a very different ranking system, one based on their identification as citizens. Needless to say, this is an extraordinary requirement. The earliest and strongest identifications formed by human beings are shaped by family life and by the broader ethnic, class, and religious community within which the family, in turn, gains its identification. These identifications are woven into the very fabric of human desire and only with great difficulty can distance from them be achieved. But, unless such distance can be achieved by significant numbers of persons, a liberal democracy cannot even be established, let alone flourish. Factions will destroy it. Every liberal democracy, therefore, must generate some form of countervailing civic culture that has the power to create and sustain civic identities. Further, educational processes must be invented that will insure the effectiveness and reproduction of that civic culture.

When we (i.e., we citizens of North Atlantic liberal democracies) speak of culture, civic or otherwise, we are speaking of a sphere of human interaction in which what we traditionally identify as the rhetorical or persuasive power of speech assumes central importance. Culture encompasses the world views, ranking systems, concepts of virtue, and standards of excellence that shape human behavior and self-understanding. Brute force applied to individuals or groups can succeed in procuring from them behavior that meets desired specifications, but it cannot, by itself, secure their adherence or commitment to norms or to a concept of the good life. To gain and retain such adherence, an ongoing process of persuasion is necessary. This ongoing process of persuasion takes different institutional, representational, and discursive forms in different types of communities. But whatever forms such processes of persuasion take, they are all subject to analysis and criticism in rhetorical terms (i.e., in terms of their logical, ethical, and emotional appeals, as well as their style, occasion and intention).

What is true of the sphere of culture in general has special application to the specific form of culture I have called civic culture. A very special kind of persuasive process is required to gain and retain adherence to the norms proper to the standpoint of liberal democratic citizenship. As I have noted, a civic culture is a type of countervailing culture. Liberal democracy as a form of political association is defined by the rather unusual assumption that the citizens of any particular liberal democracy will disagree fundamentally in their concepts of the good life. As members of the civic community, citizens will also be members of one or more particularistic cultural communities. A civic culture, then, has a very special sort of persuasive task and must have a very special sort of persuasive force. A civic culture consists of a set of institutional, representational, and discursive means of persuasion. As such, it must be conceived of in terms of its rhetorical intention and effect. As in the case of all efforts of persuasion, the persuasive means available to any civic culture are addressed to a specific audience, an audience defined by a specific set of historical, economic, and social circumstances. But, generically, the sort of audience that any civic culture must address is one composed of persons who already adhere to some specific concept of the good, some specific totalizing world view or way of life. The task of any civic culture is to win the adherence of that sort of audience to a secondary set of norms that must, necessarily, stand in a relationship of tension with the primary set of norms to which the audience remains committed.

The first step toward successfully addressing the crisis produced by the contemporary demise of modernist liberal civic culture is to understand clearly the sort of persuasive or rhetorical effort involved in gaining adherence to any particular form of civic culture. A full understanding of this sort of rhetorical effort requires us: (1) to recall, at every step, the rhetorical character of the inquiry about civic culture that we are now undertaking, and (2) to grasp clearly the rhetorical character of the modernist liberal doctrines whose failing credibility is at the root of the contemporary crisis of civic culture. Let us briefly address, in a general way, both of these tasks.

The rhetorical self-understanding proper
to any inquiry about civic culture

The most deadly possible misunderstanding regarding the nature of any inquiry about civic culture, including this one, is that such an inquiry is some sort of exercise in pure theory (i.e., an attempt simply to state what is the case, for its own sake). An exercise in pure theory, by definition, leaves all rhetorical considerations behind—or at least makes all rhetorical considerations a matter external to the subject matter, a question of the greater or lesser charm of the language in which the truth is clothed. Claims of truth produced by a purely theoretical inquiry, however they may be expressed, carry the force and implications of the hard metaphysical "is" of traditional Western propositional logic. Characteristic of such truth claims, which express the hard metaphysical "is," is the assumption that both the truths being asserted and the subject matter being discussed exist independently of any audience. Pure theoretical discourse, in other words, does not understand itself primarily as a rhetorical activity, an activity aimed at winning the adherence of a particular audience for a particular purpose, an activity whose outcome is valid or invalid (i.e., whose conclusions are "true") only to the extent that it wins audience adherence. Construed as an assertion bearing the hard metaphysical "is," for example, a statement like, "The liberal doctrine of the priority of the right over the good is a political and not a metaphysical doctrine," would be read as claiming that the doctrine in question is, and always was, a political doctrine, regardless how it may ever have been otherwise understood.

Inquiry about civic culture, however, can never be properly understood as an exercise in pure theory. Civic culture itself, like every other form of culture, is created, transformed, and reproduced by processes of persuasion. The norms proper to civic life must be embraced and internalized by citizens as a matter of conviction, a conviction produced by the rhetorical power of the persuasive resources available to some specific form of civic culture. The truth claims asserted in any inquiry about civic culture must not be understood as asserting audience-independent truths about an audience-independent subject matter. The "is" proper to inquiries about civic culture is not the hard metaphysical "is" of pure theoretical discourse, but rather the soft metaphorical "is" of rhetoric. A metaphor is an act of linguistic aggression through which a speaker seeks to transform his or her audience's understanding and behavior by means of a redescription of the subject matter at hand. If the audience buys the metaphor, and transforms their speech and behavior accordingly, the subject matter is thereby transformed. The above statement, about the political nature of the liberal doctrine of the priority of the right over the good, should be construed in this way. It should be construed as embodying a soft metaphorical rather than a hard metaphysical "is," as an attempt to transform the understanding and behavior of an audience through an aggressive act of redescription. If the discourse supporting this act of redescription is successful, the very subject matter that the discourse addresses will be transformed. Thus, an inquiry about civic culture has for its goal not changing minds so that they will conform more exactly to the nature of things, but rather changing minds in such a way that new ways of talking about and behaving, with respect to civic norms, come into being.

If in this way all inquiry about civic culture must itself belong to the sphere of civic culture, and therefore to the sphere of persuasive speech, then such inquiry is subject to all the usual categories of rhetorical analysis. The basic categories of rhetorical analysis are determined by the basic components of the rhetorical situation—speaker, audience, rhetorical intention, and occasion. A rhetorical analysis of any discourse can ask about the self-definition of the speaker and the speaker's standpoint, the characteristics of the audience addressed by the speaker, the rhetorical effect the speaker wishes to achieve, and the specific circumstances that shape the occasion of the discourse. Such categories of analysis are irrelevant to the content of a purely theoretical discourse that aims only to state what is the case. A purely theoretical discourse is addressed to a particular audience on a particular occasion only accidentally. The subject matter addressed by a purely theoretical discourse is viewed as existing independently of audience and occasion. On the other hand, for a proper understanding of discourse about civic culture, analysis of the discourse in terms of rhetorical categories is crucial. Regarding any particular discourse about civic culture, we must ask about the speaker's definition of the rhetorical situation—the speaker's self-defined standpoint, intention, and definition of the audience and occasion.

These categories of rhetorical analysis are of course no less essential to a proper understanding of this present inquiry about civic culture. To address the crisis produced by the contemporary demise of modernist civic culture is to adopt a specific standpoint, to define a specific audience, to offer an interpretation of the occasion for the inquiry, and to intend to produce a specific transformation of the subject matter at hand. The description of our present circumstances as a "crisis produced by the contemporary demise of modernist civic culture" is thus properly understood not as a claim about some audience-independent state of affairs, but rather as a definition of the rhetorical situation that must be taken up and affirmed by its intended audience in order to exist in any sense at all. One central task of this inquiry is to make this description of our current situation a plausible one. The aim of this inquiry is to mark out a path of response to this crisis. If the redescription of our contemporary circumstances as a crisis of civic culture remains implausible, then the proposed response to it will obviously have no application.

Furthermore, the standpoint from which any such response is to be proposed must be appropriate to both occasion and intent. If we citizens of North Atlantic liberal democracies face a crisis of civic culture today, then we face that crisis not as members of some particular ethnic, class, or religious community or as scholars pursuing one or another professionalized field of inquiry, but rather as citizens. The standpoint from which this crisis is addressed must therefore be defined simply as the idealized or normative standpoint of citizenship itself. In this present discourse, the appropriate self-definition of both speaker and intended audience is that which is proper to all citizens of contemporary liberal democracies—even though, needless to say, all citizens will not be equally preoccupied with the purely conceptual dimensions of the cultural crisis that concern us here. The aim of the present discourse, then, is to redescribe and thereby to transform fundamentally the very standpoint that both speaker and audience of the discourse occupy within the intended rhetorical situation (i.e., the normative standpoint of liberal democratic citizenship). To the extent that this redescription is successful, the standpoint of liberal democratic citizenship itself will be transformed in such a way as to make possible a creative response to the cultural crisis first identified by this redescription.

Foundationalism as a rhetorical strategy

A self-conscious understanding of this present inquiry's rhetorical topography is necessary for two reasons. First, the demise of Enlightenment concepts of reason and knowledge calls into question the very possibility of a purely theoretical discourse (i.e., a discourse asserting audience-independent truths about an audience-independent subject matter, merely for the sake of asserting those truths). We must subject this inquiry to rhetorical analysis because, in the emerging post-Enlightenment period of American and European culture, every inquiry must be so subjected. This requires of us all a new sort of rigor, a new intellectual discipline of which we are still scarcely capable. Second, a clear understanding of the rhetorical character of this inquiry is necessary because the modernist liberal concept of civic culture that it seeks to replace was defined above all by a systematic denial and concealment of its own rhetorical character. The description of our present situation as a crisis of civic culture—indeed, the very notion of civic culture as it emerges here—gains plausibility only to the extent that we begin to perceive the anti-rhetorical stance of modernist liberalism as an unacknowledged rhetorical strategy.

As we have seen, a civic culture is a body of narratives, representations, and discourses that serve to render intelligible and support the effective internalization of the norms proper to liberal democratic citizenship. The norms themselves clearly belong to the sphere of culture (i.e., they belong to the sphere of personal and shared collective conviction). When a civic culture is effective, large numbers of nominal citizens actually develop the capacity to adopt the standpoint of citizenship, the capacity to treat themselves and others effectively as free and equal individuals. On the other hand, a civic culture is a countervailing culture. It is a culture that requires citizens at least occasionally and temporarily to step out of the perspectives from which they normally view the world, and to see things from a different point of view. The narratives, representations, and discourses that make up the civic culture of a particular historical period provide a specific interpretation of that shift of viewpoint. In offering this interpretation of the

standpoint of citizenship, a civic culture also provides a particular set of resources for motivating citizens effectively to
assume that standpoint. This clearly involves a persuasive
process.

Modernist liberal political theories are constitutive components of a body of discourses that for more than three hundred years have defined modernist civic culture. As such,
modernist liberal political theories offered an interpretation
of the standpoint of citizenship, an interpretation that also
served as a justification and motivation for the adoption of
civic norms. Modernist liberalism, in short, was a central component of the process of persuasion by which modernist civic
culture succeeded in producing and cultivating civic attitudes
and values.

My goal here is to make clear the central importance of
the unusual rhetorical means used by modernist liberalism in
its contribution to this process of persuasion. Modernist liberal political theories, as discursive components of modernist
civic culture, offered an interpretation of the normative standpoint of liberal democratic citizenship. But, to a very large
degree, these doctrines succeeded in achieving their intended
rhetorical effect by claiming a status that denied their rhetorical character. Modernist liberal political theories, in other
words, presented themselves as sets of purely theoretical
propositions about the nature of human political association,
the nature of human reason, and the nature of the world
itself. I hope that it is evident by now that, when I characterize
modernist liberalism in this way, I am not making some sort of
new theoretical claim about the history of modern culture. To
say that modernist liberalism achieved its rhetorical effect by a
certain dissemblance, by a masking of its own rhetorical character and function, is to offer a genealogical diagnosis of our
present cultural crisis. I am saying that it is good for us, as citizens of late 20th-century North Atlantic democracies, to learn
to redescribe modernist liberalism in this way and to make the
appropriate inferences. It is good for us because it will help
us, as citizens, to maneuver with less confusion and panic
through the landscape of the post-Enlightenment cultural
world that is now emerging. With this goal in view, then, let

me briefly elaborate the redescription of modernist liberalism that I am recommending.

If a civic culture is bound to be a countervailing culture, one whose norms and perspectives to some degree stand in a relationship of opposition to and tension with the values and world views that otherwise shape the lives of citizens, the question is: how did the discourses of modernist liberalism support that countervailing culture? How did they achieve their intended rhetorical effect? Let us keep in view the general characteristics of the doctrines that we identify today as defining modernist liberalism. For our purposes, it is fair to classify modernist liberal political theories into two general types. Both varieties of modernist liberalism sought to support liberal democratic norms by offering arguments that, in a broad sense, could be described as foundationalist (i.e., modernist liberals offered theoretical discourses designed to show that liberal democratic norms are founded upon or derived from universal principles and objective truths). The two varieties of modernist liberal political theory differed from one another only with respect to the particular foundationalist style they adopted for carrying out this derivation.

To honor the most notable practitioners of each style, let us call one of these styles "Lockean" and the other "Kantian." Lockean liberal theorists generally sought to deduce the standpoint proper to citizenship (i.e., the standpoint of the free and equal individual) from what they conceived to be the universal condition in which all human beings find themselves prior to political association: the so-called state of nature, or natural condition. The utilitarian variation on this style usually took a naturalistic/psychological turn, and derived norms proper to civic life from the natural laws governing human sensation and the universal human experience of pleasure and pain. On the other hand, Kantian liberal theorists found reference to historical narratives, supposed states of nature, or psychological laws to be inadequate as sources of a sufficiently strong moral obligation to motivate development of civic attitudes and submission to the standards of civic justice. Kantian liberal theorists generally favored a more tightly logical, *a priori* style, and sought to deduce the norms proper to liberal democratic citizenship from some concept of universal human reason—in some cases following Kant himself in discovering those norms in the principles of pure practical reason and later, in other cases, following Hegel in discovering those norms in the manifestations of reason's irresistibly progressive self-realization in history.

Whichever of these styles (or mix of these styles) modernist liberal theorists favored at one time or another, the important point for present purposes is that they all saw as their task the production of purely theoretical discourses designed to justify or legitimize the norms proper to citizenship by grounding those norms upon supposedly universal metaphysical or epistemological principles. A theoretical discourse, as I have characterized it, is one that intends more or less self-consciously to set forth, merely for the sake of doing so, a set of audience-independent truths about an audience-independent subject matter. In other words, to a theoretical discourse the categories of rhetorical analysis apply only externally, if at all. A theoretical discourse aims not at persuasion, but rather at stating what is the case.

Surely it is apparent that there is something strange here. Civic norms exist only by being effectively internalized and faithfully adhered to in practice. Such internalization and adherence must be motivated, particularly when we are speaking of norms that, to some extent, must always stand in a relationship of tension with values rooted in totalizing ethnic, class, or religious world views. But do the norms proper to civic life become any more intelligible or attractive as a result of being derived from the state of nature, or from the principles of pure practical reason, by a theoretical discourse? Furthermore, if we already find civic norms attractive and are thereby committed to the form of political association that embodies them, do we really care whether those norms can be justified theoretically? If it turned out that there is some logical mistake in the theoretical justification, would that lessen our commitment to liberal democratic values? It would seem, at first glance, that the universalist theoretical discourses of modernist liberal political theory would offer rather meager rhetorical resources to a persuasive process aimed at motivating a particular audience at a particular time to develop and exercise the capacities proper to citizenship.

I maintain that it is time for us to take as our starting point the admission that the characteristically modernist project of justifying liberal democratic values theoretically is problematic. If we begin with this admission, our first question then becomes: By what mechanisms did modernist liberal political theory actually come to play such a central role in modernist civic culture? I have already stated one answer to this question as my thesis here—namely, that the foundationalist, antirhetorical posture assumed by modernist liberal political theory is itself a rhetorical strategy, a strategy that carried considerable persuasive force at the time of its adoption. Our problem is that it has, by now, ceased to carry this persuasive force. To the extent that contemporary civic culture remains dependent on this modernist rhetorical strategy, to that extent the countervailing effectiveness of contemporary civic culture is undermined and weakened. Let me briefly elaborate this diagnostic redescription of modernist liberalism.

A civic culture, as I have noted, is necessarily a countervailing culture. Liberal democracy assumes that citizens are adherents of particularistic concepts of the good life. It assumes that citizens are members of ethnic, class, and religious communities with competing interests and clashing world views. The rhetorical task of any civic culture is to win the allegiance of all citizens to a common set of civic values. This requires citizens to modify, in a certain way, and to interpret differently their commitments to the totalizing world views of their primary communities. This rhetorical task, which is proper to any civic culture, offers us a basis for understanding the rhetorical mechanisms by which the theoretical discourses of modernist liberalism managed to have persuasive impact.

Modernist liberal doctrines arose in the seventeenth century during a period of intense ethnic, class, and religious warfare. In the social and economic upheavals of the period, warring parties and factions ruthlessly struggled for power, pursuing victory for their particular causes at the expense of the common good. Language was a weapon and a captive of this civil war. Rhetoric—understood broadly as the cultural tradition, the linguistic self-consciousness, the skills and methodologies brought into play in shaping the convictions of particular audiences—was a powerful weapon in the struggle of community against community, world view against world view. Rhetoric thereby came to be viewed by the proto-liberals of the seventeenth century as the tool of particular interests and, therefore, as linguistic fuel for the fires of civic conflict. Of course, it was very easy to interpret the largely bourgeois and Protestant proto-liberals themselves as just one more party, as one more set of economic and political interests competing for power. If the liberal democratic cause was to prevail and an effectively countervailing civic culture be established, it was necessary for liberals to neutralize this perception of their own agenda as but one more particularistic, interest-driven program.

One standard rhetorical strategy, which may always be used to neutralize this sort of perception, is to present one's agenda as supported and even dictated by universal principles and timeless truth. This is the strategy that the proto-liberals of the seventeenth century adopted. Blatantly persuasive speech makes appeals to the passions and interests, the particularistic commitments and allegiances, of its audience. If the liberal democratic program was to succeed (i.e., be persuasive) and establish a common ground on which adherents of opposing interests and world views could meet, it had to distinguish its own rhetoric from the rhetoric of party and faction. It had to strip its own discourse of all appeals to passions and interests. It had to adopt the voice and persona of pure reason. It had to assume a self-consciously anti-rhetorical stance. By the mid-seventeenth century, the model for this kind of discourse—found in the writings of Galileo and Descartes—was already established and widely known. The task of the liberal party was to fit this model to the requirements of political speech.

Specifically, this meant adapting the foundationalist style of argumentation to discourses advocating the establishment of certain kinds of political institutions. The foundationalist style of argumentation required, for maximum persuasive force, the identification of one or more absolutely self-evident premises as the basis for demonstrating the timeless, "objective" truth of what were, in fact, a set of political prescriptions. While this method could be applied only with some awkwardness to political subjects, the first full-scale and self-conscious attempt at this application—Hobbes's *Leviathan,* in 1651— met at least with some conceptual success. Hobbes, though no liberal democrat himself, at least showed that political philosophy, by adopting the rhetoric of foundationalist epistemology, could credibly take on the appearance of being a purely theoretical discourse. Hobbes showed, in short, that the political rhetoric of pure theory could work.

Needless to say, I am not claiming that seventeenth-century proto-liberals adapted the rhetoric of foundationalism to political philosophy with the full awareness that it was but one rhetoric among others—a rhetoric that worked, above all, because it claimed to abstain from and constantly criticized the manipulative and ornamental tricks for which rhetoric was then notorious. No, early liberal theorists and, later, adherents of both Lockean and Kantian varieties of liberal political philosophy no doubt actually believed that the rhetoric of pure theory was not a rhetorical strategy at all. They really believed that, with the right cognitive method, they could in fact adopt a standpoint toward political affairs and the world in general from which they could issue discourses whose truth claims were not conditional upon the assent of some particular historically situated audience, discourses that set forth for all times the audience-independent truth. Seventeenth-century proto-liberals were supported in this belief by the entire array of assumptions that we now identify as basic to the cultural project of the Enlightenment. Enlightenment concepts of reason and knowledge were built upon the rejection of what was taken in the seventeenth century to be the cognitive inadequacy of explicitly rhetorical modes of speech. As partisans of pure reason, seventeenth century proto-liberals laid the groundwork for modernist civic culture by affirming the possibility of a mode of speech free of the cognitive and moral defects of self-consciously rhetorical speech, a purely theoretical mode of speech issued from a standpoint that could, in principle, be adopted by any human being at any time in any place.

Were these partisans of pure reason simply self-deluded? Were they simply incorrect, mistakenly using the words "reason" and "knowledge" to refer to things that were nonexistent, or at least other than that to which those words properly refer? Hardly. To characterize Enlightenment concepts of reason and knowledge in this way, as mistaken or incorrect, would be to reaffirm the very assumptions that we must seek to put aside today. In the context of seventeenth and eighteenth-century social and economic struggles, the invention of a standpoint of pure reason provided the basis for a rhetorical strategy that, from our point of view today, worked (i.e., worked to influence events and shape lives in ways that we approve of). While we might be inclined today to look upon this modernist rhetorical strategy as appropriate only to a more innocent and less self-critical age, or perhaps even as a bit mendacious, we must not forget that any such judgment is a reflection of our own rhetorical situation, our own cultural and political exigencies. The cultural project of the Enlightenment, after all, constituted a powerful historical form of belief that served the interests of freedom and equality for almost three hundred years.

The only basis for criticism of Enlightenment concepts of reason and knowledge is that, today, they at best serve these interests badly. We citizens of North Atlantic liberal democracies have been shaped by Enlightenment culture and by modernist liberalism. It is with eyes that were given vision by Enlightenment culture that we look back upon modernist liberalism, and find its anti-rhetorical stance naive and mendacious. Such a judgment does not constitute a rejection of the Enlightenment, but rather signifies arrival of what, in Nietzsche's vocabulary, we can describe as the Enlightenment's moment of self-overcoming. It is time now to find new rhetorical resources to support and motivate the cultivation of civic freedom and equality, resources not so subject to easy refutation, and even ridicule, as are those that were generated by the modernist rhetoric of pure theory.

In the effort to discover such resources, however, we are

not able simply to turn our backs on modernist liberal political theory and move on. This project—the project of inventing a postmodern, post-Enlightenment civic culture—must confront at every step the continuing influence and lingering effects of the earlier successes of the modernist rhetoric of pure theory. The ideas of modernist liberalism were centrally important components of modernist civic culture. As we have seen, a particular historical form of civic culture has two functions: it provides cultural resources that serve: (1) to render intelligible to citizens the values and standpoint proper to liberal democratic citizenship, and (2) to provide citizens with motivation to develop the moral capacities required for citizenship. Modernist liberalism carried out both of these functions effectively—but in a way that, from the standpoint of our late twentieth-century experience of citizenship, is bound to create continuing problems, both for the task of rendering the standpoint of citizenship intelligible, and for the task of motivating the development of civic capacities and values. In the remainder of this chapter, I will briefly outline and examine a few of these problems of intelligibility and motivation that are the consequences of modernist liberalism.

Consequences of modernist liberalism

The specific historical form of civic culture shaped by the ideas of modernist liberalism gives rise, as we have seen, to problems of intelligibility and motivation as Enlightenment concepts of reason and knowledge lose their credibility. These problems of intelligibility and motivation derive directly from the adoption by modernist liberalism of the modernist rhetoric of pure theory. Adoption of this rhetorical strategy by modernist liberals generated an interpretation of the countervailing character of civic culture that linked, in various ways, the normative standpoint of liberal citizenship to Enlightenment concepts of reason and knowledge. This link must be broken if we are to succeed in gaining a new and a renewed insight into what liberal citizenship demands of us today. Let us examine first the problems of intelligibility produced by

this link, and then the problems of motivation that flow from
these problems.

Problems of intelligibility

In discussing the problems of intelligibility and motivation we
inherit from modernist liberalism, it is important to keep in
view the rhetorical task specific to any liberal democratic civic
culture.

A civic culture is composed of discourses, narratives, and
representations of various sorts that are invented by and
addressed to citizens for the purpose of rendering intelligible,
and motivating attainment of, the normative standpoint of citizenship. A civic culture is necessarily a countervailing and
secondary culture. Liberal democracy as a form of political
association assumes, and even requires, that citizens adhere to
one or more particularistic concepts of the good life. Liberal
democracy assumes that citizens are first, and will always
remain, members of particular ethnic, class, and religious
communities. It assumes that the identities of citizens are first
defined, and will continue to be shaped, by the totalizing
world views and value systems associated with those primary
communities. On the other hand, in order for liberal democratic political institutions to function properly, citizens—as
members of particular ethnic, class, and religious communities—must also internalize the values proper to the encompassing civic community. A liberal democracy is an association
of free and equal individuals. In order to qualify as citizens in
the full cultural sense, the members of particularistic cultural
communities must develop the capacity to view themselves
and others as free and equal individuals and to act accordingly—even as they maintain their primary adherence to the
beliefs and practices of the particularistic cultural communities to which they belong.

Attainment of this capacity is the central cultural and
moral task that citizenship imposes on all members of the liberal democratic political community. It is a cultural and moral
task of great complexity. It requires citizens to develop and
cultivate identities that involve standpoints intrinsically

opposed to one another, and which must be distinguished as clearly as possible. Every citizen must develop and cultivate not only an identity shaped by the values or ranking systems of some particularistic cultural community, but also the identity of a free and equal individual (i.e., an identity defined by a certain kind of independence from any particularistic set of values). Let us call the first type of identity a *communitarian identity*, and the second a *civic identity*.

To complicate matters further, citizens who have achieved the identity of a free and equal individual exercise that identity primarily through participation in activities related to the public sphere of their particular civic community. The public sphere of any particular liberal democracy is roughly defined by those types of interests, interactions, activities, and discourses in which the norms—the standards of excellence, the virtue concepts, the obligations—proper to citizenship apply. This sphere is never defined once and for all. Rather, its parameters are always a matter of dispute and consensus, growing and shrinking as social, cultural, and economic conditions change. Definition of its exact boundaries at any given time is, in fact, one of the most fundamental issues that citizens enter the public sphere in order to decide. In the process of participating in the political processes that define the boundaries of the public sphere, citizens must be able to call into play both their civic identities and their communitarian identities. As bearers of a civic identity, they must be concerned to uphold the norms of civic justice wherever they apply. As bearers of a communitarian identity, they must be concerned to defend particularistic cultural beliefs, values, and practices against possible intrusive action by the liberal democratic state on behalf of some temporary electoral majority.

Thus, to develop a capacity for liberal democratic citizenship is to develop a capacity for maintaining, cultivating, distinguishing, and exercising both civic and communitarian identities, as appropriate. Citizenship requires persons to strike some kind of precarious balance between these two opposing standpoints. The rhetorical task of any liberal democratic civic culture is to provide resources that can be used to persuade citizens that this precarious cultural balancing act is not only possible, not only desirable, but even obligatory. To the extent that any particular historical form of civic culture effectively carries out this rhetorical task, a viable liberal democratic public sphere or civil society is constituted and liberal democratic political institutions can function as intended. Modernist liberal political theory, as a component of modernist civic culture, generated discourses that provided a characteristic set of resources and strategies for carrying out this rhetorical task. It provided a very specific interpretation of the relationship between civic and communitarian identities.

Modernist liberal political theory, presented in foundationalist theoretical discourses, defined the standpoint of citizenship in essentialist terms (i.e., they defined the civic standpoint of free and equal individuality as the essential or natural standpoint proper to every human being). In this essentialist interpretation, modernist liberalism in fact reversed the developmental relationship between the standpoint proper to citizenship and non-civic standpoints—leading to, among other things, the characteristically modernist failure to recognize the importance of a civic culture for the support of liberal democratic political institutions.

Lockean varieties of modernist liberal political theory, for example, defined the standpoint proper to citizenship as prior in an historical or anthropological sense. Social contract theories of the liberal state and of political obligation derived their concepts of civic norms from narratives that supposedly described the first establishment of political association. In social contract narratives, liberal theorists represented individuals living under natural or pre-political conditions, meeting together to decide upon mutually advantageous conditions of political association. Such negotiations, of course, would be carried on by free individuals (or at least family heads) subject to no common power, individuals whose identities would therefore be shaped by their natural condition alone, rather than by a set of historically contingent political arrangements. The primary question all parties would face in such negotiations would be how much of their natural liberty to relinquish for the sake of maximizing the benefits of association. Such negotiators would, of course, insist upon placing strict limits on governmental authority and the state's power to coerce. They certainly would not grant to the state the power to institute any sort of regime that would impose on citizens a particular concept of the good life. In other words, such negotiators would definitely insist on constitutional recognition of their natural liberty to pursue happiness as they saw fit.

The graphic clarity and simplicity of such contract narratives had great rhetorical force. Those narratives gave plausibility to the notion that the natural human condition—the universal condition of all human beings prior to political association—is a condition of liberty, a condition of free individuality unencumbered by limits imposed or obligations incurred by membership in particularistic ethnic, class, or religious communities. However any particular liberal theorist represented the outcomes of this imagined negotiation, the social contract narrative itself gave an aspect of self-evidence to the general idea of the priority of human liberty. The social contract narrative licensed claims affirming natural human rights (i.e., claims that certain legal protections and entitlements were mandated by the original, or pre-associational, condition of human liberty). As in the earlier tradition of natural law, which was influenced by classical metaphysical concepts of nature, the standard of justice or the principle of right was affirmed by modernist liberal political theory as existing prior to the establishment of every particular historical regime. But, in the case of Lockean varieties of modernist liberalism, this priority was conceived of historically rather than metaphysically, in terms of a narrative of cultural and material progress. The principle of right was derived from the purported natural or spontaneous form of life that would be followed by human beings, were they not subject to the power of governments. Since the establishment of a government would then be a voluntary act, it must be represented as an improvement upon the natural condition, as a story of progress. These were the minimal narrative rules imposed upon Lockean, or contractarian, varieties of liberal political theory.

Thus, Lockean varieties of modernist liberal political theory attributed to the normative standpoint of citizenship (i.e., the standpoint of free and equal individuality) an historical or anthropological priority with respect to other cultural stand-points. Once again, this attribution of priority was very effec-tive, as a rhetorical strategy, in the context of seventeenth and eighteenth-century political struggles. It allowed liberals to claim that civic values were grounded in human nature and in nature generally, as opposed to the artificial and arbitrary val-ues of court and church. But it also interpreted the stand-point of citizenship in a very specific way—as a standpoint that was universally accessible and available to all human beings, provided certain impediments to its development were removed. Properly understood, social contract narratives were educational devices that helped persons formed by various ethnic and religious cultures to imagine what it would be like to be the free and equal individuals who were described as parties to the social contract. Ideally, by imagining themselves in that role, they could imaginatively strike the attitudes and demand the political arrangements compatible with it. But, paradoxically, social contract narratives could have this educa-tional and empowering impact only by denying their rhetori-cal status as educational devices, and by claiming the status of theoretical discourses about the nature and origins of political association. To admit that the social contract narrative was merely an educational device—a component of civic culture—would have been to admit that the standpoint of citi-zenship was a constructed and an acquired cultural stand-point, just like any other. To admit the artificiality of that sta-tus would have been to lose the rhetorical edge gained by the claim that civic values, unlike those of court and church, were grounded in the nature of things.

This successful modernist rhetorical strategy has today become a liability. Our primary task, as citizens of developed North Atlantic liberal democracies, is no longer to fight for the initial establishment of liberal political institutions, using all the ideological weapons available against the entrenched power of court and church. Rather, our task today is to main-tain a supportive liberal democratic civic culture, one capable of strengthening in ourselves and others the dispositions and attitudes proper to citizenship. In short, our task consists in creating cultural means for the effective reproduction of cultural values. Modernist liberal political theory, to the extent that it attributed to the normative standpoint of citizenship an historical and anthropological priority, does not serve us well in the pursuit of this task. By claiming this sort of priority for the standpoint of free and equal individuality, modernist liberalism suggested that the primary obstacles to the development and reproduction of civic values are cultural and political in nature. It suggested that a civic identity is somehow the native and original identity of persons, and that civic identity somehow emerges spontaneously, once impediments derived from accidental cultural and political circumstances are removed. Because it at least implicitly assigned to civic identity a metaphysical status, modernist liberalism systematically discouraged reflection about civic identity as a cultural construction. It also systematically discouraged reflection about the sort of cultural resources that are required for the development and maintenance of civic identities.

This is one way in which modernist liberal political theory, to the extent that it continues to influence our understanding of liberal democratic citizenship, generates for us what I have called problems of intelligibility. An effective civic culture must provide resources for rendering intelligible to citizens the tasks involved in developing the values and attitudes proper to citizenship. With respect to this function, modernist liberal political theory today produces confusion rather than clarity. It produces confusion, above all, by its denial that the process of developing the capacities proper to citizenship is a particularistic cultural process requiring particularistic cultural support. By representing the standpoint of citizenship, the standpoint of free and equal individuality, as the universal standpoint of all human beings in their natural or pre-associational condition, modernist liberalism represented the standpoint of citizenship as a standpoint stripped of all particularistic cultural attributes. The process of developing a civic identity was thereby defined as a process of stripping away the culturally accidental in order to arrive at a supposedly culture-neutral, natural, and universal standpoint.

This way of understanding the developmental and anthropological relationship between civic and communitarian identities not only misrepresents our contemporary experience of citizenship, but also positively impedes our efforts to insure the cultural reproduction of civic values and attitudes. Today we regularly encounter in the media the inescapable facts of global cultural diversity. Awareness of this cultural diversity makes it all too clear to us that civic values and civic identities are particularistic cultural constructs that have emerged from, and which are still largely local to North Atlantic European traditions. Modernist liberal political theory reversed the actual developmental and anthropological priorities when it represented the standpoint of the free and equal individual as the natural and universal standpoint of all human beings prior to political association. The civic standpoint of free and equal individuality, where it is widely attained at all, is one that presupposes and emerges from historically specific communitarian cultural standpoints. It can be successfully attained by large numbers of persons only under the most favorable cultural, economic, and political conditions. This understanding of the culturally contingent and particularistic nature of citizenship must be incorporated into the civic culture that succeeds modernist liberal civic culture. If one of the central tasks of any liberal democratic civic culture is to render intelligible liberal democratic citizenship as an ideal to be realized, a postmodern civic culture must represent and affirm citizenship as an ideal that is contingent, particularistic, and culturally constructed.

If modernist liberal political theory continues to generate problems of intelligibility because of its doctrinal content (i.e., by virtue of its representation of the normative standpoint of citizenship as historically and anthropologically prior to other cultural standpoints), it also continues to generate problems of intelligibility because of the conceptual and rhetorical common ground it shared, from the beginning, with modern foundationalist epistemology. That common ground was defined by the doctrine of the autonomy of reason. Foundationalist epistemologists conceived of the faculty of reason itself as the origin of the critical standards it brought to bear in the assessment of cognitive claims. For them, reason was autonomous in the assessment of truth claims, subject to no authority other than itself. Modernist liberal political theory saw the theoretical justification of political arrangements as work that was proper to this autonomous faculty of reason, in its practical application. More importantly, modernist liberals sought to establish a connection between the standpoint of autonomous reason and the attitudes, dispositions, and values proper to liberal democratic citizenship. They sought to extend the notion of a rationally autonomous "knower" from the cognitive into the political realm, and to use it to define the normative standpoint of liberal democratic citizenship. Modernist liberalism thus not only attributed to the standpoint of citizenship an historical and anthropological priority, but also an autonomy in matters of political morality that was analogous to the autonomy of reason in matters of truth. This historical and conceptual link between modernist liberal political theory and foundationalist concepts of knowledge continues, today, to generate confusion about the nature of liberal democratic citizenship. This sort of confusion still compels some people to view adherence to civic values as groundless and unjustified, if those values cannot be shown to be the expression of an autonomous and universal faculty of reason.

In order to free ourselves from such confusions, it is important for us to see that the modernist liberal concept of liberal democratic citizenship, as a function of an autonomous faculty of reason, was not just a mistake. It is quite possible to construct an illuminating analogy between the normative standpoint of citizenship and the purported standpoint of an autonomous rational faculty. But while this analogy may have played a useful role in the context of modernist civic culture, today, in view of the contemporary demise of the modernist doctrine of the autonomy of reason, it invites only misunderstanding. The project of inventing a viable postmodern civic culture requires that we find a new way of understanding the nature of liberal democratic citizenship, one that no longer commits us to viewing citizenship as involving the exercise of reason in some metaphysically or epistemologically privileged sense. The modernist liberal concept of the citizen as "man" of reason was grounded in a metaphor that has lost its power to illuminate the practice of citizenship. But to free ourselves from the influence of this metaphor, it is important to understand how it could have ever been illuminating.

The modernist doctrine of the autonomy of reason received its first, and most influential, formulation as the methodological point of departure for Descartes' project of providing the new mathematical physics with an absolutely secure metaphysical foundation. That project arose in the early seventeenth century, partially in response to the ethnic, class, and religious warfare that erupted in Europe following the Reformation. By 1620, Europe had suffered over one hundred years of civil strife provoked by disputes about religious doctrine and authority. One cultural response to these conflicts over opposing truth claims was the reemergence of a Pyrrhonian skepticism regarding all truth claims. This skepticism—identified today, above all, with Montaigne—was steeped in the spirit of tolerance and openness that the rhetorical culture of the Renaissance engendered. Descartes' response took a quite different tack. Skepticism and religious warfare seemed, to him, to feed off one another. If reason can provide no criterion for assessing opposing doctrinal truth claims, then rational discourse is useless in the resolution of doctrinal disputes—and force can plausibly be seen to have a legitimate role in resolving socially divisive disputes over matters of truth. Descartes' project was to rehabilitate rational discourse through an attack on skepticism. He set out to show that reason, by itself, does indeed provide a criterion for assessing opposing truth claims, a criterion that infallibly distinguishes true statements from false and the knowable from the unknowable.

Descartes discovered that infallible criterion of truth by giving free rein to skepticism, permitting himself to doubt every truth claim that in any way proved to be anything less than fully self-validating. If, after letting skepticism have full sway, he could indeed identify a proposition immune to skeptical argument, a proposition whose truth all who consider it must acknowledge, then Descartes could declare skepticism to be defeated and reason to be in possession of a criterion of truth. The self-validating proposition that Descartes claimed to have discovered was, of course, "I think, therefore I exist." Descartes took this proposition to be a statement about the world, a statement affirming the actual existence of a particular entity, a particular thinking being. He took it to be a true proposition whose truth depended in no way upon any contingent state of affairs or personal religious commitments, a proposition that is necessarily true each time it is affirmed, regardless of the time and place of its affirmation—for to affirm a proposition is in fact an act of thinking, and no act can exist without an existing agent. For Descartes, the truth of this proposition was necessarily self-evident to every human being capable of affirming any proposition whatever. Perception of its truth did not depend on the possession of prudence, special experience, or any other quality that persons possessed only by virtue of membership in one or another ethnic, class, or religious community. Perception of the truth of this proposition depended only on the capacity to inspect carefully the content of any proposition without regard to the pleasurable or painful consequences of affirming it, or the particular authorities asserting its truth, or the veneration in which it is held by friends and relatives—that is to say, without regard to its rhetorical dimension or the rhetorical situation it addresses. This was a capacity for a special kind of reflection, a capacity for inspecting the content of a proposition without taking into account the context of its utterance, a capacity requiring the deliberate adoption of a standpoint imagined to be external to every particular rhetorical situation, and therefore unaffected by any particular set of cultural assumptions. For Descartes, this was the "natural light," the standpoint intrinsic to reason itself.

This standpoint of pure reflection provided Descartes with the absolutely autonomous criterion that he needed in order to distinguish: (1) statements that in fact carry truth claims from those that do not, and (2) among statements actually bearing truth claims, the true from the false. Applying this criterion, the only propositions that carry truth claims are those whose content can be clearly and distinctly conceived from the culture-neutral standpoint of pure decontextualized representation. Only such propositions are candidates for admission into the realm of cognition. Statements advanced as true only for certain purposes, or in certain contexts or for certain audiences (e.g., a particular community of religious belief), thus do not, strictly speaking, carry truth claims at all. Discourses consisting of such statements do not qualify as cognitive discourses. Such discourses are to be measured by other standards, standards derived from the external contexts and accidental circumstances to which they are addressed. Those standards are arbitrary and dependent. When such standards are applied in evaluating statements, reason is not being used autonomously. The standards are drawn from rules and principles external to reason itself.

Accordingly, if statements carry truth claims only if they can be conceived clearly and distinctly from the context-free, culture-neutral standpoint of autonomous reason, the truth or falsity of such statements must be determined solely by reference to the rules and principles inherent in that standpoint—the rules, as we would say today, of deductive and inductive logic. These rules are inherent in reason itself, in the sense that they are rules for connecting sentences to one another intelligibly without regard for their contexts of utterance, and without regard to rhetorical considerations of speaker, audiences, intent, and circumstances. Thus, implicit in the methodological starting point of Descartes' project of overcoming skepticism is an unambiguous affirmation of the doctrine of the autonomy of human reason.

Once this notion of an absolutely autonomous faculty of reason gained some credibility and acceptance, it was then used to license a whole range of new cognitive discourses that appealed to autonomous human reason as their sole basis and claim to authority. As we noted earlier, Hobbes was the first to extend the vocabulary and style of argument proper to these new cognitive discourses into the field of political affairs—the first to attempt the construction of a political and moral science that based normative political claims on criteria purportedly drawn from reason alone. But it was Kant, perhaps, who provided the most perspicuous expression of the modernist linkage of liberal political norms to the doctrine of the autonomy of reason.

In his famous article, "What Is Enlightenment?" Kant answered the question posed in its title in such a way that his audience could have no doubt that liberal political norms were dictated by, and alone consistent with, the exercise of autonomous human reason. "*Sapere aude!* 'Have courage to use your own reason!'—that is the motto of enlightenment." Needless to say, Kant here was not identifying "enlightenment" with just any person's capacity to think clearly about his or her particular interests and welfare as a member of a particularistic cultural community. Of course, members of particular ethnic, class, and religious communities differ in their ability to master the vocabulary and apply the ranking systems that prevail in their particular communities. The application of general concepts grounded in particularistic cultural world views definitely involves what we now call reasoning skills, and some people develop these skills to a greater degree than others. But Kant's call to enlightenment was clearly not a call to develop reasoning skills of that sort. He was not interested in encouraging persons to become more thoroughly self-consistent and self-critical Lutherans, Prussians, or peasants. For Kant, as for all modernist liberals, the use of human reason in the honorific sense involved the use of critical standards that were drawn not from particularistic loyalties and commitments, but rather from reason itself. To the extent that a person strives to think in an orderly way about any subject matter, merely as a member of a particular ethnic, class, or religious community, that person is not, in Kant's vocabulary, using his or her own reason. Such a person, for Kant, would not be enlightened. To be enlightened, one must think and speak from a very different standpoint or identity, one no longer subject to particularistic ethnic, class, or religious ranking systems and world views.

Kant's injunction to use "one's own reason" thus implies the existence of a critical standpoint external to all historically conditioned and particularistic world views. To think for oneself (i.e., to think independently of the rules laid down by Pope, prince, employer, class, profession, village, and nation) is to adopt this standpoint. It is this standpoint that Kant identifies with the faculty of reason. To whom, then, is the Kantian injunction addressed? It is certainly not addressed to any person, insofar as he or she is the bearer of what we have called a communitarian identity. A person bears a communitarian identity insofar as he or she accepts or answers to descriptions using the vocabulary and ranking systems proper to a particular ethnic, class, or religious community. Kant's injunction to use "one's own reason" is thus an injunction to regard the reasoning in the pursuit of particularistic concepts of the good life as not "real" reasoning, and therefore as not one's own—which is to say, it was an injunction to regard one's communitarian identity as external to one's "real" self. What then is "real" reasoning, and what is it that defines the "real" self?

Of course, the answer that Kant gives in his article, "What Is Enlightenment?" is famous. Enlightenment is about the free use of reason. Reason is free only when subject to its own rules and criteria. The free use of reason is the use made of it by the scholar. The scholar issues purely rational discourses (i.e., discourses governed by the criteria derived from reason alone). As discourses governed by reason alone, the scholar's speech is genuinely cognitive speech. The scholar is one who possesses knowledge that is universal. The scholar speaks not as a member of one or another ethnic, class, or religious community, but rather as one who stands outside all such particularistic communities. The scholar is the quintessentially public person. To use "one's own reason," therefore, is to speak as a scholar to the public. It is to speak to the whole community as a world community, a community of persons not differentiated by particularistic ranking systems and world views. It is to speak from what we have called one's civic identity (i.e., one's identity as a member of the civic community).

In this famous article, Kant clearly takes as a given the metaphorical link between the autonomous standpoint of pure reason and the normative standpoint of citizenship. The social embodiment of autonomous reason is the autonomous scholar or intellectual. The autonomous scholar is another name for the autonomous citizen. Here the faculty of cognition and the capacity for political liberty are defined as mutually implied and interdependent. Here, too, civic identity is given a new sort of priority over communitarian identity. Just as social contract narratives attributed to the normative standpoint of citizenship an historical and anthropological priority, the metaphorical assimilation of the standpoint of citizenship with the standpoint of autonomous reason attributed to civic identity the sort of priority over communitarian identity that, in the defunct language of foundationalist epistemology, the transcendental ego had to the empirical ego. Just as the Kantian transcendental ego is the ground or underlying permanent reality of the conditioned and finite empirical ego, so too the civic self is the ground or underlying permanent reality of the conditioned and finite communitarian self. As the discourses that are genuinely cognitive and as the world that is genuinely known take priority over subjective impressions and the world of popular opinion, so also does civic identity take priority over communitarian identity. In this article, this peculiar cognitive/metaphysical common ground shared by modernist epistemology with modernist liberal political theory could not be more obvious. The doctrine of the autonomy of human reason in the sphere of cognition, when translated into the political sphere, mandates the doctrine of political liberty. The normatively free citizen is also the cognitively free thinker—in Kant's terms, the scholar or intellectual. The foundationalist epistemological arguments that underwrite claims to objective truth also ultimately underwrite demands for the rights of citizenship.

This analogy between the standpoints of the ideally autonomous citizen and the ideally autonomous knower defined modernist liberal political theory and determined the character of the modernist form of civic culture that it generated. Like all great metaphors that succeed in shaping history, it gave rise to a comprehensive interpretation of the world by equating two very unlike things in a way that, nevertheless, illuminated and gave a new kind of intelligibility to both. The modernist concept of the purely objective and autonomous knower was drawn from classical concepts of the contemplative life. The modernist liberal concept of the normative citizen was drawn from classical concepts of the political or active life. But in the seventeenth century, for whatever historical reasons, these two ideals were intertwined in ways entirely unfamiliar to classical philosophy. Whereas, for Aristotle, pursuit of the contemplative life led the philosopher to turn away from political affairs, for modern philosophy the standpoint of the pure, contemplative knower became a model for the standpoint of the active citizen. It might be the case that this modern appropriation of the classical ideal of pure theory may tell us something about the concealed political significance of the contemplative life, as it was classically understood. Without doubt, however, it tells us something important about the nature of modern citizenship.

Classical republicanism and classical concepts of the political life presupposed a community united by a shared concept of the good. Modern liberalism presupposes the opposite. Modern concepts of citizenship assume that the civic community will be composed of a number of diverse ethnic, class, and religious communities defined by conflicting world views and ranking systems. Membership in such a civic community makes very different demands on citizens. Citizens must strive to attain a far greater degree of detachment from their particularistic value commitments. In order to address one another as free and equal individuals within the liberal democratic public sphere, citizens must cultivate a far greater critical distance from their communitarian identities than classical citizenship required. The model for this extreme detachment became the detachment of the pure philosophical knower, the transcendental ego—the standpoint of a person who has embraced an identity completely separate from all particularistic commitments and beliefs in order to gain a knowledge of universal truth. This is what is illuminating about the modernist liberal identification of the normative citizen with the pure knower: it makes clear the degree of detachment that modern citizenship requires from adherence to totalizing particularistic beliefs and values. This identification also served well as the basis for a form of civic culture. It provided a clear measure of, and clear direction for, development of the capacities proper to modern citizenship. In effect, modernist liberal civic culture invited citizens of liberal democracies to become citizens in the full cultural sense by learning to adopt the standpoint of the pure knower (i.e., the universal standpoint of one who has resolved to adopt only those criteria of truth that are applicable to all persons, without regard to their membership in particular ethnic, class, or religious communities).

While this identification between ideal citizen and pure knower produced and supported a most effective form of civic culture for more than three hundred years, it has now become a liability. The cognitive enterprise that originated with Galilean mathematical physics has by now become an enterprise that would no longer be recognized even by its founders. The Cartesian doctrine of the autonomy of human reason was designed as an explanation and defense of that earlier cognitive enterprise. But in an age when science is anything but the province of autonomous knowers, when cognitive enterprises have become well-financed, internally complex, multi-audience, nationally organized, economically necessary, and militarily vital professionalized research enterprises, the doctrine of the autonomy of human reason is simply obsolete—marginally useful today, perhaps, only as an ideology supportive of the independence of research institutions. Science, in short, has become something vastly different from anything that Descartes could have imagined. The myth of an autonomous faculty of human reason has retained whatever currency it continues to hold because it has played such a central role in modernist civic culture. This doctrine has, so far, been the most effective cultural support for the production and reproduction of civic values in contemporary liberal democracies. But its usefulness is now at an end. For us today, the doctrine of a universal and autonomous faculty of human reason has lost its credibility. The analogy between the ideal citizen and the pure knower no longer illuminates our contemporary experience of citizenship. Today, we must think beyond this analogy if we are to succeed in the invention of a new form of liberal democratic civic culture that will succeed the old. But this analogy, up until now, has provided the basis for the political vocabulary identified with liberalism, as such. The first task in the project of reinventing liberalism must be to free liberalism, as a concept of citizenship and political life, from this modernist vocabulary. Because of the origins of that vocabulary in the myth of an autonomous faculty of reason, the reinvention of liberalism requires a radical shift in the way we speak not only about citizenship, but also about reason and cognition.

Problems of motivation

In any civic culture, the linguistic and representational resources that help make the normative standpoint of citizenship intelligible to citizens also provide resources for motivating them to make the effort required to develop civic identities and to cultivate civic virtues. An effective civic culture must make clear not only what it means to be a citizen, but also why it is good to be a citizen. The civic culture shaped by modernist liberal political theory provided motivational resources supportive of citizenship that were drawn from its peculiar interpretation of citizenship. As we have seen, on the question of the nature of citizenship, modernist liberalism answered in two ways: (1) with respect to political authority, citizenship is a political standpoint analogous to the standpoint that might be imagined to prevail among free and equal individuals in the natural condition, prior to their voluntary submission to political authority; and (2) with respect to beliefs and values, citizenship is a political standpoint analogous to the radically detached cognitive standpoint of the pure theoretical knower.

In both of these ways of defining the nature of citizenship, modernist liberal political theory represented the normative standpoint of citizenship in essentialist terms. It represented civic identity as the anthropologically and metaphysically prior identity of persons. The answer offered by modernist liberalism to the question of motivation—the question of why anyone should go to the trouble of developing civic identities and cultivating civic virtues—was dictated by its essentialist concept of citizenship. Its answer was that free and equal individuals, those with radically autonomous minds, define what all human beings everywhere really are. Thus, for the civic culture shaped by modernist liberal political theory, the motivation to develop civic identities and cultivate civic virtues was defined as a type of self-realization, where the move from communitarian identity to civic identity was represented at once as a move from the generic to the individual, and as a move from the particular to the universal.

The two wings of modernist liberal political theory—Lockean and Kantian—tended to offer slightly different versions of this essentialist and universalist interpretation of the ethics of citizenship. However, the effect of both versions of civic ethics was to undermine the validity of, and even to disparage, particularistic cultural world views and value systems. Lockean forms of liberalism tended to specialize in representing the move from communitarian identity to civic identity as a move from the generic to the individual (i.e., as a move from the subjection of persons to various kinds of group authority and norms, to the standpoint of the free-standing individual imagined in social contract narratives). For this reason, forms of modernist civic culture heavily influenced by Lockean liberal theory—in particular, the civic cultures of England and America—tended to motivate the development of civic attitudes by motivating the development of a kind of individualism that easily conformed to the logic of market systems of production—where economic competition licensed behavior that often placed individual self-interest above loyalty to local cultural community.

At the extreme, Lockean forms of civic culture became virtually indistinguishable from the culture of possessive individualism. On the other hand, Kantian forms of liberal theory tended to specialize in representing the move from communitarian identity to civic identity as a move from the particular to the universal (i.e., as a move from the immersion of persons in merely contingent and local cultural world views, to the standpoint of the all-embracing and purely self-determining individual identified with the autonomous, objective knower). For this reason, forms of modernist civic culture that were heavily influenced by the Kantian, or rationalist, style of liberal theory—say, the civic culture of France—tended to motivate development of civic attitudes by motivating a quest for a condition of pure, universalist self-determination. This quest was no less hostile to the restrictive laws of the market than to the constrictive values of local ethnic, class, and religious cultures.

What is important for us today is that both Lockean and Kantian varieties of modernist liberal political theory generated forms of civic culture whose motivational resources tended to undermine the validity of, or even to disparage, particularistic cultural concepts of the good life. Modernist liberal civic culture tended to present the culture of citizenship as a totalizing culture to which all particularistic ethnic, class, and religious cultures were subordinate, both cognitively and morally. The contemporary consequence of this subordination is that—as the Enlightenment world view, which gave modernist liberal concepts of citizenship their persuasive power, progressively loses its credibility—we are now experiencing in reaction a reassertion and resurgence of particularistic cognitive and moral belief. The impact of modernist liberal civic culture upon religious communities was to weaken orthodox claims to the possession of exclusive doctrinal truth and absolute moral standards. The impact of modernist liberal civic culture on ethnic and class communities was to weaken particularistic identification. But today, as modernist liberal civic culture gradually loses its motivational power, we see the emergence everywhere of a new politics of orthodoxy and a new politics of ethnic and class identity, wherein demands are raised that particularistic cultural values be given priority over civic values. It is this development that presents possibly the most daunting challenge to the project of inventing a viable postmodern civic culture. The first step we must take toward meeting this challenge is to identify clearly the way in which modernist liberal political theory attributed to the culture of citizenship an entirely inappropriate motivational primacy over cultures grounded in particularistic ethnic, class, and religious world views.

Civic culture influenced by Lockean forms of liberal theory motivated the development of civic attitudes by sanctioning purely self-interested and acquisitive motives—motives imagined to be consistent with those of the solitary individual in the natural condition of perfect liberty. Lockean liberalism attributed to these motives historical and anthropological priority. They were conceived of as authentic human motives (i.e., authentic by comparison with the arbitrary, artificial, and often hypocritical motives that govern the behavior of individuals as members of particular cultural communities). Civic culture influenced by Lockean liberal political theory thus tended to support what I shall call a civic "ethics of authenticity." In the civic ethics of authenticity, the normative standpoint of citizenship was represented as the authentically human standpoint. To be a citizen in the full cultural sense was to be a fully authentic human being—a human being whose identity was firmly grounded in the original and inevitable human standpoint of the natural condition, the condition of all human beings prior to their subjection to the artificial limits imposed by the arbitrary authority of particularistic cultural and political communities. The civic ethics of authenticity represented the motives and standpoint proper to the citizen (i.e., to the free and equal individual) as the motives and standpoint native to all human beings, those that would be left after all particularistic cultural accretions have been stripped away. Of course, different theorists of the civic ethics of authenticity conceived of the content of authenticity differently, depending upon their concept of the state of nature. For Hobbes, human authenticity was identified with the competitive struggle for physical survival; for Locke, with industrious labor aimed at the accumulation of property; for Rousseau, with the primeval innocence and spontaneity of animal life. The point is that, however the ideal of the authentically free and equal individual was conceived in any particular case, realization of that ideal definitely required the citizen to consider all obligations and identifications derived from membership in particular ethnic, class, or religious communities as secondary, superficial, dispensable, and even spurious.

Civic culture influenced by Kantian forms of liberal theory tended to invalidate and disparage particularistic cultural values in a slightly different way. Kantian liberal political theory represented the relationship between civic and communitarian identities as analogous to the relationship between the autonomous, rational self-consciousness and the conditioned, empirical self-consciousness of foundationalist epistemology. Just as the quest for certainty in modernist epistemology was represented as a quest for self-determination—a quest to escape the realm of belief grounded only upon tradition and the authority of others—so too, for Kantian varieties of liberal political theory, the project of developing civic attitudes was represented as a quest for moral independence—a quest to attain freedom from motivations deriving only from the accidental circumstances of biology, upbringing, and fortune. While Lockean forms of liberalism characterized the process of achieving full cultural citizenship as a stripping away of cultural accretions to reach an original core individuality, Kantian forms of liberalism characterized the process as an ascent from a conditioned, particularistic identity to an autonomous, universalized identity.

Civic culture influenced by Kantian liberal theory thus tended to support what I shall call a civic "ethics of autonomy." In the civic ethics of autonomy, the normative standpoint of citizenship was represented as the only fully self-determining human standpoint, the only standpoint available to persons who wish to escape subjection to historically contingent communitarian identities. Those historically contingent communitarian identities, as viewed by the civic ethics of autonomy, were shaped not only by arbitrary, but also by hopelessly particularistic moral standards—standards promoting rivalry and conflict among the different cultural communities adhering to them. To be a citizen in the full cultural sense, then, was to take over individual responsibility for one's own identity and moral standards—but in such a way that the self-determining individuality thereby attained was one that was free of all historical particularism and, for that reason, constituted the sole hope for moral unanimity and social peace.

The civic ethics of autonomy thus called into question the moral validity of particularistic concepts of the good in an even more powerful way than did the civic ethics of authenticity. Just as the modernist doctrine of the autonomy of reason had the effect of discrediting all truth claims that could not be supported by the cognitive methodology it mandated (the "scientific method"), so also the civic ethics of autonomy had the effect of discrediting all moral standards that were identified with particularistic cultural traditions and which could not be justified by appeal to the metaphysical ideal of moral autonomy. This meant that persons who were motivated to become citizens in the full cultural sense, under the influence of the civic ethics of autonomy, were faced with a difficult choice. To the extent that their lives were given direction and meaning by moral ideals and world views associated with some particularistic cultural community, they were forced either to abandon those ideals and world views or to reformulate them in ways that stripped them of their historically contingent and particularistic content.

Schleiermacher's reinterpretation of Christian theology, which was heavily influenced by Kantian thought, became the model for this sort of doctrinal reformulation. In his project of making adherence to Christianity once again intellectually and morally respectable in the eyes of its cultured despisers, Schleiermacher stripped Christian doctrine of all elements that were not, in principle, accessible to all human beings everywhere—identifying Christianity not with a set of truth claims regarding events that occurred during the Roman occupation of Judaea, but rather with a privileged personal experience that was analogous to, if not identical with, personal experiences available to members of all religions. Members of particular cultural communities who were not willing to reformulate their local moral ideals and world views in this way seemed, as a result, not only to be excluded from full cultural citizenship, but also to be excluded by the civic ethics of autonomy from the cultural mainstream, and condemned as cultural and political sectarians incapable of both responsible citizenship and self-determining individuality.

In this way, the civic ethics of autonomy pressured all particularistic culture communities to conform to its cultural rule, on pain of being vilified as enemies of reason, freedom, equality, moral progress, and social peace. But the civic ideal of individual autonomy also introduced an even more potent and insidious way of undermining the authority of particularistic moral standards: by introducing an ascetic theme into modernist civic culture.

Any sort of ascetic impulse was comfortably alien to the civic ethics of authenticity. The civic ideal of authenticity motivated persons to achieve full cultural citizenship by throwing off the restraints upon their desire and behavior produced by particularistic moral standards. The goal was represented as a return to the imagined standpoint of the free-standing individual who inhabited the state of nature, the condition of perfect liberty. The civic ideal of authenticity was thus entirely compatible with an affirmation of unbridled material self-interest and this-worldliness.

The civic ethics of autonomy, on the other hand, was laced through with a sense of the futility and vanity of particularistic desire. For the civic ethics of autonomy, human contingency and finitude were the real enemy. To the extent that the civic ethics of autonomy expressed this ascetic impulse, living a life in pursuit of some particularistic ethnic or religious concept of the good was viewed as an activity akin to polishing the door-knobs on the Titanic. All historically conditioned concepts of the good expressed only inclinations and interests governed by particularistic biological, psychological, social, and economic needs. From the standpoint of the civic ideal of moral autonomy, all such needs were faceless and merely generic. Action governed by them stripped human life of the dignity and worth proper to fully individualized human life (i.e., the ideal life of the citizen). In view of this ascetic evaluation of contingent and finite human life, particularistic moral ideals and world views thus could be judged not only as divisive and irrational, but even as intrinsically futile and meaningless.

In different ways, and to different degrees, both Lockean and Kantian forms of modernist liberalism—both the civic ethics of authenticity and the civic ethics of autonomy[1]— called into question the validity of particularistic moral ideals and world views. Both Lockean and Kantian varieties of modernist liberal political theory represented the normative standpoint of citizenship in essentialist and universalist terms. This essentialist and universalist concept of civic identity certainly provided cultural resources for motivating citizens to undertake the difficult work of developing the intellectual and moral capacities proper to citizenship. Modernist civic culture, influenced by the civic ethics of authenticity and the civic ethics of autonomy, affirmed civic identity as anthropologically and metaphysically more fundamental than communitarian identity. This generated a motivation to develop civic identity that identified the pursuit of civic identity as an inward search for a "true" self. Communitarian identity was thereby defined as a "false" self, a self distracted from its real vocation by the conformity to arbitrary moral ideals and world views demanded by particularistic cultural communities as the price of membership. The motivational resources offered by modernist civic culture, powerful as they were, thus tended to define the relationship between civic and communitarian identity as one characterized by hopeless conflict between mutually exclusive, totalizing standpoints.

This is the consequence of modernist liberalism that will no doubt prove the most difficult to overcome as we, today, undertake to lay the basis for a postmodern liberal democratic civic culture. This is not to say, of course, that a liberal democratic civic culture can ever be free of the conflict between civic identity and communitarian identity. Given the moral and intellectual demands of liberal democratic citizenship, such conflict is inevitable. As I have noted, attainment of the nor-

---

[1] Two of the most influential and original projects in recent political philosophy may be fairly described as attempts to breathe new life into what I have called the civic ethics of authenticity and the civic ethics of autonomy. Charles Taylor, in his books *Sources of the Self: The Making of Modern Identity* (Cambridge, Mass.: Harvard University Press, 1989) and *The Ethics of Authenticity* (Cambridge, Mass.: Harvard University Press, 1992), undertakes to retrieve and reaffirm the pursuit of authentic selfhood as a moral ideal supportive of liberal democratic citizenship. Similarly, one aspect of Jürgen Habermas' decades-long project of constructing a theory of communicative action involves an attempt to retrieve and reaffirm a version of the civic ethics of autonomy—see, in particular, *Moral Consciousness and Communicative Action* (Cambridge, Mass.: MIT Press, 1990). Both of these projects of retrieval seek to retain some remnant of the universalist and totalizing character of earlier formulations of the ethics of authenticity and the ethics of autonomy. To that extent, both of these projects, in my view, fail to address in its full scope what I have called the contemporary crisis of liberal democratic civic culture.

mative standpoint of citizenship requires persons to develop a capacity to put aside, whenever they enter the public realm, the moral ideals and world views that define their communitarian identities. Citizens must be able to distance themselves from the most basic commitments that otherwise govern their actions and give meaning to all aspects of human life.

This balancing act is truly a fantastic requirement—a requirement that relatively few citizens in any particular liberal democracy will satisfy with great distinction. But modernist liberal civic culture made that balancing act even more difficult by representing the relationship between civic and communitarian identity as something approximating an either/or choice. If a viable postmodern civic culture is to be invented, this needless difficulty must be removed. In our rethinking of liberalism as a form of political association, we must come to see the relationship between civic and communitarian identity—whatever its ineradicable difficulty—as a mutually supportive, rather than competitive, relationship. Perhaps the most important contemporary contribution to this rethinking of liberalism has been made by John Rawls, in his work published since 1980. Before we can begin to build on that contribution, we must first turn briefly to an examination of the new concept of liberalism—"political liberalism"—that Rawls has begun to formulate.

2 Rawls and the Shaping of a Postmodern Liberalism

Addressing the consequences of modernist liberalism

A postmodern civic culture will no doubt differ in many significant ways from the form of civic culture that developed under the influence of modernist liberal political theory. But in whatever other ways a postmodern civic culture may differ from its predecessor, it definitely must differ in two respects:

1. It must provide a new concept of the nature of liberal democratic citizenship, one that can successfully address the intelligibility problems produced by modernist liberalism.
2. It must provide new rhetorical resources for motivating citizens to develop civic identities, resources that can successfully address the motivational problems produced by modernist liberalism.

We must keep in mind what these two tasks specifically require.

First, in order to address the intelligibility problems pro-

duced by modernist liberal political theory, a postmodern
civic culture must provide a concept of citizenship that is thoroughly independent of foundationalist epistemological modes
of thought. As we have seen, modernist liberalism, in its
rhetorical use of Enlightenment concepts of reason and
knowledge (i.e., in its use of the anti-rhetorical rhetoric of
pure theory) established and worked from an analogy
between the normative standpoint of liberal democratic citizenship and the standpoint of the autonomously rational,
objective knower. This connection generated an essentialist
and universalist concept of the standpoint of citizenship that
represented civic identity as anthropologically and metaphysically prior to communitarian identity.

Among the negative consequences of this twofold attribution of priority were, first, the systematic neglect of civic culture as a factor in the production and reproduction of civic
values and, second, the widespread belief that civic moral
ideals were somehow dependent, for their legitimacy, on a
proof demonstrating their deductibility from timeless and
universal principles—whether these principles be drawn from
some imagined natural human condition or from the imagined traits of the faculty of pure practical reason. A postmodern civic culture must sever once and for all this connection
between the normative standpoint of citizenship and the
standpoint proper to an autonomous faculty of reason. A postmodern civic culture will no longer require the services of
epistemologists or metaphysicians. It will take as its point of
departure a rejection of the anti-rhetorical rhetoric of pure
theory—or, more positively, it will embrace rhetorical practice
and analysis as instruments and resources for the production
and reproduction of civic values. In short, a postmodern liberalism must take a rhetorical turn. It must start from a rejection of the essentialist and universalist concept of the normative standpoint of citizenship, identified with modernist
liberalism, and an affirmation of the historically situated and
particularistic nature of civic values.

Second, in order to address the motivational problems
produced by modernist liberal political theory, a postmodern
civic culture must offer resources for motivating citizens to

develop civic identities and capacities that are no longer dependent upon the essentialist and universalist concept of citizenship proper to modernist liberalism. As we have seen, this essentialist concept of citizenship had the effect of undermining and disparaging particularistic concepts of the good life. The communitarian identities shaped by particularistic concepts of the good were represented by modernist liberalism as arbitrary and groundless. This basic strategy of motivation was embodied in the two most influential moral standpoints generated by modernist liberal political theory: what I have called the civic ethics of authenticity, and the civic ethics of autonomy. These moral ideals differed from the moral ideals identified with particular ethnic, class and religious communities not only by their claim to universality, but also by their peculiarly formal nature.

The civic ethics of authenticity—largely associated with Lockean styles of modernist liberalism—motivated citizens to achieve the normative civic standpoint of free and equal individuality by representing as an ideal the free-standing individual of the pre-political natural condition. But the free-standing individual of the natural condition is represented in social contract narratives as motivated only by the goal of self-interest in general. A person motivated to pursue only his or her own self-interest is not motivated to pursue any specific goal or move in any specific direction. From the admonition to be authentic alone, no specific concept of the good or ranking system or concept of excellence can be inferred. The same formalism also characterizes the civic ethics of autonomy. The civic ethics of autonomy—largely associated with Kantian styles of modernist liberalism—motivated citizens to achieve the normative civic standpoint of free and equal individuality by representing as an ideal a pure self-determination analogous to that of the autonomous, rational knower. Once again, the purely self-determining individual is conceived of only as an autonomous chooser. The actual content of the choice remains undetermined. From the admonition to be autonomous alone, no specific concept of the good or ranking system or concept of excellence can be inferred.

Thus, both the modernist civic ethics of authenticity and

autonomy were characterized by a peculiar formalism or lack of specific content. As moral ideals, they mandated not a particular way of life, but rather universal ways of choosing and living a particular way of life. This formalism was expressed in modernist liberal political theory in the doctrine of the priority of the right over the good. In different ways, both the civic ethics of authenticity and the civic ethics of autonomy embodied this doctrine. They were non-teleological: they mandated a particular *how* of action rather than a particular *why* or *end* of action. At the extreme, as we have seen, these moral ideals even called into question the value of all particularistic concepts of the good—affirming the priority of the right by calling attention to the contingent and arbitrary character of all particularistic and historically conditioned concepts of the good.

At the extreme, then, the moral ideals generated by modernist liberal civic culture represented the worst of both worlds. They required citizens to develop a skeptical attitude toward the values of the particular ethnic, class, and religious communities to which they belonged and to adopt as their primary stance in life the purely formal and vacuous identity of an authentic self or an autonomous chooser. A postmodern civic culture must take as its point of departure a rejection of this modernist concept of the priority of the right over the good. It must begin with the affirmation of the ideal of citizenship as a particularistic moral ideal capable of giving life particularistic content and direction. As a particularistic moral ideal, it is not a merely empty and formal mandating of a particular how of choice, but rather the mandating of a specific what (i.e., a specific life ideal, a specific concept of the good life). In short, a postmodern liberalism must take a teleological turn. It must reinterpret the modernist liberal doctrine of the priority of the right over the good in a way that both gives the notion of moral rightness specific ethical content and, at the same time, makes the affirmation of moral rightness compatible with respect for and the pursuit of particularistic cultural concepts of the good.

Thus, a postmodern civic culture must be defined at least by a rhetorical turn (i.e., a turn away from the universalism of the modernist rhetoric of pure theory), and by a teleological turn (i.e., a turn away from the formalism of the civic ethics of authenticity and autonomy). In his work since 1980, as summed up in his recent book, *Political Liberalism*,[2] John Rawls points the way toward a reinterpretation of liberal doctrine that is both rhetorical and teleological, although he himself moves along that way only so far. Let us now briefly examine how Rawls formulates and how far he takes the rhetorical and teleological turns toward a genuinely postmodern concept of liberal doctrine.

The rhetorical turn: from political theory to civic culture

In 1971, Rawls published *A Theory of Justice (TJ)*.[3] That book presented a theory of the principles of social justice, which he called "the theory of justice as fairness." Rawls began by assuming that reasonable human beings are capable of correctly evaluating the justice of particular social arrangements, even though they are often not able to provide a theoretical account of the criteria they apply in arriving at their evaluation. Further, Rawls believed that the intuitive judgments reasonable persons made regarding justice were frequently at odds with the judgments licensed by utilitarianism, the dominant academic theory of political morality at the time (in the 1950s and '60s). The fact that reasonable persons intuitively judged questions of social justice differently than mandated by utilitarianism constituted, for Rawls, a *prima facie* case that utilitarianism, as a theory of social justice, was untrue.

In *TJ*, Rawls set out to uncover, make explicit, and refine the principles of justice that he believed were operative in the moral intuitions of reasonable persons. A theory of justice would encompass, at least, a statement of those principles, along with an argument in their support. A correct theory of

---

[2] John Rawls, *Political Liberalism* (New York: Columbia University Press, 1993).

[3] John Rawls, *A Theory of Justice* (Cambridge, Mass.: Harvard University Press, 1971).

justice would be one whose principles yielded judgments that conformed to the moral intuitions of reasonable persons. This test for determining the truth of a theory of justice determined the methodology that Rawls adopted in *TJ*. The theory would be arrived at through engaging in a process of mutual adjustment between stated principles and the intuitive judgments of reasonable persons. When a state of reflective equilibrium between moral intuitions and stated principles had been achieved, the resulting principles would be established as the content of the true or correct concept of social justice. This true concept of social justice could then be applied or appealed to in disputed questions of political morality. This is roughly how Rawls conceived of his philosophical project in 1971.

For present purposes, the actual principles of justice that Rawls arrived at, in his 1971 inquiry, are less important than his concept of the theoretical enterprise itself, and how that concept has changed since then. Although Rawls now rejects this interpretation, there is no doubt that most readers of *TJ* understood the book to present a theory of the essence of political morality. If true, the theory of justice as fairness would state the criteria by which the justice or injustice of any political regime, existing at any place and time, are to be judged. In other words, using Rawls's later vocabulary, most readers interpreted *TJ* as offering a metaphysical, rather than a political concept of justice (i.e., a concept of justice claiming universal truth, known for its own sake). Admittedly, there are many passages in the book that support this interpretation. Even now, as I shall note later, Rawls himself has not yet completely broken free, at least, of a certain style of thought that supports a metaphysical interpretation of his work. Nevertheless, the book's central argument, as well as its peculiar methodology, resist this metaphysical interpretation, and point in the direction that Rawls has followed in his published writings since 1980.

This new direction was signaled most conclusively in 1985, when Rawls published an essay entitled, "Justice as Fairness: Political not Metaphysical."[4] In this essay, Rawls disassociated himself decisively from earlier metaphysical interpretations of

his project and offered a very different concept of it. His starting point remained the intuitive judgments of reasonable people regarding what is just and unjust. The subject matter for
analysis remained the implicit principles underlying those
judgments. But both starting point and subject matter were
reinterpreted by Rawls in such a way as to place his entire
inquiry within a radically new context, and to give the results
of that inquiry a radically different character and status.

In that 1985 article (whose content was largely incorporated later into his book, *Political Liberalism*) Rawls defined the
"reasonable people," whose intuitions provided the subject
matter and standards for the method of reflective equilibrium
as those persons whose self-understanding and moral standards had been shaped by the institutions and political culture of a modern constitutional democracy. The moral intuitions that serve as both data and control for his project were
thus no longer to be understood simply as the moral intuitions of reasonable people in general, without regard to any
particularistic or historically conditioned assumptions that
may influence them. On the contrary, the relevant moral intuitions were identified as precisely those that had been produced by an historically specific political culture: they were
identified as the moral intuitions specifically of those persons
who had been shaped by the civic culture of contemporary
liberal democracies and who, as a result, had in some degree
developed the intellectual and moral capacities proper to citizenship. Given this reinterpretation of the starting point of
Rawls's project, its subject matter and goals had to be reinterpreted accordingly. If the relevant data are the historically
conditioned intuitions of members of a specific type of political regime, then the principles underlying those intuitions are
no less historically conditioned. The theory of justice as fairness therefore cannot be understood as a statement of the
principles of justice as such, as a claim about the universal
essence of political morality, or as a revelation of the truth
about an objective moral order. Rather, the theory of justice

---

[4] John Rawls, "Justice as Fairness: Political not Metaphysical," *Philosophy and Public Affairs* 14 (1985).

as fairness seeks to articulate only those principles and assumptions actually operative in the intuitions of persons influenced by the public culture of modern constitutional democracies.

This 1985 essay marked a decisive shift in Rawls's philosophical project. One sign of this shift is his dropping of the word "theory." Rawls today speaks of offering not a theory of justice that claims to be true, but rather a concept of justice that claims to be reasonable.[5] Consider for a moment what might be implied (from the standpoint of modernist epistemology) by the very notion of a "theory" of justice. The notion of theory deriving from modernist philosophy is roughly understood to refer to a discourse that seeks to provide a uniquely satisfactory (as determined by logical considerations alone) explanation of the patterns actually observed in some field of data. The data are understood to be "givens." Their patterns are stable and they are logically independent of the theory explaining those patterns. A theory pertaining to a field of data continuously in a state of flux (i.e., showing no observable patterns) would have nothing to explain. A theory pertaining to a field of data whose patterns can be described only through the use of the theory could not be said to be a correct account of that field. The theory would then constitute its subject matter rather than provide a true explanation of it—the sort of relationship between theory and observation familiarly associated with the work of Thomas Kuhn and Paul Feyerabend.

Furthermore, the modernist notion of theory suggests that this discourse is undertaken from a purely impartial standpoint, one that aims at "getting it right" (i.e., arriving at the one true or correct understanding of its subject matter)— truth for its own sake. This notion of theory assumes that there is a "fact of the matter" and that the facts can and ought to be finally coercive with respect to both the theoretical discourse and its audience. The criteria for ranking rival theories, in terms of the degrees to which they give a satisfactory explanation of the data, must be determined by the rules of

---

[5] Rawls, *PL*, p. xx.

inductive and deductive logic alone. On the basis of purely logical considerations alone, then, if one particular theory, among all its competitors, offers the most satisfactory account of the facts, the theory can be affirmed as true whether any particular audience happens to affirm its truth or not.

In Rawls's original concept of his project, the theory of justice as fairness could plausibly be interpreted as a theory in roughly this sense. The field of data consisted in the set of intuitive judgments made by reasonable people regarding disputed questions of social justice. It assumed that these data were "given" independently of any particular theory of justice, and that the goal of every theory of political morality was to provide a satisfactory account of the patterns evinced in our intuitive moral judgments. But Rawls's revised concept of justice is clearly not a theory in this sense. Can there be a correct theory about the historically conditioned principles used by members of a specific type of historically conditioned community to decide disputed questions of political morality? In this case, the field of data itself is clearly unstable and subject to variation. The moral intuitions of the better citizens of constitutional democracies are not fixed once and for all, but can be changed through persuasion, and may even be influenced by Rawls's theoretical discourse itself or by the discussion it produces. This means that no theory-independent set of intuitional patterns or regularities exists about which a correct theory could be objectively "correct."

Moreover, a theoretical discourse is thought to aim at truth for its own sake. It assumes that there is a "fact of the matter," and the goal of the discourse is to get those facts right. A theoretical discourse is thus to be distinguished from discourse seeking to persuade, discourse that aims at producing a certain rhetorical effect upon its audience. A theory can be true whether or not any particular audience has been persuaded of its truth. But can the concept of justice as fairness, in the light of Rawls's 1985 reinterpretation of it as a political and not a metaphysical concept, be viewed as a theory in this sense? Could we affirm its truth, even if an audience made up of the most insightful citizens of constitutional democracies does not find it to be a persuasive account of the principles of justice? Would we be willing to say that the members of such an audience are mistaken about their own assumptions and intuitions, that they are victims of false consciousness? And what if the theory of justice as fairness not only were rejected by this audience, but also produced among its members such a negative reaction that they were led to embrace a new set of assumptions, and therefore a new pattern of intuitive judgments radically incompatible with it? Would we be willing to say that this change in the patterns of intuitive judgments, because it produces patterns different from those explained by the theory, shows that the audience has "fallen away" from the correct principles and its members are in need of reformation? In short, can there be anything that we would call a theory (i.e., in the traditional modernist sense) about a subject matter that the theory itself can decisively influence and that must win the actual adherence of an audience in order to be considered acceptable as a product of inquiry?

It seems obvious that, understanding the term "theory" in its modernist sense, Rawls quite properly no longer speaks of offering a theory of justice. Not only would the data (i.e., the moral intuitions of reasonable citizens of modern constitutional democracies) of any such "theory" be variable and historically conditioned, but the explicit goal of inquiry would be to win the acceptance of those reasonable citizens and not simply to arrive at a statement of what is the case. How are we to classify the status of Rawls's political concept of justice as fairness, then? A practical political proposal? An attempt to influence public judgment by proposing a set of principles that reasonable persons who disagree about matters of social justice might find acceptable as a means of settling disputes? This is the interpretation of his project that Rawls embraced in his 1985 article:

> Now suppose justice as fairness were to achieve its aim and a publicly acceptable political concept of justice is found. Then this concept provides a publicly recognized point of view from which all citizens can examine before one another whether or not their political and social institutions are just... It should be observed that, on this view, justification is not regarded simply as valid argument from list-

ed premises, even should these premises be true. Rather, justification is addressed to others who disagree with us, and therefore it must always proceed from some consensus, that is, from premises that we and others publicly recognize as true; or better, publicly recognize as acceptable to us for the purpose of establishing a working agreement on the fundamental questions of political justice.[6]

Thus, in 1985, although he himself didn't describe it in these terms (and, for that matter, no doubt still wouldn't), Rawls in effect reinterpreted his philosophical project as a project belonging to the cognitive realm of rhetoric. Traditionally, rhetorical reason defined its cognitive realm as the realm of *pistis*, or belief, as opposed to the cognitive realm claimed by philosophy, the realm of episteme or science. Belief, or *pistis*, is the state of being persuaded. To the extent that any discourse aims at producing belief (i.e., the uncoerced adherence of its intended audience), to that extent it belongs to the cognitive domain of rhetoric. This is the way it seems that Rawls, since 1985, has conceived of his inquiry into the principles of justice. His aim is no longer (if it ever was) to arrive at a timelessly true statement of the universal principles of social justice, but rather to offer a statement of the principles of justice that might win the uncoerced adherence of the reasonable citizens of a modern constitutional democracy. The principles of justice produced by Rawls's inquiry are to be judged cognitively not by the traditional standard identified with philosophy (i.e., the standard of timeless truth), but rather by the traditional standard identified with rhetoric (i.e., the standard consisting in the successful establishment of a body of uncoerced shared belief). This reinterpretation by Rawls of his philosophical project as a project whose goal is consensus and the adherence of a specific audience, then, I call his rhetorical turn. It is this rhetorical turn that constitutes the first defining mark and guiding maxim of postmodern liberalism.

There is no question that, at least since 1985, Rawls has adhered rigorously to this reinterpretation of his project as

---

[6] Rawls, "Political not Metaphysical," p. 229.

one offering a political, rather than a metaphysical concept of
justice and of liberal doctrine in general. However, there is
also no question that he has failed to adhere rigorously to the
full conceptual, stylistic, and methodological implications of
that reinterpretation. The rhetorical turn requires the abandonment of the modernist rhetoric of pure theory that characterized modernist liberal political theory. It requires that
the doctrines of liberalism be comprehended and analyzed in
terms of the categories proper to a rhetorical concept of
inquiry. Liberal doctrine, that is to say, must no longer present itself as a body of truth-claims about an audience-independent subject matter, presented by means of a purely theoretical discourse addressed to no one in particular. Rather, if
liberalism is to be conceived of consistently as a body of political (as opposed to metaphysical) doctrine, its proponents
must embrace explicitly an appropriately rhetorical understanding and analysis of its content. They must embrace fully
an analysis of the content of liberal doctrine in terms of the
rhetorical categories of speaker, audience, occasion and
intended rhetorical effect.

Rawls stops considerably short of this. This failure leads, in
the case of Rawls, to: (1) a certain abstractness or rhetorical
indeterminacy in his reconstruction of liberal doctrine, and
(2) a tendency to incorporate into that reconstruction far
more of the conceptual baggage of modernist liberal political
theory than is consistent with his project. These consequences
of Rawls's reluctance to embrace fully a consistently rhetorical
self-understanding and concept of his inquiry are instructive.
Let us briefly examine some of these consequences.

(1) First, consider the rhetorical indeterminacy that characterizes Rawls's post-metaphysical thinking and writing. Any
speech or discourse is rhetorically indeterminate when its
form and content offer no clear definition of the rhetorical
situation to which it is addressed (i.e., no clear definition of
its intended audience, its occasion, or the role adopted by the
speaker or writer). Speaking and writing are communicative
actions. Language has a pragmatic, or what Austin called an
illocutionary, dimension. Linguistic communication is not
merely a matter of transmitting meanings from one mind to

another. Speech achieves its communicative effects through its embedment in social and institutional contexts. Speech coordinates interaction within those contexts, and does so more effectively to the degree that particular speech acts make explicit, in one way or another, the sort of interactional effects their speakers intend. When a speaker intends a particular utterance, say, as a request, the standard way of making the pragmatic or illocutionary dimension of that utterance as explicit as possible is by labeling the utterance accordingly: "I hereby request that..." Speech or writing in which the illocutionary or pragmatic dimension of its content is sufficiently clear I call "rhetorically determinate" speech or discourse. Of course, in the case of most speech or writing, various features of context, style, and medium are sufficient to make the content rhetorically determinate.

Discourse governed by the rhetorical imperatives of modernist philosophy—the anti-rhetorical rhetoric of pure theory—represents a somewhat paradoxical instance of this. The rhetorical imperatives of modernist philosophy required any discourse claiming genuine cognitive status to be as rhetorically indeterminate as possible. Modernist philosophy sought to distinguish itself, as the superlatively cognitive or theoretical discourse, from other forms of literature whose success was measured by the capacity to affect audiences in certain ways. Literature governed by the intention to move or affect a specific audience in specific ways cannot be indifferent to the pragmatic or illocutionary dimension of speech. Such literature cannot afford to strip itself of any internalized reference to the rhetorical situation it addresses.

Modernist philosophy, on the other hand, claimed a superior cognitive status. As pure theory, philosophy claimed to be governed only by the intention of stating the timeless and audience-independent truth about a timeless and audience-independent reality. For any discourse to qualify as philosophical discourse, therefore, it had to exhibit a certain style, a style characterized above all by an absence of rhetorical adornment and an absence of any internalized reference to any specific rhetorical situation. Thus, paradoxically, modernist philosophical discourse defined and identified itself rhetorically by its own striving for rhetorical indeterminacy. I think most readers of Rawls's *TJ* would agree that the book was characterized by this sort of rhetorically indeterminate style. Whatever its message, stylistically it clearly aspired to meet the anti-rhetorical standards proper to purely theoretical discourse, in the modernist sense. Even if the book's content might be interpreted non-metaphysically (i.e., as offering something approaching a political, as opposed to a metaphysical concept of justice), its style was metaphysical through and through.

Rawls's *Political Liberalism (PL)* is characterized by the same rhetorical indeterminacy. But in this case the incongruity between the book's relatively post-metaphysical content and its quasi-metaphysical style is far more noticeable. It is as though Rawls, while rejecting modernist liberal political philosophy's claims to cognitive essentialism and universalism, nevertheless continues to speak in the voice of pure theory. For example, in *PL,* it seems indisputable that Rawls's project, at least in part, is one of political advocacy. He speaks in the voice of an active citizen who has entered the public sphere to propose for the consideration of his fellow citizens the concept of social justice he calls "justice as fairness." In *PL,* Rawls acknowledges that his proposed concept of justice is not to be measured by the cognitive standards of truth and falsity.[7] He claims only that it is a reasonable concept, one that deserves to win the support of reasonable citizens. Further, he seems to understand clearly that justice as fairness is only one of perhaps several other concepts of justice that reasonable citizens might consider endorsing—rival concepts that are equally consistent with a political interpretation of liberal doctrine and can claim equally to be drawn from ideas prevalent today in the public culture of constitutional democracies.[8] The most controversial element of Rawls's proposed concept of justice is the "difference principle." This principle states roughly that, to be considered just in a liberal democratic society, social and economic inequalities or differences must

---

[7] *PL,* p. xx.

[8] See, for example, p. 167.

provide the greatest benefit to the least advantaged of its members. Needless to say, the difference principle, viewed by some critics as amounting to an open invitation to unlimited statist intervention in the marketplace, conflicts with the moral intuitions of many reasonable citizens today.

As a political advocate, then, as an active citizen proposing a set of basic rules for social cooperation, Rawls continues to face a very tough sell. But, in *PL*, does Rawls actually speak in the voice of a political advocate? Does he define and directly address the issues raised by the controversy? Does he present arguments that really engage, even at the most general and abstract levels, the sort of objections that might be raised against justice as fairness? Is there any evidence that he even understands his proposed concept as a practical political matter at all—as a proposal that might at some point have to be worked out concretely in actual political activity, in actual dialogue with the various warring factions of some particular flesh-and-blood liberal democracy? Hardly. What we find instead, in *PL*, is the voice of a Kantian constructivist, concerned with the "procedure of construction" by which a political concept of justice is put together, and offering a "family of concepts" to be used in that procedure.[9] But the outcome of a procedure of construction is rhetorically very different from a proposal for a concept of justice. A Kantian constructivist is rhetorically very different, in persona, from an advocate of a controversial political agenda. It is almost as if Rawls really believed that, by showing justice as fairness to be the outcome of a procedure of conceptual construction, the opponents of the difference principle would abandon their opposition and all reasonable citizens would embrace it. It is almost as if Rawls really believed that partisans of rival concepts of justice could not present their own proposed concepts as the products of a similar procedure of construction, based upon their own families of favored concepts drawn from the public culture of contemporary liberal democracies.

Thus, while it seems to me indisputable that Rawls, in the aftermath of his rhetorical turn, must view his role at least par-

---

[9] See *PL*, p. 43.

tially as that of a political advocate seeking to convince fellow
citizens of the superior reasonableness of his proposed concept of justice, he nevertheless, in *PL,* refuses to adopt the
appropriate rhetorical voice and persona. He continues to
speak as though the process of adopting basic rules for social
cooperation is a process of conceptual derivation, rather than
an actual political process aimed at achieving an overlapping
consensus among diverse social, economic, and cultural
groups. Rawls's abstract and rhetorically indeterminate attitude toward the subject matter is expressed even grammatical-
ly. *PL* is written in a peculiar style, with abstract nouns pre-
dominating as agents and the passive voice given an
overwhelming presence. Justice as fairness "adopts" an idea of
social cooperation, a family of concepts has been "worked
up," citizens "are viewed" as free and equal, ideas "are introduced," a principle of justice "is constructed." Given this predominance of the passive voice and, when the active voice
appears at all, the predominance of abstract nouns as agents,
the reader of *PL* not only loses any sense of political advocacy,
but any sense of authorial agency as well. It seems that political concepts simply unfold, that principles construct themselves, and that the reader is little more than a witness to these
magical and anonymous conceptual processes. I believe that
this is more than a mere stylistic quirk. I believe that Rawls's
refusal to assume explicitly the rhetorical voice and role proper to political advocacy is itself a rhetorical appeal, an effort to
retain the cultural authority of the modernist cognitive ideal
of pure theory, while at the same time denying that ideal conceptually. It is ironic that, in *PL,* the anti-rhetorical cognitive
ideal of the Enlightenment lives on today as little more than a
linguistic trick.

Whether or not Rawls is willing to adopt fully the voice
and persona of political advocacy, then, his project in its post-
metaphysical phase must in part be conceived of in those
terms. But, in PL, that aspect of his project takes a back seat to
another aspect. If Rawls as an advocate of the principles of justice as fairness assumes, at least implicitly, the role of active
citizen, in *PL* Rawls pursues a related but nevertheless, in
rhetorical terms, quite different sort of project, one that in

fact places him in a quite different role with respect to his audience. In *PL*, Rawls speaks primarily as a reflective citizen whose aim is to offer his fellow citizens new and better ways to think about liberal democratic citizenship, and about the ideas and ideals of liberal democracy. In other words, PL is much less an attempt to sell justice as fairness than it is a contribution to civic culture. Of course, it is not as if these two different rhetorical projects are totally unrelated. After all, Rawls's analysis of the nature of liberal democratic ideals and citizenship can generate *topoi,* to be drawn upon in the invention of arguments advocating public acceptance of his favored concept of justice. Nevertheless, the criteria of success proper to these two rhetorical projects are quite different. Rawls's reflections on the nature of liberal democratic citizenship and the epistemological status of liberal doctrine may well serve to enlighten the self-understanding and the political practice of his fellow citizens—even if citizens unanimously disagree with the concept of justice that, in the context of advocacy, he might use those reflections to support.

Once again, however, Rawls's continuing commitment to the anti-rhetorical ideals of modernist philosophical discourse prevents him from explicitly assuming the role and voice proper to the project of public enlightenment. He seems to conflate completely the two very different projects of political advocacy and public enlightenment—or, rather, to remain entirely innocent of any such distinction, and to view the entire "family of concepts" that he offers as belonging to one single project aimed at the conceptual construction of a set of principles of justice. Unfortunately, this general obliviousness to the rhetorical or illocutionary dimension of his inquiry places limits on the contribution that he makes toward the reconstruction of contemporary liberal democratic civic culture.

This unmindfulness of the illocutionary dimension of his inquiry is not complete. He does at times seem to have some limited sense of the rhetorical distinctness of his project of public enlightenment. He begins *PL* with a reference to the rhetorical occasion of his inquiry. He points out that basic reassessments and reinterpretations of liberal democratic ideas and ideals are necessary when we are faced with deep

conflicts of cultural and political values.[10] Indeed, he identifies
one specific conflict to which his reflections are addressed—
the conflict within modernist liberalism between partisans of
the "liberties of the moderns" and partisans of the "liberties
of the ancients"—the conflict between concepts of liberal
democratic citizenship that give precedence to the doctrine of
negative freedom (today identified largely with "con-
servatives"), and those that give precedence to the doctrine of
positive freedom (today identified largely with "liberals").[11]
The conflict Rawls identifies has been, and continues to be, a
real and fundamental one. But even more significant today is
a second cultural conflict that has become interwoven with
the first—namely, the conflict between the culturally "progressive" and the culturally "orthodox."[12] These two conflicts
together, in their complex relationship to one another, seem
to constitute the rhetorical occasion that Rawls addresses in
his role as reflective citizen, or as critic and reformer of civic
culture.

To the extent that Rawls in *PL* addresses the first conflict
at all (i.e., the conflict between the partisans of "negative freedom" and the partisans of "positive freedom"), he seems to
view these opposed concepts of freedom only as pure theories, as elements of comprehensive or metaphysical versions of
liberal doctrine associated with Locke or Mill, in the case of
negative freedom, and Rousseau or Kant, in the case of positive freedom. Rawls's strategy with respect to these two conflicting metaphysical concepts of freedom is basically to distance himself from both, and to insist that liberalism must be
understood to be a political doctrine, a doctrine that remains
neutral with respect to all metaphysical questions about the
essence of human liberty. But as a response addressed to the
issues raised for civic culture by these two opposed concepts
of liberty, Rawls's response is inadequate. By viewing these two

---

[10] Rawls, *PL,* p. 44.

[11] Rawls, *PL,* p. 5.

[12] For a discussion of this new conflict and its relationship to previous
ideological conflicts, see James Davison Hunter, *Culture Wars: The Struggle to
Define America* (New York: Basic Books, 1991).

opposed concepts of liberty merely as philosophical theories, without regard to their role they played in modernist liberal civic culture, Rawls fails to grasp their full significance for his project of liberal reconstruction.

The concept of freedom as "negative freedom" provided the basis of what I have called the civic ethics of authenticity. The concept of freedom as "positive freedom" provided the basis of what I have called the civic ethics of autonomy. In modernist civic culture, both concepts of freedom, whatever other ideological roles they played as philosophical "theories,"[13] provided important motivational resources for the cultivation of civic identities and values. As moral ideals, there were not merely theories adhered to by one particular community among others—say, the community of metaphysical liberals. Rather, they were addressed to members of all particularistic cultural communities equally, and provided countervailing weight in support of civic values against the pull of particularistic world views. The task of any critic or would-be reformer of contemporary civic culture is, at least, to point in the direction of possible new motivational resources to replace those formerly provided by the ethical ideals of authenticity and autonomy. Rawls not only fails to do this, but, in his role of reflective citizen, fails even to grasp the issue itself.

To the extent that Rawls in *PL* addresses the second conflict at all (i.e., the current culture war between the "progressive" and the "orthodox"), he does so only tangentially, even though this conflict seems to be the one to which his reconstruction of liberal doctrine is most relevant. Rawls begins *PL* with a statement of the fundamental question to which the book is addressed: "How is it possible for there to exist over time a just and stable society of free and equal citizens, who remain profoundly divided by reasonable religious, philosophical and moral doctrines?"[14] His strategy, as he puts it, is to apply the principle of toleration to philosophy itself.[15] This

---

[13] With concepts of negative freedom, for example, providing justification for laissez-faire capitalism and concepts of positive freedom providing justification of state intervention in markets.

suggests that philosophy was previously not subject to this principle, that modernist liberal political philosophy conceived of liberal doctrine as dogmatically presupposing the truth of now controversial metaphysical theories. These theories are now controversial because affirmation of their claims to truth seems to require rejection of religious beliefs and moral concepts dear to the hearts of many citizens. This is the sort of complaint against liberalism that the culturally "orthodox" have long made against the culturally "progressive" or "liberal." Implied in Rawls's attempt to apply the principle of toleration to philosophy itself, then, seems to be a recognition of and a response to the conflict between the "progressive" and the "orthodox." Rawls's reconstruction of liberalism aims at driving a wedge between liberal moral ideals and controversial modernist metaphysical commitments, thereby removing this source of political conflict and promoting the development of a new form of liberal civic culture more hospitable to cultural difference. This is the import of what I have called Rawls's rhetorical turn.

Unfortunately, Rawls's reluctance to embrace fully the implications of his application of the principle of toleration to philosophy itself limits his success in achieving this goal. Even though *PL* seems to be inspired by the project of recasting liberal doctrine in such a way as to make it compatible with a real cultural pluralism, throughout the book Rawls adopts the voice and persona, not of a reflective citizen making a contribution to the reconstruction of liberal civic culture, but rather of a Kantian constructivist concerned with setting forth a rhetorically undifferentiated "family of concepts" from which the principles of justice as fairness can be derived. In fact, Rawls's formulation of the fundamental question the book addresses is stated in such a way that it invites a Kantian misinterpretation of the project. When Rawls asks "how is it possible" for there to exist a genuinely pluralistic liberal democratic society, this could be construed as some sort of quasi-transcendental question about the conditions of such a

---

[14] Rawls, *PL*, p. 4.
[15] Rawls, *PL*, p. 154.

society's possibility (i.e., about the ideas, the inevitable presuppositions we must accept if such a society is to be established or fully realized).

In fact, where Rawls continues to identify his approach as a form of "Kantian constructivism," he remains largely under the influence of this sort of misinterpretation of his project. But the question about the possibility of a pluralistic liberal democratic society should be interpreted in a very different way. The question is not one about how democratic pluralism is possible in general, but about whether it is possible for *us* — that is, whether it is possible for us, as late twentieth-century Americans or, at most, for us as citizens of existing North Atlantic liberal democracies, to reconceive and reconstitute liberal democratic civil society and civic culture in such as way as to make the civic ideals of freedom and equality compatible with a strong affirmation of cultural pluralism. When the question of the possibility of liberal democratic pluralism is understood in this way, as a matter requiring public reflection in very specific historical and cultural circumstances, then all the subtle methodological questions surrounding the adaptation of Kantian constructivism to the "construction" of a concept of political justice simply lose their relevance. There are places in *PL* where this sort of interpretation of the question does in fact shine through, and momentarily brightens the otherwise rather dreary and austere Kantian construction project. For example, at one point Rawls properly characterizes his notion of the original position not just as a "device of representation" in a "procedure of construction," but, far more importantly, as a heuristic device, a resource for civic education, a means of public reflection and self-clarification.[16] This is the voice that should have prevailed in *PL*. This is the voice that is alone consistent with Rawls's rhetorical turn, with his application of the principle of tolerance to philosophy itself.

(2) Thus, Rawls's reluctance to adopt fully a rhetorical concept and analysis of his inquiry limits his effectiveness, both as a political advocate of a particular concept of justice and as a contributor to the contemporary reconstruction of

---

[16] Rawls, *PL,* p. 26.

liberal democratic civic culture. But this reluctance also places limits on the scope and depth of his rethinking of classical liberal doctrines. As we have noted, Rawls wishes to make liberal democracy more hospitable to cultural difference by offering an interpretation of liberal doctrine and a liberal concept of justice stripped of the truth claims and metaphysical commitments associated with modernist forms of liberal political theory—truth claims and metaphysical commitments that can conflict with religious beliefs and moral ideals that are adhered to by members of particularistic cultural communities within liberal society. Modernist liberal political theory grounded liberal political principles and moral ideals in totalizing and universalistic philosophical systems, making it seem that acceptance of those principles and ideals demanded acceptance of some particular comprehensive view of the world.

In *PL*, Rawls wants to offer a version of liberalism that avoids any such suggestion, one that clearly identifies liberal doctrine as a set of ideas addressing only a part and not the whole of life, a set of ideas whose validity extends only as far as the living consensus that supports it. In his concept and execution of this project, Rawls has cleared the path that all postmodern liberal political philosophy must take. My only criticism is that he himself takes that path not nearly far enough. Rawls, in his effort to free liberal principles and ideals from their embedment in the conceptual and ideological matrix of modernist philosophy, remains all too faithful, not only to the rhetorically indeterminate style and voice of modernist philosophy, but also to attenuated versions of some of its basic metaphysical assumptions.

The continuing operative presence of those modernist assumptions are nowhere more evident than in Rawls's concepts of reason and rationality. First, fully operative in *PL* is a standard version of the characteristically modernist prejudice against rhetoric: "Now all ways of reasoning...must acknowledge certain common elements: the concept of judgment, principles of inference, and rules of evidence, and much else otherwise they would not be ways of reasoning but perhaps rhetoric or means of persuasion. We are concerned with reason, not simply with discourse."[17] Here Rawls contrasts rhetoric with reasoning in a way completely consistent with the modernist anti-rhetorical rhetoric of pure theory. He identifies rhetoric with means of persuasion that exclude reasoning, that exclude logical judgment, principles of inference, and rules of evidence. In this sort of contrast, frequently encountered in everyday speech, rhetoric is identified only with the most blatant and crass appeals to emotion and interest for the sake of achieving impact on an audience (i.e., rhetoric is pretty much identified with sophistry, or at least salesmanship). Even rhetoric's greatest enemy, Plato, knew better than this.

Such a concept of rhetoric shows little familiarity with the traditions of classical rhetoric. For example, of the three traditional means of persuasion in Aristotelian rhetorical teaching—*logos, ethos* and *pathos—logos,* or argumentative reason, is given the greatest possible weight. Where rhetorical teaching does in fact differ from the concepts of reason found in modernist foundationalist philosophy is in its awareness of reasoning as a dialogical activity, even when it is a silent and solitary activity. The rhetorical tradition always viewed judgments, inferences and the critical examination of evidence as addressed to an audience, even when that audience is not present. Rawls's adoption of this characteristically modernist way of contrasting reasoning and rhetorical discourse naturally inclines him toward the acceptance of characteristically modernist monological and formalist concepts of reason. Given that this modernist assessment of rhetoric is taken over by Rawls without question, his reluctance to embrace fully and explicitly his own rhetorical turn is little wonder.

This inclination to conceive of reasoning and rationality in modernist terms puts definite limits on Rawls's project of rethinking liberal doctrine in non-metaphysical terms. As we have noted, the significance of the rhetorical turn in liberal political philosophy lies in its contribution to the intelligibility of liberal doctrine and of the moral ideal of liberal democratic citizenship. Recall that a liberal democratic civic culture

---

[17] Rawls, *PL,* p. 220.

must provide resources to perform two related tasks. It must provide discourses, narratives, and representations that: (1) make the normative standpoint of liberal democratic citizenship intelligible to citizens, and (2) motivate citizens to cultivate civic identities and values. Rawls's rhetorical turn (i.e., his project of reinterpreting liberalism as a political doctrine, as opposed to a metaphysical doctrine) opens the way to a new understanding of the normative standpoint of citizenship, one that is far more consistent with our contemporary awareness of the indispensable role played by particularistic forms of culture in the production and support of civic identities and civic values. A rhetorical concept of reason always keeps clearly in view the cultural or dialogical dimension of rationality. It is not inclined to place critical reasoning and persuasive discourse in radical opposition to one another. Because a rhetorical concept of reason views critical reasoning as an activity that is always culturally and historically situated, it is not inclined to view as rationally defective the particularistic cultural supports of civic values—such as religious belief—and it is not inclined to ignore the actual particularistic cultural processes by which civic identities are produced and reproduced. Unfortunately, largely because of Rawls's continuing attachment to modernist monological concepts of reason, what we find in *PR* is the complete absence of any useful account of the ways in which civic values actually have been or can, in the future, be culturally produced. What is missing in *PR*, in other words, is the very concept of what I have called a civic culture. When Rawls refers, as he often does, to the public culture of a liberal democracy, he conceives of it as little more than a repository of ideas to be used in projects of conceptual construction.

This lack of the very concept of an effectively countervailing civic culture places *PR* squarely within the tradition of modernist liberal political theory. As I observed in chapter 1, modernist liberal political theory attributed to the normative standpoint of liberal democratic citizenship both an anthropological and a metaphysical priority. In different ways, both Lockean and Kantian styles of liberal theory made the standpoint of the citizen, the standpoint of free and equal individuality, appear to be the natural and essential human standpoint. Further, given the links between modernist political theory and foundationalist epistemology, both Lockean and Kantian liberals, in different ways linked the normative standpoint of citizenship with the modernist principle of the autonomy of reason, viewing a capacity for autonomous rationality as the universally distinguishing mark of the human. The result of this attribution of anthropological and metaphysical priority to civic identity and civic values was the systematic disregard of the role of particularistic cultural forms in their production. Modernist liberal political theory tended to regard the standpoint of free and equal individuality as a given. Where no evidence of the operation of this standpoint was found, modernist liberals viewed its absence as something to be explained, usually by political suppression or by a lack of complete civilization.

Rawls, in *PL*, perpetuates this characteristically modernist disregard of the particularistic cultural supports required for liberal democracy. Of course Rawls, in the wake of his rhetorical turn, would reject any attribution of metaphysical priority to the normative standpoint of citizenship. But the peculiarities of his favored method of Kantian constructivism allow him to grant civic identity and civic values a certain methodological priority that has virtually the identical impact. Kant himself, the original Kantian constructivist, derived his own concept of the principle of morality from ideas that he understood to be pervasively operative in, and essential to, all rational beings. Kant was a metaphysical liberal. Rawls, in his own version of Kantian constructivism, draws the ideas he uses in his "procedure of construction" from the prevailing public culture of modern liberal democracies. Among those ideas he finds a certain concept of personhood, concepts of the moral powers that distinguish persons from non-persons and concepts of the reasonable and the rational that are associated with those powers. While Rawls makes no claim that any of these concepts are grounded in the nature of things, his "procedure of construction" allows him to treat these concepts as if they were.

In his construction of a concept of civic justice, Rawls

starts off simply by attributing to real flesh-and-blood human beings the moral and intellectual capacities specified by the concept of political personhood he has discovered in the public culture. While he is not thereby committed to any metaphysical view of human nature, he is thereby licensed by his constructivist method to treat those intellectual and moral capacities proper to political personhood simply as givens, as if they were in fact essentially human faculties in the metaphysical sense. So, throughout *PL*, reasonableness and rationality, the capacities for a sense of liberal justice and for the pursuit of a particularistic concept of the good, simply "are attributed" to citizens. Rawls does not ask how they got there. He does not ask how they can be produced or maintained. In short, Rawls's method of Kantian constructivism lends itself, no less than did the methods and assumptions of modernist metaphysical liberals, to the same disregard of the role of particularistic forms of culture in the production of civic identities and values.

Rawls's continued attachment to modernist concepts of reason and rationality impedes, in an additional way, his effort to reconstruct liberal doctrine in non-metaphysical terms. Rawls himself traces his own distinction between the reasonable and the rational to Kant's distinction between the categorical and hypothetical imperatives and, therefore, to a Kantian concept of practical reason.[18] Rawls defines reasonableness as a capacity to propose and act in accordance with fair terms of cooperation. He defines rationality as a capacity to define and act in accordance with a set of priorities governed by an overall concept of the good.[19] However, Rawls's readiness to assimilate his concepts of the reasonable and the rational (i.e., his concepts of the intellectual and moral capacities proper to liberal democratic citizenship) to a Kantian concept of practical reason betrays his own project. Kantian concepts of both theoretical and practical reason are notoriously formalist in nature. They draw a radical distinction between form and content, between the universally valid logical patterns of

---

[18] Rawls, *PL*, p. 49.
[19] Rawls, *PL*, pp. 50–51.

reasoning and the particular subject matter reasoned about. For Kant, the principles of theoretical and practical reason are applied to particular content—representations and actions—but those principles themselves remain external to all historically conditioned content, grounded in the universal faculty of human reason.

Rawls falls into this same sort of formalism. For example, in his distinction between reasonable comprehensive doctrines (i.e., those totalizing particularistic world views and moral ideals that are judged to be consistent with a liberal social order) and unreasonable comprehensive doctrines, Rawls defines reasonable comprehensive doctrines in characteristically Kantian formalist terms. A reasonable comprehensive doctrine is one that uses both theoretical and practical reason (i.e., makes both truth claims and moral demands that are universal in logical form) and that draws upon a tradition of doctrine.[20] The problem with this definition of what constitutes a reasonable comprehensive doctrine is the same problem that afflicts Rawls's concept of the reasonable in general—namely, it provides no guidance at all when applied to particular cases. Virtually any comprehensive doctrine can be construed and articulated so as to conform to the definition Rawls offers, just as, with a little ingenuity, any action can be construed and described so as to conform to Kant's categorical imperative. But that doesn't mean that every comprehensive doctrine meeting these formal requirements is actually consistent with the proposal and acceptance of fair terms of cooperation (i.e., is actually consistent with participation in a liberal social order). This means that reasonableness (i.e., the capacity of the citizen to act in accordance with the principles of liberal justice) cannot be properly understood as a capacity merely to act in accordance with a set of formal rules or to meet certain formal requirements. More is involved in what Rawls calls reasonableness than an exercise or application of Kantian theoretical and practical reason.

Reasonableness—the capacity for liberal democratic citizenship—is a capacity that involves transformation of content,

---

[20] Rawls, *PL,* p. 59.

whether the content in question be the concrete self-understanding or identity of an individual, or the doctrines and practices specific to a particularistic cultural community. This is what I mean by "transformation of content." The citizens of a liberal democracy are first, and always remain, members of particular class, ethnic, and religious communities. Their identities are shaped by the ranking systems, virtue concepts, and standards of excellence transmitted by the cultural traditions embodied in those communities. The first and primary identity of any citizen is thus what I have called a communitarian identity. This is the identity that must be transformed in the process of developing a civic identity. The normative standpoint of citizenship stands in a relationship of tension with the standpoint proper to membership in a particularistic cultural community. To achieve citizenship in the full cultural sense, a person must develop a capacity to adopt, cultivate, and act from both of these opposing standpoints. The development of this capacity requires a transformation, a radical revision of the self-understanding associated with communitarian identity. It requires no less than a fundamental rethinking and reinterpretation of the doctrinal content and practices proper to the cultural traditions supportive of communitarian identities. Such transformations cannot in principle be understood as a matter of meeting the formal requirements of Kantian theoretical and practical reason.

In chapter 4, I will argue that this transformation of content is produced by the development and cultivation of linguistic and moral capacities that are not conceived of by modernist philosophy as capacities for reasoning at all. I will argue that what Rawls calls reasonableness is a capacity that can be produced only through the exercise of certain forms of narrative imagination and self-understanding.

The point here is that, due to his continuing attachment to modernist, and specifically Kantian, concepts of reason and rationality, Rawls can carry out his reconstruction of liberal doctrine in non-metaphysical terms only so far. It seems that Rawls simply cannot free himself from excessively formalist and quasi-transcendental modes of thought. The project of inventing a postmodern civic culture requires a far more consistent and complete execution of the rhetorical turn that Rawls gives us in *PL*.

The teleological turn: citizenship as highest-order interest

If Rawls's continuing attachment to modernist concepts of reason and rationality has the effect of limiting the success of the project he undertakes in *PL,* it also imposes a further and perhaps even more significant cost. Rawls sets out to free liberalism, as a moral ideal, from its associations with any comprehensive doctrine or totalizing world view. Liberal ideals of freedom and equality need no longer be justified by demonstrations deriving them from pure reason or the natural condition. But Rawls, in conformity with the spirit if not with the letter of the modernist principle of the autonomy of reason, nevertheless seeks to derive liberal moral ideals from a freestanding "procedure of construction" that tells us nothing about the countervailing cultural processes that are actually needed to create and support civic identities and values. As Rawls carries out, or at least talks us through, this "procedure of construction" in *PL,* what I find notably lacking is any sense of the pathos of liberal democratic citizenship as a form of life, any sense of how liberal moral ideals could ever be or become objects of impassioned aspiration. The moral of this observation is that Kantian constructivism seems not to be the method of choice for an inquiry seeking to understand and to communicate how attainment of a capacity for reasonableness—a capacity for citizenship in the full cultural sense—can ever actually become, for someone, a good worth seeking for its own sake.,

The issue I am raising here speaks to the second major task that any liberal democratic civic culture must perform: it must provide resources for motivating persons who enjoy the legal status of citizens, or nominal citizenship, to develop the capacities proper to full cultural citizenship. What I have called the "rhetorical turn" in postmodern liberal political

philosophy speaks to matters of intelligibility. Citizens cannot
aspire to the realization of ideals they don't understand. The
rhetorical turn opens the way to a new understanding of the
moral ideal of citizenship, one no longer encumbered by
analogies and metaphors drawn from now discredited traditions of modernist epistemology and metaphysics. But the
issue of motivation remains. Once we have gained a new
understanding of the moral ideal of citizenship, one no
longer burdened by the multitude of confusions produced by
modernist liberal political theory, we still must generate from
this new understanding resources for motivating citizens to
pursue realization of that moral ideal. What sort of motivational resources might be offered by a post-metaphysical interpretation of liberal doctrine?

Needless to say, Rawls does not himself pose the question
in these terms. Nevertheless, his writings since 1980 do suggest, I believe, something like the beginnings of an answer to
it. In order to appreciate the novelty and to grasp the promise
of what we might take as Rawls's response to the question of
motivation, we must keep in mind the general features of the
characteristic way this issue was addressed by modernist liberalism. As we noted in chapter 1, modernist liberal political
theory generated two primary motivational visions of the normative standpoint of citizenship—what I have called the civic
ethics of authenticity, and the civic ethics of autonomy. These
two civic moral ideals must be distinguished carefully from
the sort of moral ideals generated by particularistic cultural
world views—or, what we might call communitarian moral
ideals. These modernist civic moral ideals differed from communitarian moral ideals in two noteworthy ways—first, in the
way that all civic moral ideals differ from communitarian
moral ideals (i.e., by virtue of the very different cultural tasks
civic and communitarian moral ideals perform), and second,
by virtue of the specific historical content and character of
modernist civic moral ideals. Let us examine these differences
briefly.

First, modernist civic moral ideals must be distinguished
from communitarian moral ideals in general because, like all
civic moral ideals, they had a very different sort of cultural

task to perform. The task of a civic moral ideal is to present the normative standpoint of citizenship—the standpoint of free and equal individuality—as an ideal worthy of realization, an object of desire worthy of attainment. This is a tougher sell than it might seem. Liberal democratic civic culture is always a countervailing culture. It is addressed to citizens who have already been shaped in their desire and self-understanding by the moral standards of the particularistic cultural communities to which they belong. The inculcation of communitarian moral ideals begins virtually at birth, in the context of family life. Because families generally belong to larger ethnic, class, and religious communities, the values and world views proper to those communities are transmitted by the earliest processes of socialization. They are learned along with the learning of a first language and begin to shape desire, feeling, and self-understanding long before powers of critical reflection develop. By comparison, civic educational processes generally begin to be felt (if at all) relatively late. The language associated with civic moral ideals is always a second moral language and, as is always the case in the learning of a second language (unlike the learning of a first language), the effort involved in learning it requires special justification.

Thus, civic moral ideals are a tough sell because they always address an audience previously and continuously shaped by diverse and conflicting communitarian moral ideals. But they are a tough sell for a more important reason as well. Civic moral ideals are not designed to replace communitarian moral ideals. The process of adopting and internalizing civic moral ideals is not a process of conversion from one totalizing concept of the good life to another. Rather, civic identity exists only as a modification of communitarian identity. The secondary moral language associated with civic moral ideals is parasitic upon the primary moral language associated with communitarian moral ideals. The secondary moral language presupposes and remains dependent upon the primary, but renders that primary moral language richer, more complex, and more ambiguous. Full attainment of a civic identity requires the adoption of a standpoint and a set of norms that remain in a more or less permanent state of tension and conflict with the standpoint and values proper to communitarian moral ideals. For liberals, this state of tension and conflict is good. Explaining to non-liberals why it is good is something else.

Civic moral ideals are not designed to replace communitarian moral ideals because the normative standpoint and moral language proper to citizenship pertains only to membership and participation in the public sphere of a liberal democratic political community, a community that encompasses a multiplicity of diverse cultural communities. Such a political community comes into existence in order to achieve and maintain the conditions for a just and free pursuit of happiness. It would be pointless for such a civic community to come into existence only then to force upon its members a particular ideal of happiness. A liberal democracy leaves that question largely undecided. It does not require its members to pursue any specific totalizing concept of the good life. On the other hand, the opposite is true in the case of particularistic cultural communities. They are defined by a global way of life, governed by an encompassing concept of the good, united by a common sense of what is important in life and what is not. Their traditions of belief and practice provide an interpretive framework within which the fundamental issues of human life—sex, friendship, work, suffering, sin, death and salvation—are given specific order and meaning. From the viewpoint of the civic community, such cultural communities exist in order to nurture, direct and support the pursuit of happiness. Such communities generate moral ideals, ranking systems, hierarchies, virtue concepts and standards of excellence that shape and order human desire. It is always to an audience whose desire and self-understanding has previously been and is continuously being shaped by such communities that civic moral ideals must persuasively speak. The message that they must successfully deliver is not an easy one either to hear or to accept.

The members of particular ethnic, class, and religious communities are first of all, say, French, bourgeois, and Catholic. Such communitarian identities are inseparable from the communitarian moral ideals and local traditions that have produced them. The moral language proper to such identities and moral ideals is teleological (i.e., it defines the most basic and encompassing perspective of life as a field of aspiration, in terms of a hierarchy of ends). It assigns meaning and rank to human qualities and actions by referring these to a final good. This moral language provides the vocabulary and generates the descriptions that guide everyday life. Civic identities and civic moral ideals differ above all in this respect. The civic community exists in order to secure the conditions for a just and free pursuit of happiness. The moral language associated with civic moral ideals is a moral language that provides the vocabulary and generates the descriptions appropriate to this political purpose. It is the moral language proper to the public sphere of a liberal democracy. Within the public sphere, citizens, who are otherwise members of particularistic cultural communities, meet and cooperate in order to realize and maintain the conditions for a just and free pursuit of happiness. As participants in the liberal democratic public sphere, citizens must not understand themselves primarily as French, bourgeois, and Catholic (or whatever), but rather as free and equal individuals. In order to become citizens who are qualified to participate in the public sphere, and to act positively to achieve the goals proper to it, they must learn to treat themselves and one another as free and equal individuals (i.e., as persons whose identity and rank is not wholly, exhaustively, or finally determined by identities and ranks assigned to them within particularistic cultural communities). The task of civic moral ideals is to provide the motivational resources that nurture, direct, and support this civic transformation of desire and self-understanding.

As we have noted, this is a large order. The dispositions and attitudes that a civic moral ideal must nurture and support require of citizens a complex moral, intellectual, and linguistic balancing act. While affirming and remaining deeply committed to their communitarian identities and moral ideals, they must be able to externalize or put aside those identities and ideals sufficiently to speak to, respect, and act in concert with fellow citizens whose communitarian identities and ideals differ greatly from theirs. Attainment of this capacity to put aside, or to unplug, the primary moral language and moral identity that give meaning and direction to everyday life is an extraordinary moral and linguistic accomplishment. The struggle to achieve the insight and judgment necessary to develop this capacity fully is fraught with danger and difficulty. This struggle is the source of the moral pathos of citizenship. The rhetorical task of a civic moral ideal is to produce in citizens a desire for this accomplishment strong enough to permit them to persevere in this struggle.

Second, modernist liberal civic moral ideals—assigned this task proper to any civic moral ideal—naturally possessed a character very different from communitarian moral ideals. Civic moral ideals serve in the cultural production of free and equal individuality. Accordingly, both the civic ethics of authenticity and the civic ethics of autonomy were silent on the question of what sort of happiness to pursue or what the nature of the good life ultimately is. Both mandated only that happiness be pursued in a certain way—namely, as a pursuit whose object was freely chosen by the individual. Communitarian moral ideals, identities, and concepts of the good life are ordinarily not first perceived as objects of choice. Ordinarily, they are understood as ways of being rather than as matters of choice. The communitarian identity of a person is simply who he or she is. The communitarian world view simply describes the world, as such. The moral language associated with a particular communitarian moral ideal is simply identified with the language, as such, that is spoken by the community.

Full cultural citizenship, however, requires the introduction of difference in all these spheres. It requires persons to develop the capacity to make a distinction between communitarian and civic identities, between their particularistic cultural world view and the world as such, between the primary moral language that they speak and the language that they share with citizens who speak different primary moral languages. But the capacity to perceive and apply these distinctions does not amount to the adoption of a new concept of the good or a new comprehensive world view. Accordingly, neither the civic ethics of authenticity nor the civic ethics of autonomy mandated acceptance of a specific concept of the good. What they did mandate was the development of a capacity to speak a primary moral language from a standpoint external to every primary moral language—the standpoint of the free individual, the standpoint of a speaker capable of viewing every primary moral language as if it were a freely chosen second language.

This general feature of all civic moral ideals accounts, in part, for the peculiarly abstract and reflective character of the civic ethics of authenticity and autonomy. The civic ethics of authenticity required of its followers not the choice of a specific concept of the good, but rather a choice of a concept of the good that conformed to their own intrinsic individual natures or selves. This promoted, of course, a belief in the existence of an intrinsic individual nature or self, and encouraged the pursuit of its discovery. In the same way, the civic ethics of autonomy required of its followers not the choice of a specific concept of the good, but rather a choice of a concept of the good whose pursuit could be rendered consistent with the principles or rules inherent in pure theoretical and practical reason. This promoted, of course, a belief in the existence of such universal human faculties, and encouraged attempts to discover their principles.

At this point, we begin to bring into view what made the civic ethics of authenticity and autonomy distinctive, and distinctively modernist, as civic moral ideals. What made these moral ideals distinctively modernist was the interpretation of the normative standpoint of citizenship that they drew from modernist liberal political theory. As I pointed out in chapter 1, modernist liberal political theory attributed to the normative standpoint of citizenship an anthropological and a metaphysical priority. Lockean versions of modernist liberalism viewed the standpoint of free and equal individuality as the standpoint proper to the natural condition (i.e., the condition of all human beings prior to political association and, in some versions, prior to any form of association at all). Kantian versions of modernist liberalism viewed the standpoint of free and equal individuality as the standpoint proper to the autonomous faculty of human reason (i.e., the standpoint

governed only by the universally binding laws of pure theoretical and practical reason). In both cases, the relationship
between civic identity and communitarian identity was
defined as a relationship between the humanly essential and
the accidental.

This way of attributing anthropological and metaphysical
priority to the normative standpoint of citizenship governed
formulations of modernist liberal political theory's most general and distinctively modernist moral doctrine—the doctrine
of the priority of the right over the good. In different ways,
the civic ethics of authenticity and autonomy both embodied
this doctrine. This doctrine states that the free pursuit of happiness must be subject to limits, as defined by law that is
applicable equally to all individuals as individuals. This doctrine is designed to rule out, morally, any political and legal
order in which moral rightness (i.e., an action's conformity to
law) is defined by the conformity of action with some particularistic concept of the good. Every cultural community is governed by a set of rules to which all members are subject.
These rules, usually informal and unspoken, coordinate and
direct the action of community members in their common
pursuit of a particularistic concept of the good. These rules
derive from and express the totalizing world view and life
ideal that all community members share. In a monocultural
political community (i.e., a community that is culturally
homogeneous), there is usually no distinction between the
legal order and the moral order grounded in particularistic
cultural values and rules. In such a monocultural political and
legal order, moral rightness, as the conformity of action to
law, is determined by the conformity of action to a particularistic concept of the good and a particularistic cultural world
view. Think, for example, of traditional Islamic law or of any
other regime in which the legal order rests upon a foundation
of particularistic religious belief.

The doctrine of the priority of the right over the good
establishes and requires a distinction between moral rightness
and the conformity of action to a particularistic concept of
the good. Liberal democracy assumes cultural heterogeneity.
A civic community is generally a multicultural, rather than a

monocultural, community. For this reason, a liberal democratic political and legal order must apply a criterion of moral rightness distinct from criteria derived from, or dependent upon, any of the particularistic world views adhered to by the cultural communities that comprise it. The doctrine of the priority of the right over the good, then, affirms the priority of this criterion of moral rightness over all criteria derived from communitarian moral ideals and world views. But because the liberal democratic criterion of moral rightness is not derived from or based upon communitarian moral ideals, every liberal democracy must offer some account of precisely how the specifically liberal criterion of moral rightness is to be explained and justified. Modernist liberal formulations of this doctrine linked the criterion of moral rightness to philosophical theories that attributed an anthropological and metaphysical priority to the normative standpoint of citizenship. Modernist liberal political theory thus claimed to derive the liberal democratic criterion of moral rightness from the nature of things. It identified the civic standpoint of free and equal individuality as the universal and essential standpoint of all human beings, whether that standpoint be defined in Lockean terms, as the standpoint proper to the natural condition, or in Kantian terms, as the standpoint proper to the faculty of autonomous reason. For modernist liberalism, then, the liberal doctrine of the priority of the right over the good was to be read as a doctrine affirming nothing more controversial than the philosophically obvious priority of the humanly universal and essential over the humanly arbitrary and accidental.

The civic ethics of authenticity and autonomy offered different interpretations of this reading of the doctrine. On the one hand, Lockean styles of liberal political theory conceived of the humanly essential (i.e., the natural condition) as a condition of liberty, a condition free of all cultural and legal constraints on individual will. But if the natural condition is a condition of liberty, then, in order to claim derivation from that condition, any legal constraints on the free-standing individual's will could be imposed only by gaining the individual's uncoerced consent. For Lockean styles of liberalism, then, the individual's uncoerced consent became the ground of the principle of right. The basic content of the liberal criterion of moral rightness was then defined as the basic rules of cooperation that an individual in the natural condition of liberty would freely accept as binding. In accordance with the doctrine of the priority of the right over the good, adherents of the civic ethics of authenticity would then be licensed to pursue the concept of the good consistent with their own intrinsic individual natures (i.e., the qualities that would emerge spontaneously in the condition of natural liberty), subject only to the constraints imposed by the rules of association that would be voluntarily adopted by all free-standing individuals pursuing the same formal goal of authentic self-realization.

On the other hand, Kantian styles of liberal political theory conceived of the essential (i.e., a faculty of pure reason subject only to its own logical and practical laws) as a condition of pure self-determination, a condition free of all constraints except those dictated by reason itself. But if pure self-determination is the mark of the faculty that constitutes human nature, then, in order to claim the authority of autonomous reason, any legal constraints on the individual's will must be consistent with the principles of pure theoretical and practical reason. Thus, for Kantian styles of liberalism, conformity with the rules intrinsic to the universally human faculty of autonomous reason becomes the ground of the principle of right. The content of the liberal criterion of moral rightness can be determined by an examination of the principles of pure practical reason. A will that accepts the constraints imposed by a criterion of moral rightness derived wholly from the principles of pure practical reason actually obeys only itself, and thereby remains autonomous. In accordance with the doctrine of the priority of the right over the good, then, adherents of the civic ethics of autonomy would be licensed to pursue any particularistic concept of the good at all, so long as, in their actions, they observed the limits imposed by a legal order grounded in the principles of pure practical reason (i.e., grounded in the basic rules that the autonomous will gives to itself).

Thus, the civic ethics of authenticity and the civic ethics of autonomy amounted to two different universalist and essentialist interpretations of the liberal doctrine of the priority of the right over the good. Both of these civic moral ideals offered powerful rhetorical resources for motivating the development of civic attitudes and virtues, rhetorical resources drawn mainly from their essentialist and universalist philosophical underpinnings. The aim of both of these civic moral ideals was to produce in citizens the capacities proper to full cultural citizenship. Persons who have developed the capacities proper to citizenship are those who understand and act in accordance with the liberal doctrine of the priority of the right over the good. In their judgments and actions, such persons apply the liberal criterion of moral rightness and give precedence to it over any competing criterion of moral rightness deriving from particularistic concepts of the good.

In order to understand, let alone apply, a liberal concept of moral rightness, however, citizens must first achieve an understanding of themselves as free and equal individuals. If persons who have become citizens in the full cultural sense can be identified by their acceptance and application of the liberal criterion of moral rightness, the condition for their attainment of full cultural citizenship is the attainment of a civic identity, the attainment of a standpoint involving a certain detachment from or externalization of their communitarian identities and moral ideals. The task of a civic moral ideal is to provide rhetorical resources powerful enough to persuade citizens that this detachment from, and externalization of, their primary moral identity and moral language is a goal worth pursuing. The essentialism and universalism of modernist liberal political theory provided the civic ethics of authenticity and autonomy with two powerful and simple themes that could be exploited in this persuasive effort.

Unfortunately, these themes could be exploited effectively for persuasive purposes only by drawing a contrast between civic and communitarian moral ideals that, at least implicitly, tended to depreciate and disparage particularistic cultural beliefs and practices. Given the anthropological and metaphysical priority attributed to the normative standpoint of citizenship by modernist liberal political theory, modernist civic moral ideals could claim that the ideals of authentic and autonomous individuality were written into human nature itself. To be an authentic individual meant to choose a way of life or concept of the good that conformed to the essential properties of one's own real self (i.e., those properties that would presumably have emerged spontaneously in the natural condition of liberty, a condition free of all arbitrary cultural and political constraints). To be an autonomous individual meant to choose a way of life or concept of the good that conformed to the universal principles of pure practical reason and, therefore, to take one's direction and bearings not from prince, Pope, habit, or appetite, but rather from laws deriving from principles inherent in one's innermost metaphysically real self. Further, to the extent that persons had become either authentic or autonomous in these senses, they could claim also to pursue a way of life free of all cultural particularity or ethnocentricity, a way of life not only accessible to all human beings equally, regardless of the accidents of ethnicity, class, and religion, but also expressing most purely the universal nature of humanity as such.

This essentialist and universalist concept of the ideals of authenticity and autonomy provided ample and powerful means of persuasion to modernist civic culture. These modernist civic moral ideals represented free and equal individuality not as a cultural requirement for full membership in a particular contingent and very unusual sort of political community, but rather as a standpoint conforming both to human nature, as such, and to the individual nature of each human being—a perfect wedding of the universal and the particular. Thus, in becoming an authentic or an autonomous individual, a person could claim not only to have fully realized his or her innermost metaphysically real self, but also to have thereby achieved identification with all human beings everywhere.

On the other hand, the civic ideals of authentic and autonomous individuality painted a rather grim picture of those who failed to realize these ideals. If authentic individuals are those who have discovered and realized their own true selves, then inauthentic individuals are those who have been shaped passively by the social and cultural environment, those who have mistaken as their real selves the internalized descriptions applied to them by others. If autonomous individuals are those who are governed by rules issuing ultimately from their own intrinsic rational nature, then heteronomous individuals are those who are governed by rules imposed by external and arbitrary authority—those who are, in effect, metaphysically enslaved by accidental cultural and political arrangements. There is little doubt that citizens who were exposed to, and who took seriously, moral discourses employing these modernist distinctions between authentic and inauthentic, autonomous and heteronomous, individuality had little trouble in telling which of the presented alternatives was most desirable.

Thus, the modernist civic moral ideals of authenticity and autonomy offered abundant rhetorical resources for motivating citizens to achieve full cultural citizenship. But they carried disadvantages and dangers as well. Both the civic ethics of authenticity and the civic ethics of autonomy were subject to self-destructive dialectics or confusing paradoxes rooted in their essentialist and universalist claims. In their claims to universality, for example, both of these civic moral ideals made ethnocentrism or cultural particularism a *bête noire*. Yet nothing could be more ethnocentric than Western claims to cultural universalism. Persons motivated to attain authentic or autonomous individuality, because they were attracted by the universality of this ideal, were thus defeated at the very moment when they achieved their goal. Again, in their claims to embody only the essential, both of these civic moral ideals impugned the culturally arbitrary and circumstantial. Yet the ideals of authentic and autonomous individuality were purely formal. They mandated only a way to be and not specifically what to be. In choosing specifically what to be (i.e., a specific concept of the good or a specific way of life), a person has only limited options, options that just happen to be available at a particular place and time—that is to say, options that are arbitrary and circumstantial. Persons motivated to attain authentic or autonomous individuality, because they were attracted by its claims to embody only the essential, were thus defeated at the very moment when they achieved their goal.

These paradoxes reflected more fundamental contradictions and more dangerous implications lurking deep within the universalist and essentialist logic of modernist civic moral ideals, contradictions and implications whose culturally and politically destructive impact are only now beginning to be widely felt. As we have seen, for the moral ideals of authenticity and autonomy, the paradigm of the authentic and autonomous individual is the person who no longer recognizes as final the authority or legitimacy of any culturally particularistic moral ideal, recognizing instead only those claims to moral authority based upon purely universal principles. Given this understanding of authenticity and autonomy, it follows that the paradigm of the inauthentic and heteronomous person is the one who in fact does recognize, as final and sufficient, claims to moral authority based only upon particularistic cultural beliefs and practices. The problem is that the vast majority of human beings on this planet happily fits this paradigm of inauthenticity and heteronomy. The remainder (i.e., adherents of the moral ideals of authenticity and autonomy), also fits this paradigm, although unhappily, insofar as the claims to moral authority asserted by those modernist civic moral ideals are also based upon particularistic cultural beliefs and practices—the cultural beliefs and practices of modernist Western liberal democracies.

Thus, the universalist and essentialist logic of the modernist civic moral ideals of authenticity and autonomy carried within itself the seeds of a blanket condemnation and depreciation of all moral ideals, both communitarian and civic, as inauthentic and heteronomous. The more seriously the universalist and essentialist claims of modernist civic moral ideals were taken, the more suspicion was generated about the cultural particularism of even those moral ideals. During the last fifty years, with the discrediting of Enlightenment concepts of reason and knowledge, we have added to this internally generated suspicion the full weight of a growing skepticism about the purely intellectual foundations of modernist civic moral ideals. The net effect of these developments today—the net effect of the three hundred-year hegemony of the modernist civic ideals of authenticity and autonomy—is a growing doubt about the value of all moral ideals, a doubt whose entire strength is drawn paradoxically from the culturally particular-istic modernist belief that moral ideals in general, to be theo-retically justifiable and therefore worthy of respect, must be grounded upon purely universal principles. Thus today, at the end of the roughly three hundred-year reign of modernist lib-eral political theory, the continuing influence of the civic ethics of authenticity and autonomy pushes us in the direc-tion of a generalized cultural nihilism, a generalized sense of the groundlessness and unjustifiability of all moral ideals. Ironically, the very ideas that for three hundred years served to motivate development of the capacities proper to citizen-ship, now serve to confuse and undermine the pursuit of any moral ideal whatever. It is this consequence of modernist lib-eralism that, above all, must be addressed by the project of inventing a postmodern civic culture.

Rawls, in *TJ*, said little that spoke to this set of issues. That book was largely received as a contribution to modernist liber-al political theory. Rawls was not yet a full-blown "political" liberal. He had not yet made what I have called his rhetorical turn. His ambition in that book seemed to be to arrive at a statement of the correct theory of social justice—in his terms, the theory of social justice that could rightly claim to produce a reflective equilibrium between our moral intuitions and a set of stated principles or criteria of justice. In this project, Rawls drew on the conceptual and stylistic resources of both Lockean and Kantian versions of modernist liberal political theory. But, in his hands, those resources were pretty much stripped of their motivational power.

Consider, for example, the ideas of the natural condition and the social contract. As we have observed, modernist liber-als imagined the natural condition of all human beings prior to political association to be a condition of more or less com-plete liberty. Persons in the state of nature were represented as subject to no cultural or legal constraints. They were repre-sented, in effect, as embodiments of the civic ideal of free and equal individuality. We may recognize today that free and equal individuality has much more to do with the moral ideals of liberal democracy than with anything like the natural human condition. Nevertheless, there is little doubt that, as

the ideological basis for the civic ethics of authenticity, this
modernist identification of the normative standpoint of citizenship with the natural human condition wound up providing powerful motivational resources to modernist civic culture. Again, consider the idea of an autonomous faculty of
practical reason. Kantian liberals imagined all human beings
to possess such a faculty. This faculty was rational in that it
prescribed universal rules for conduct. It was autonomous in
that the rules it prescribed were rules originating entirely in
itself, independently of any external cultural authority. Persons who lived by those rules could then claim that they lived
autonomously—that their lives were governed by rules dictated not by prince, Pope, habit, or appetite, but rather by their
own faculty of pure practical reason, their own innermost
metaphysically real self. Once again, we may recognize today
that, in this notion of rational autonomy, Kantian liberals misread the normative standpoint of liberal democratic citizenship as a condition of metaphysical self-determination. But
here too there is little doubt that, as the ideological basis of
the civic ethics of autonomy, this misreading offered powerful
motivational resources to modernist civic culture.

In *TJ*, Rawls went just about as far as he could to downplay
the anthropological and metaphysical claims associated with
the modernist liberal notions of social contract and rational
autonomy. The result was the development of a version of
those ideas that diminished dramatically the persuasive power
of the civic moral ideals based on them, while adding little
that was new to modernist liberal concepts of citizenship. In
place of the modernist anthropological concept of the state of
nature, Rawls introduced the methodological concept of an
"original position"—a counterfactual state of affairs that
required us to imagine the negotiators of the basic terms of
political association carrying out their negotiations behind a
"veil of ignorance," having no knowledge of their individual
life circumstances in the society whose rules of association
they were negotiating. The task given to these hypothetical
negotiators was to arrive at an uncoerced consensus regarding
the principles of justice. Under such negotiating conditions,
the reasoning of the negotiators (having nothing else to go

on) would be governed supposedly only by the purely formal logic of game theory (Rawls's version, in *TJ*, of a pure or autonomous practical rationality). As a result, the rules of association or principles of justice arrived at by such negotiators would presumably embody an impartial or neutral stance toward all particularistic concepts of the good life, favoring no particular ethnic, class, or religious cultural community at the expense of any others, and insuring that the basic social, political, and economic arrangements would be fair to all.

Thus, in *TJ*, all the basic metaphors, images, and arguments familiarly employed in modernist liberal political theory are called into play. Legitimacy is claimed for a specifically liberal criterion of moral rightness by demonstrating that such a criterion would be the outcome of a discussion among free and equal individuals, governed only by the logic of a culture-neutral rationality. While Lockean liberals tended to focus on the circumstances of the discussion and Kantian liberals on the reasoning allowed, Rawls's deduction of his own favored version of liberal justice incorporated both concerns—he makes sure that his own demonstration gives a lot of attention both to the free and equal status of discussion participants (a.k.a. "natural liberty") and to their determination to let a certain kind of culture-neutral reasoning (i.e., the rules of game theory) alone decide the outcome (a.k.a. "rational autonomy"). But the most striking continuity between Rawls's version of this modernist liberal style of argument and those of his precursors is also the most fundamental and important. Modernist liberal political theory was anxious to make it appear that there was nothing arbitrary or contingent about liberal democratic political norms and moral ideals. Modernist liberal theorists couldn't just come out in favor of those norms and ideals, and then go on to make a case for their favorite concepts of them. No, they had to make it appear that the concepts of liberal justice and civic values they offered marched irresistibly forth from the state of nature itself or from the bowels of pure reason. So, in order to make sure that their demonstrations and theories would have a happy conclusion, they built their favorite concepts of liberal moral ideals into their accounts of the social contract and of autonomous reason.

Rawls, in *TJ*, felt this same compulsion. In his version of the show, it seems obvious that the standpoint of the negotiators built into his description of the original position represents, in part, Rawls's own concept of the normative standpoint of citizenship. The negotiators of the terms of political association are described by Rawls as operating behind a veil of ignorance. This means that, in the discussion of those terms, particularistic cultural perspectives, personal interests and commitments, individual circumstances, and other such appeals must be ruled out. But why not just say so directly? Why bother with the tedious "device of representation" known as the original position? Why not just say that citizens in the full cultural sense are those persons who have gained the capacity to externalize their primary moral identities, to unplug their primary moral vocabularies, to step behind the "veil of ignorance" when appropriate, and to treat fellow citizens fairly as free and equal individuals? Again, instead of "constructing" the difference principle from an assumption-loaded account of the original position, why didn't Rawls just make a compelling case for his view that citizens who are winners in the existential lottery should care about and help those less fortunate? Why couldn't Rawls just come out and say, as Rorty does, something like "liberals are the people who think that cruelty is the worst sort of thing we do."[21]

The answer to these questions is that for whatever reason, Rawls in *TJ* somehow still felt the need, characteristic of most modernist liberal political philosophers, to portray liberal political morality as if it were not a matter of particularistic belief and practice, but rather as a set of claims whose truth or validity could be demonstrated. But in order to increase his chances of producing a successful demonstration, Rawls felt that he had to jettison the more controversial aspects of modernist liberal political theory—its tendency to claim anthropological and metaphysical priority for liberal moral ideals. Unfortunately, it was just this aspect of modernist liberalism that provided liberal doctrine with its motivational clout and

---

[21] Richard Rorty, *Contingency, Irony and Solidarity* (New York: Cambridge University Press, 1989), p. xv.

rhetorical fireworks. In stripping liberal doctrine of its metaphysical pretensions while retaining its literary form, Rawls came up with the worst of both worlds. A citizen will look in vain in the pages of *TJ* for a vision of the world or of human life that might have the power actually to move him or her to embrace liberal moral ideals more gratefully and enthusiastically. The version of liberal doctrine he produced in *TJ* was a rhetorically impoverished one. It was a liberalism without passion, an arid procedural liberalism that expressed, if anything, the gray bureaucratic spirit of the culturally-neutralist liberal welfare state. In short, Rawls in *TJ* initiated a form of liberal political philosophy that has probably done more to worsen than to resolve the motivational crisis of contemporary civic culture.

When we get to *PL*, however, things are beginning to be quite different. The first step away from the attenuated modernist liberalism of *TJ* was Rawls's more or less determined embrace of an explicitly political or rhetorical concept of liberal doctrine. This move settles once and for all the question about the source and status of liberal moral and political values. It decisively rules out any sort of universalist and essentialist interpretation of the normative standpoint of liberal democratic citizenship. It thereby eliminates the need or compulsion to justify liberal principles by showing that they can be deduced from the universal natural human condition or from the principles of pure practical reason. For Rawls in *PL*, liberal doctrine is affirmed as a partial political, and not a comprehensive metaphysical, doctrine. The source of liberal democratic moral ideals is to be found in the public culture of modern constitutional democracies. These ideals just happen to have won many adherents in certain North Atlantic political communities. They are contingent products of history. Their status is defined accordingly. Liberal democratic moral ideals will continue to have adherents as long as those adherents continue to be persuaded of the desirability of liberal democracy as a form of political association and as a way of life. If the moral ideals of particularistic ethnic, class, and religious communities are arbitrary and accidental historical artifacts, then liberal democratic moral ideals are no less so.

More or less implied, then, in Rawls's reinterpretation of liberal doctrine as political and not metaphysical doctrine, is this denial of the modernist assumption that liberal democratic moral ideals, to be justifiable, must be somehow written into the very fabric of things. But this denial, of course, constitutes only the first step toward a renewal of liberal belief. The next step is perhaps the more interesting and difficult one.

Rawls, in his writing published since 1980, takes this next step also, or at least points in its general direction. Modernist liberal political theory characteristically distinguished between civic moral ideals and communitarian moral ideals so as to identify civic moral ideals with the humanly universal and the essential, and communitarian moral ideals with the humanly particular and the accidental. But, as we noted earlier, linked to these contrasts was another one. Civic moral ideals were viewed as embodying a certain formal concept of moral rightness that carried a special kind of moral obligation. The modernist civic ideals of authenticity and autonomy, for example, required conduct to assume a certain form rather than to have a specific content. They mandated a way to be rather than a what to be, leaving to individual desire to determine the what (i.e., the particular concept of the good to pursue). Communitarian moral ideals, on the other hand, were matters of desire, inspired by and grounded in totalizing concepts of the good. The cultivation and direction of desire were the work of families and of particularistic cultural traditions. Modernist civic moral ideals, however, were to find their work elsewhere. Their job was to establish and support obligatory constraints on desire—obligatory constraints on the pursuit of happiness—that were in accord with liberal principles of justice.

This sort of contrast and division of labor between civic and communitarian moral ideals make sense, as long as it is believed that civic moral ideals have a metaphysical origin and therefore don't really need to be attractive objects of desire. But once we have abandoned the notion that principles drawn from some imagined natural condition of liberty or faculty of autonomous reason dictate liberal constraints on the pursuit of happiness, then the contrast and division of labor mentioned above ceases to make sense. The distinction between civic and communitarian moral ideals as a distinction between matters of formal obligation and substantive desire collapses. Liberal moral ideals, too, must be thought of as substantive shapers of desire, as final goods defining not only the how, but also the what of life. In short, the rhetorical turn— the turn from metaphysical to political liberalism—implies a second reorientation of liberal political thought. This second reorientation involves a fundamental rethinking of the liberal doctrine of the priority of the right over the good. The liberal principle of right must be redefined in substantive, particularistic, and teleological terms. The liberal doctrine of the priority of the right over the good must be recast as a doctrine of the priority, under certain circumstances, of a special object of desire over other objects. The rhetorical turn in postmodern liberal political thought thus calls forth what I want to call a teleological turn.

This teleological turn is first announced in Rawls's Dewey Lectures[22] in 1980. In those lectures, Rawls introduced a concept of moral personhood according to which moral personhood is defined by the possession of two moral powers, along with two highest-order interests in the full development and exercise of those powers. The two moral powers defining moral personhood, according to Rawls, are: (1) a capacity for an effective sense of justice, and (2) a capacity "to form, to revise, and rationally to pursue a concept of the good."[23] Further, these moral powers carry two highest-order interests in their full development and exercise. For Rawls, to call these interests "highest-order" interests is to say that they "are supremely regulative as well as effective. This implies that, whenever circumstances are relevant to their fulfillment, these interests govern deliberation and conduct."[24]

The significance of this concept of the powers and interests proper to moral personhood, for present purposes,

---

[22] Published in John Rawls, "Kantian Constructivism in Moral Theory: The Dewey Lectures, 1980," *Journal of Philosophy* 77 (1980).

[23] Rawls, "Kantian Constructivism," p. 525.

[24] Rawls, "Kantian Constructivism," p. 525.

becomes evident above all when the passage is taken in conjunction with the thesis presented in his 1985 essay, "Justice as Fairness: Political not Metaphysical." As long as we understand the concept of moral personhood in the passage above as a political and not a metaphysical concept, we will read it properly. To say that it is a political concept is to say that, in putting it forward, its author seeks to win the acceptance of his audience (i.e., his fellow citizens of North Atlantic liberal democracies) regarding the issue at hand. The issue at hand is the question of how the normative standpoint of liberal democratic citizenship can be most profitably understood. In his Kantian constructivist mode, Rawls's concept of moral personhood plays a role in his design of the original position. But, as noted previously, the standpoint of the hypothetical negotiators of the original position actually amounts to a heuristic definition and representation of the idealized standpoint that citizens are required to adopt as they participate in civic discourse and public life. Within his concept of moral personhood, therefore, Rawls is in fact offering us his concept of the normative standpoint of citizenship. Rawls is telling us that, in his view, citizenship in the full cultural sense requires the development of two new moral powers and two new highest-order interests. As elements of a political concept, these powers and interests are not to be taken as part of human nature, or as universally present as faculties in all human beings. They are powers and interests that, if they are to exist at all, must be culturally produced in persons in order to enable those persons to be full participants in a liberal democratic political community.

Given this interpretation of Rawls's concept of moral personhood, what is novel and important is the content of the concept itself. According to this concept, citizens in the full cultural sense must develop and exercise: (1) a capacity for an effective sense of justice, and (2) a capacity to form, revise, and pursue rationally a particular concept of the good. Furthermore, they must possess an interest in developing and exercising these powers that, in relevant contexts, overrides all other interests. To say that the development and exercise of these powers are highest-order interests is to say that they are experienced as goods and that, in some contexts, they are experienced as final goods whose attainment takes precedence over all goals. It is to say, in short, that the development and exercise of these powers are objects of desire. Here we have the basic ingredients of what I have called the teleological turn in postmodern liberal political philosophy. In Rawls's concept of moral personhood (i.e., in his post-1980 concept of the normative standpoint of citizenship), citizenship is regarded as an end, as a matter of desire, and not merely a matter of following rules and meeting formal obligations. Liberal morality mandates a specific substantive content of life, and not merely a form. The ideal liberal democratic community (i.e., one whose citizens all have achieved full cultural citizenship) is itself a particularistic cultural community, one united by virtue of a shared pursuit of a contingent and particularistic concept of the good.

The next question, then, naturally would be: what is the nature of this civic good? If a civic community is a community united to pursue a particularistic concept of the good, what is the relationship between this concept of the civic good and the various happiness ideals and ways of life pursued by the particularistic cultural communities that constitute the encompassing civic community? On these and many related questions, Rawls himself offers little help. Yet it is Rawls, perhaps despite himself, who has opened the perspectives that allow these questions to be asked. If it is true that today—in the aftermath of the wreck of the Enlightenment and the demise of modernist liberalism—we face a motivational crisis in the sphere of civic culture, resources for the resolution of this crisis may be discovered somewhere in the new perspectives that Rawls has opened. Our contemporary task is not just to invent new ways of understanding the ideal of liberal democratic citizenship, but, more importantly, to invent new ways of motivating citizens to realize it in their own lives. The teleological turn speaks to this second, and perhaps most difficult part of our task. It turns us in the direction of new issues and questions, new ways of thinking about liberal political morality. It invites us to begin to think of liberal democratic citizenship as about something more than formal rights and duties.

It invites us to begin to think of citizenship in terms of desire and aspiration. It seems to me that only this kind of thinking can effectively speak to the contemporary moral crisis of liberal democracy.

3   The De-Totalization
of Politics

The rhetorical and teleological turns evidenced in the recent work of John Rawls set the agenda for contemporary liberal political philosophy. This reorientation of liberal thought is required for the postmodern reconstruction of liberal democratic civic culture. The task is to invent new cultural resources capable of producing in as many citizens as possible the insight and the motivation required for attainment of full cultural citizenship. What I have called the rhetorical turn in postmodernist liberal thought addresses primarily the issue of the intelligibility of liberal political morality in a post-Enlightenment cultural context. What I have called the teleological turn in postmodernist liberal thought addresses primarily the issue of motivation—the issue of whether means of persuasion can be found sufficient to motivate citizens to develop and exercise the capacities proper to citizenship, once we have come to terms with the historical contingency and cultural particularism of liberal moral ideals. In this chapter, I want to take up the first issue—the issue of intelligibility—and to work out more fully the implications of the rhetorical turn in postmodern liberalism. In the following chapter, I will explore the second issue—the issue of motivation—and will focus on the implications of the teleological turn, the question of whether a concept of citizenship can be invented that possesses the persuasive power and normative authority necessary to support an effective postmodern civic culture.

The rhetorical turn and the intelligibility
of liberal democratic citizenship

First, let us make sure that we understand the connection between the rhetorical turn in liberal political philosophy, and the issue of the intelligibility of the standpoint and norms proper to liberal democratic citizenship. As I observed in chapter 1, liberal democracies make extraordinary cultural demands on their citizens. They require that citizens develop and cultivate attitudes, dispositions, identities, and moral capacities that do not occur spontaneously among human beings. These qualities must be produced in citizens by a special sort of countervailing culture—what I have called a civic culture. A civic culture is composed of discourses, narratives, and representations of various sorts that are designed to promote among citizens the development and cultivation of civic capacities. Any civic culture has two functions, in particular, that it must successfully carry out:

(1) It must provide cultural resources for rendering the normative standpoint of citizenship intelligible to citizens.
(2) It must provide cultural resources for motivating citizens to develop and exercise the capacities proper to citizenship.

Among the cultural resources available to modern forms of liberal democratic civic culture is the sort of discourse known as political philosophy. The rhetorical turn is a development affecting that particular discursive resource of liberal democratic civic culture.

I have called this development a "rhetorical turn" in order

to characterize the sort of shift that has occurred. Other terms could be used. Rawls, as we have seen, characterizes this reorientation of liberal political philosophy as a shift from a metaphysical liberalism to a political liberalism. At this point, no characterization can be final, since the process of reorientation is still in its infancy. In my view, the description of this reorientation in political philosophy as a rhetorical turn has some advantage right now, in that it establishes a contrast between old and new suggestive of new directions for inquiry. Modernist metaphysical liberalism, in both its literary form and content, defined itself in opposition to rhetorical concepts of reason and knowledge. Rhetorical concepts of reason and knowledge, on the other hand, are characterized by an affirmation of the audience-directedness of all discourse and the audience-dependence of all subject matter. Modernist metaphysical liberalism embraced the anti-rhetorical rhetoric of pure theory. In its literary form, it presented itself as a purely theoretical discourse, a discourse seeking to articulate the audience-independent truth about an audience-independent subject matter. Characterizing the contemporary reorientation of political philosophy as a rhetorical turn, then, helps to keep in focus not only the crucial issues raised by this reorientation, but also where it is leading us.

In any case, whatever terms we use for it, it should be clear how a shift of this magnitude, affecting an important component of civic culture, could produce problems. We should not exaggerate the importance of metaphysical liberalism as a cultural support for liberal democracy. Until the beginning of this century, for example, Protestant Christianity probably played a more crucial role in the effective civic culture of the United States than did modernist liberalism. But, as the cultural diversity of American society has increased and the influence of Protestant Christianity has diminished, civic culture in America has become more dependent upon the universalist and essentialist ideas of modernist liberal political philosophy as its primary resource for rendering intelligible to citizens the nature of liberal democratic citizenship. The influence of modernist liberal ideas has been particularly evident during the last thirty years in discussions of universal human and civil rights, and in concepts of the cultural neutrality of the liberal democratic state. This means that, to the extent that American civic culture has been effective in actually producing citizens in the full cultural sense, citizenship will be understood by such citizens today in large measure through the use of a vocabulary shaped by the universalist and essentialist world view of modernist liberalism. The shift from modernist metaphysical liberalism to political or rhetorical liberalism, therefore, entails significant changes in the vocabulary that citizens must use to understand and reproduce in others the civic capacities they have achieved. This is what I have referred to as the intelligibility crisis in contemporary civic culture. The old vocabulary of citizenship is now defunct. The new one has yet to be coined.

The project of inventing a postmodern civic culture is the project of inventing this new vocabulary. The difficulties and dangers involved in this project are hard to underestimate. To the extent that modernist liberal political theory has indeed been influential in forming culturally effective concepts of citizenship, our understanding of what it means to be a citizen is bound up with the totalizing and universalist vocabulary of modernist European culture in general. The vocabulary of a political or rhetorical liberalism will be radically different. The perspectives underlying that vocabulary will be even more alien. Universalist and essentialist concepts of liberal moral ideals will disappear. The new vocabulary of citizenship will be shaped by concepts of liberal moral ideals that emphasize their cultural particularism and their partial nature. To some, the reorientation within liberal political thought will seem, as a result, like a rejection of liberal moral ideals altogether. The shift from modernist metaphysical liberalism to political or rhetorical liberalism thus amounts to a cultural transformation, not merely of generational, but even epochal proportions.

This shift requires a rethinking of virtually every aspect of liberal democratic citizenship. One of the most difficult tasks involved in this project is the reinterpretation of the capacities and attitudes proper to citizenship as qualities pertaining to only a partial aspect of life. Rawls gives special emphasis to this feature of the shift from metaphysical to political liberalism. Modernist metaphysical liberalism presented itself as what Rawls terms a "comprehensive" doctrine. According to Rawls, a comprehensive doctrine is a doctrine that, at the extreme, applies to all subjects. It is a doctrine including "concepts of what is of value in human life, ideals of personal virtue and character...that are to inform much of our nonpolitical conduct (in the limit our life as a whole)."[25] On the other hand, according to Rawls, political liberalism is a doctrine that is partial—that is, it is "worked out for a specific subject, namely, the basic structure of society."[26] As such, it is a doctrine that pertains to a specific part (i.e., the political part, our lives as citizens) and not to the whole of life.[27] Rawls thus distinguishes modernist metaphysical liberalism from political or rhetorical liberalism in two ways. First, while metaphysical liberalism was universalist and essentialist doctrine—a doctrine claiming to pronounce the truth about the very essence of political morality—political or rhetorical liberalism is a particularistic cultural doctrine, defining only the norms proper to one particular and contingent form of political association. Second, while metaphysical liberalism, in its universalism and essentialism, was a comprehensive or totalizing doctrine, a doctrine applying to the whole of life, political or rhetorical liberalism is a doctrine that applies to only a part of life, the part concerned with the capacities and norms proper to liberal democratic citizenship.

For Rawls, then, the postmodern reorientation of liberal political philosophy should be read as a shift from a concept of liberalism as a universalist and comprehensive doctrine to a concept of liberalism as a particularistic and partial doctrine. When we speak of liberalism as a doctrine in this way, however, we should remind ourselves that we are not talking about mere "theories" of liberalism. If we understand liberal political philosophy as a component of civic culture, then we must see it as addressed to an audience (i.e., citizens) and, to the

---

[25] Rawls, "The Priority of Right and Ideas of the Good," *Philosophy and Public Affairs* 17 (1988), p. 252.

[26] Rawls, "The Priority of Right," p. 252.

[27] Rawls, "The Priority of Right," p. 253.

extent it is effective, as shaping that audience's experience of the subject matter—that is, its experience of citizenship and liberal democratic political life in general. This means that the postmodern reorientation of liberal political philosophy entails much more than a mere doctrinal shift. It entails a reorientation and reconstruction of citizenship and of the liberal democratic political sphere as such. To the extent that this reconstruction actually occurs, then, the normative standpoint of citizenship will come to be *lived* differently. It will come to be lived as a standpoint that is culturally constructed (i.e., contingent and culturally particularistic) and that pertains to only a part, and not the whole, of life.

It is above all at this point—when the postmodern reorientation in liberal political philosophy is viewed concretely at the level of its impact on everyday life—that specific problems of intelligibility arise. If the role of philosophical reflection as a component of civic culture is in part to provide resources for rendering intelligible to citizens the normative standpoint of citizenship, then postmodern liberal political philosophy must make it clear to citizens precisely what it means, precisely what difference it makes, to experience citizenship as culturally constructed and as pertaining only to a limited part of life. It is the partiality or—for lack of a better term—the nontotalistic character of citizenship that is particularly problematic. As we have seen, modernist metaphysical liberalism represented citizenship as a comprehensive or totalizing standpoint. The totalizing character of metaphysical liberalism was shaped by the totalizing character of modernist Enlightenment culture in general. Modernist Enlightenment culture generated that totalizing perspective we have come to call the "scientific world view." Modernist liberal political theory, as a component of Enlightenment culture, became an agent of the scientific world view. Its self-appointed task of "legitimating" liberal democracy really amounted to a reading of liberal democratic moral ideals in terms of the assumptions proper to a totalizing scientific naturalism. For this reason, in the characteristically modernist conflict between the opposing totalizing world views of science and religion, liberalism has generally been seen not only as friendly to the claims of scientific rationalism, but even as its political expression and embodiment. As represented by modernist metaphysical liberalism, liberal moral ideals thus have often seemed to be part and parcel of a totalizing world view that was not only in competition with other totalizing cultural world views, but also actively hostile to religious world views in particular.

If this is true, then we know roughly what it means to say that, under the regime of modernist civic culture, citizenship and the liberal democratic political sphere in general were experienced as elements of a comprehensive or totalizing world view. Liberal moral values often seemed to promote if not require a process of cultural secularization—a process in which religious communities, in order to remain civically respectable, are pressured to "liberalize" their beliefs by making them logically compatible with the scientific world view. If this sort of conflict is entailed in a comprehensive or totalizing interpretation of citizenship and liberal moral ideals, then the impact of—once again, for lack of a better term—a "de-totalizing" interpretation of those ideals would be to eliminate the possibility of any such conflict. To say that liberalism is not a comprehensive doctrine, but a doctrine pertaining only to a part of life, is to say that citizenship, liberal moral ideals, and the liberal democratic political sphere in general do not and should not entail, promote, or require any particular totalizing world view at all. If we are indeed to be affected by the postmodern reorientation of liberal political philosophy and thereby experience the reconstruction of our own understanding and practice of citizenship, then we must learn to draw new lines that distinguish very clearly between the partial civic identities and perspectives proper to the liberal democratic public sphere and the comprehensive communitarian identities and totalizing cultural perspectives proper to non-political life.

I want to focus in this chapter on this question of how and where those new lines must be drawn—on the question, that is to say, of what a non-totalistic and de-totalizing liberalism, civic identity, and public sphere might look like. I will divide the question as follows. Assuming a political or rhetorical concept of liberal political philosophy (i.e., viewing it as a discursive component of civic culture) addressed to citizens for the purpose of rendering intelligible and motivating development of civic capacities and attitudes, then we may examine and describe its character as discourse with respect to any of the relational standpoints proper to the structure of the rhetorical situation (e.g., the address itself, its general definition of the subject matter, its addresser, its addressees, its general occasion or proper context, its intended effect, and so on). In this chapter, I will focus on two of these standpoints in particular. In Section II, I will ask about the address itself—that is, I will ask about the self-understanding and rhetorical self-definition proper to a de-totalized/de-totalizing concept of liberal political philosophy. Then, in Section III, I will ask about the subject matter—that is, I will ask about the way in which the boundaries of the liberal democratic public sphere might be redrawn by such a de-totalizing liberalism.

The de-totalizing character of liberal doctrine as a component of civic culture

When Rawls defines political or rhetorical liberalism in terms of a distinction between comprehensive and partial doctrines, he often seems to suggest that political liberalism represents a retreat from comprehensive or totalizing forms of liberalism. For Rawls, comprehensive and political doctrines differ only in scope. Political doctrines are those that apply to a limited range of life issues. Comprehensive doctrines, at the limit, apply to all life issues. But comprehensive concepts of liberal doctrine, like those of Kant and Mill, tend to generate conflicts with other comprehensive doctrines or totalizing world views. Rawls's view seems to be that, for the sake of political stability, it is necessary to limit the scope of liberal doctrine in order to avoid the risk of such destabilizing conflict. Political liberalism, then, would be a form of liberal doctrine that has cut back on its claims and lowered its sights as part of a survival strategy. To the extent that this is Rawls's view, then, his turn to political liberalism is indeed a retreat. Rawls implies that, if it were possible, a comprehensive liberalism—a totalizing liberal world view adhered to by all citizens—would be preferable to him. But to secure political stability, we must settle for what is possible. To think of liberal doctrine as partial in this way would thus be to point out a defect. Partial here means fragmentary or incomplete. It refers only to the scope of a doctrine or the range of issues it addresses. It points to no quality in political or rhetorical liberalism that might be considered positive or valuable in itself.

This is the view I want to oppose. I think that Rawls, too, in his better moments, would also oppose it, although he himself does not offer much conceptually that would explain why. To distinguish political or rhetorical liberalism from totalizing or comprehensive doctrines primarily in terms of its range of application is misleading. While its range of application is indeed limited, that fact does not constitute the truly distinguishing mark of political or rhetorical liberalism. A political or rhetorical liberalism is not a stripped-down version of liberalism, put forward as a compromise in the name of social stability. Rather, it is a liberalism that has been properly understood as a component of a liberal democratic civic culture. Because the word "partial" suggests something fragmentary or incomplete, it is better to characterize political or rhetorical liberalism in different terms, in a way that brings into sight the positive significance and impact of this partiality. That is why I prefer to describe political or rhetorical liberalism as a de-totalized and de-totalizing doctrine. As a component of civic culture, liberal political doctrine positively carries out its assigned function only insofar as it is presented as a de-totalized discourse aimed at achieving a certain kind of de-totalizing effect.

As I noted earlier, a civic culture must be a countervailing culture. It addresses human beings for whom the normative standpoint of citizenship is neither a spontaneous endowment of nature, nor something whose possession is particularly longed for in its absence. Human beings are shaped in their identities and aspirations from earliest childhood by cultural perspectives that provide meaning and direction to life as a whole. The logic that drives such cultural perspectives is a totalistic and totalizing logic. In their development, such cultural perspectives move in the direction of global and exclusive competence. As interpretive and evaluative frameworks capable of indefinite extension and elaboration, they reach completion only when they can satisfactorily assign specific meaning and define a specific response to all the fundamental issues of human life—sex, friendship, work, suffering, sin, death, and salvation. Persons whose identity and values are shaped *exclusively* by any such totalizing cultural world view may be laudable in many ways, but they are not, morally and culturally speaking, citizens. Citizens in the full cultural sense are those who have developed the capacity to treat themselves and one another, when appropriate, as free and equal individuals. As we have seen, to do this requires a capacity to unplug, or put out of play, the ranking systems and totalizing interpretive frameworks that normally determine judgment and action in everyday life. For nominal citizens to become citizens in the full cultural sense, they generally need the support of a civic culture that provides a perspective capable of counteracting the effects of those totalizing interpretive frameworks. Thus, a liberal democratic civic culture, as a countervailing culture, must provide perspectives governed by a logic that is de-totalizing in its impact.

To characterize liberalism, then, as a moral doctrine that is partial, rather than comprehensive, is to call our attention to a feature of liberalism that involves much more than the question of its range of application. The moral doctrines generated by particularistic cultural world views are comprehensive doctrines, in that their cultural function is to provide meaning and direction to the whole of life. Their role is to offer a comprehensive vision of the world, an interpretive and evaluative framework that can be extended and elaborated indefinitely and that, at the limit, can provide a reading of and a strategy for dealing with the entire range of human life issues. In short, the fact that they are totalizing in their logic and scope is to be taken as neither an accident nor as a defect. There is a problem with such totalizing world views, however. This problem is not intrinsic to them, but rather exists only when their adherents also happen to be citizens of a liberal democracy.

The problem is that these totalizing world views, at the limit of their development, can generate a certain politically troublesome linguistic illusion. Particularistic cultural world views, as global interpretive and evaluative frameworks, provide vocabularies for defining and successfully addressing the basic issues of human life. These vocabularies embody the ranking systems, concepts of virtue, and standards of excellence proper to a particular cultural community. As such, they take root in and inhabit the deepest strata of identity and desire. Like all human vocabularies, these particularistic moral vocabularies are produced through processes of metaphorical transmutation. Properly spoken and heard, the descriptions of things and persons licensed by these particularistic moral vocabularies carry what I have called the soft metaphorical "is," rather than the hard metaphysical "is." A description of the world spoken and heard as carrying a soft metaphorical "is" is one that is heard and spoken as a redescription. The metaphorical "is" works (i.e., achieves its effect on thought and feeling) by virtue of an act of linguistic aggression by which an identity is asserted of two unlike things (e.g., "My love is a rose"). For a metaphor to work, its audience must retain a lively sense of the unlikeness of the things identified. In the terminology of classical rhetoric, metaphor achieves its effect by eliciting a play of difference between like and unlike, between res and verbum. A description of the world spoken and heard as carrying a hard metaphysical "is," however, imposes on things an identity devoid of difference. Res and verbum collapse into a lifeless unity. The world "is" precisely what it is described as being, and nothing else.

This is the sort of linguistic illusion that can be generated by totalizing cultural world views, and particularly by those that are most powerful and successful. It consists in a certain forgetfulness about the metaphorical origins of all human vocabularies. Such forgetfulness may or may not have a negative impact on the development of the particular cultural traditions suffering it, but it definitely poses a danger for any liberal democracy. As we have seen, for a such a regime to survive, let alone flourish, large numbers of its citizens must develop the capacity to use a second moral vocabulary in addi-

tion to their first. This second moral vocabulary is that proper
to the public sphere of a liberal democracy. It licenses
descriptions of things and persons that are compatible with a
recognition of the free and equal individuality of every citizen. As such, it embodies and defines the normative standpoint of liberal democratic citizenship. This secondary vocabulary is parasitic upon the first. Just as civic identity exists only
as a modification of communitarian identity, so also this secondary moral vocabulary gets its meaning only through its difference from primary moral vocabularies. It licenses descriptions of things and persons that gain their impact only
through their relationship of metaphorical tension to the
descriptions licensed by primary moral vocabularies—that is,
only by being spoken and heard as redescriptions.

It is at this point that the linguistic illusion generated by
successful cultural world views can come into conflict with the
cultural requirements of liberal democracy. Primary moral
vocabularies quite properly embody the ranking systems,
virtue concepts, and standards of excellence proper to a particularistic cultural community. Primary moral vocabularies
warrant descriptions of things and persons as defined and
ranked by particularistic interpretive and evaluative frameworks. It is by warranting such descriptions that particularistic
moral traditions effectively give meaning and direction to
human desire. On the other hand, the secondary moral
vocabulary of citizenship licenses very different descriptions of
things and persons—descriptions consistent with the recognition of all persons, regardless of their rank as measured by
particularistic standards of excellence or achievement, as free
and equal individuals. Competence in this secondary moral
language of citizenship, thus, really consists of a special kind
of competence in speaking a primary moral language. Speakers of a particular primary moral language must learn to apply
the descriptions mandated by that language in such a way as
to leave room for the very different descriptions mandated by
the moral language of citizenship. Citizens must gain the ability to speak and hear interpretive and evaluative descriptions
in a way that reflects a lively sense of the difference between
the evaluative principles of the two moral languages.

It may be possible, then, to speak a primary moral language simply and directly, with no sense at all that the descriptions of things and persons licensed by that language are not perfect fits. But it is not possible to speak the moral language of citizenship in that simple and direct way. The very aim of the secondary moral language mandated by citizenship is to loosen the fit between things and persons, and the descriptions of them licensed by primary moral languages. Thus, a working-class Italian-American Catholic, for example, in everyday life contexts, describes self and others in terms that reflect ranking systems proper to certain ethnic and religious cultural milieus—in terms that, say, show a certain kind of respect for family connection and religious identification. A working-class Italian-American Catholic who is also a citizen (i.e., who has attained competence in the language game of citizenship) applies the same evaluative descriptions to the world, but speaks and hears those descriptions, as it were, synecdochically, so that they take on a figurative significance. The description of a particular police officer as "the law" carries its full figurative weight and significative value only as long as its audience holds the distinction between the two—the individual police officer and the coercive legal order, in general—clearly in view. In the same way, the moral language of citizenship requires its speakers and hearers to introduce into every evaluative description a note of difference, to hold apart the *res* of free and equal individuality from the *verbum* of evaluative categorization.

Thus, persons who have attained the competence to speak their primary moral language "civilly" (i.e., with this awareness of difference) are those capable of keeping more or less continuously in view the metaphorical nature of the moral descriptions they apply to others. The "is" of attribution through which they apply those descriptions is far more likely to be spoken by such persons as a soft metaphorical "is," rather than as a hard metaphysical "is." Citizens in the full cultural sense are those who have gained this capacity to use their primary moral vocabulary with a certain ironic distance. The exercise of this capacity by many citizens accounts for the peculiar ambiguity, complexity, and power of moral discourse in a liberal democracy. However, not every cultural tradition is strong and capacious enough to acknowledge the metaphorical character of its own moral vocabulary. Ideally, when a primary moral language is spoken and heard in and through the play of metaphorical difference, it gains in power and creativity. But some cultural communities can survive only by closing the divide separating *res* and *verbum,* and by insisting that their members take the descriptions they apply to the world as simply the world itself. In a liberal democracy, such communities are likely to become isolated and even to mobilize against liberal democratic moral ideals. Such reactions are ultimately to be accounted for by the totalizing character of particularistic cultural world views. Under the most fortunate circumstances the logic of cultural totalization and the logic of cultural difference can be complementary, but more often they remain antagonistic. In a liberal democracy, this tension can never be finally overcome. The best that can be achieved is a balance of forces between the drive toward totalization, operative in particularistic cultural communities, and the de-totalizing resources of a civic culture.

A de-totalized and de-totalizing form of liberal political philosophy should be one of those resources. A de-totalized version of liberal political philosophy would be one that, in its self-definition and presentation, could not be mistaken for any sort of totalizing concept of the world. The rhetorical turn, the concept of liberal doctrine as a component of civic culture, constitutes the first step in this direction. Rhetorical modes of analysis by themselves have a de-totalizing impact on doctrinal claims of all types. The rhetorical concept of knowledge as *pistis,* or belief (as opposed to *episteme,* or demonstrably certain cognition), introduces an element of difference or otherness into every doctrinal truth claim. *Pistis* is the state of being persuaded. The cognitive state of being persuaded is very different from the cognitive state consisting of certainty or the possession of demonstrable truth. A proof is final. But what I am persuaded of, today, I may not be persuaded of tomorrow. When I reflectively label what I take to be the actual properties of things and persons as matters of persuasion (i.e., as descriptions that I am now convinced really apply to those things and persons), I implicitly recognize a distinction between my descriptions and the things and persons they describe. A rhetorical concept of knowledge, in this way, incorporates permanent recognition of the divide separating *res* and *verbum*. Thus, the rhetorical turn itself, strictly carried through, is something like an immunization against a totalizing inclination toward the metaphysical "is"—that is, toward any sort of easy identification of description and world.

In general, then, a form of liberal political philosophy that is comfortable with rhetorical modes of analysis, that understands and represents itself as an effort to persuade a particular audience at a particular time with a certain intention, is likely to offer a version of liberal doctrine that won't be mistaken for a global metaphysical vision of the nature of things—which is to say, it will be likely to offer a de-totalized version of liberalism. This tells us something about the general form or style of a postmodern version of liberal doctrine. It tells us that a de-totalized, post-metaphysical version of liberal doctrine will not present itself as a demonstration of eternal truth. But this does not answer the more specific question of what sort of tasks or types of inquiry in particular should be taken on by a de-totalized version of liberal doctrine. We might get some idea about how to answer this question by looking briefly at two paradigmatic styles of classical political philosophy, both of which understood themselves as belonging strictly to the cognitive realm of *pistis*, as opposed to *episteme*.

Can classical political philosophy provide models for post-metaphysical de-totalized versions of liberalism? I would say yes, provided we observe all the necessary caveats. Without any question, classical political philosophy of all styles was grounded in a non-liberal concept of republican political association. As we have observed, liberal democracy as a form of political association is distinguished by its presumption that citizens do, and perhaps should, disagree on the question of the ultimate meaning and purpose of life. Liberal democracy assumes that citizens are members of diverse ethnic, class, and religious communities and that each such community is defined by its adherence to a concept of the good life differ-

ent from, and often in conflict with, those of other communities. This is the assumption that is missing in classical forms of
political philosophy. Classical Greek philosophy in general
was part of a cultural project that aimed at the ethnic consolidation and political unification of Greek-speaking peoples. It
sought to articulate a perspective that could provide a cultural
common ground for all Hellenes, one strong enough to overcome the divisive particularism of local religions and tribal
loyalties. As such, classical Greek philosophy in general
embodied and expressed a totalizing cultural standpoint, a
particularistic cultural world view. However fragmented the
Greek world may have been, Greek philosophy addressed
audiences that could be expected to speak a common primary
moral language.

Thus, to the extent that classical political philosophy in all
its various styles presupposed in its audience a shared world
view and a common set of values, it was governed by an agenda and addressed issues quite unlike those proper to liberal
political philosophy. To that extent, classical political philosophy does not have much to offer the project of reconstructing
liberal doctrine. But that is not the whole story. Greek philosophy, in drawing the cognitive map through which it defined
itself and distinguished itself from its main political and educational rival, Greek rhetoric, also made some use of rhetorical categories and modes of analysis. If it is true that rhetorical
categories and modes of analysis embody in themselves a de-
totalizing understanding of political discourse, then, to the
extent that Greek political philosophy made use of them, we
may after all find some styles of Greek political philosophy
useful as models for a de-totalized form of liberalism. Rhetorical concepts of discourse and knowledge influenced the cognitive map drawn by Greek philosophy wherever Greek
philosophers made a sharp distinction between theoretical
and practical cognitive realms.

Aristotle is canonical in this respect. Aristotle distinguished practical from theoretical philosophy in terms of
both subject matter and method. Invariability and necessary
existence identify the subject matter of theoretical knowledge.
Knowledge of what exists invariably and necessarily is gained

by demonstration. On the other hand, variability, particularity, and contingency identify the subject matter of practical knowledge. Knowledge of such subject matter is gained not by demonstration, but by experience combined with good judgment. Ethics and politics are fields of practical philosophy. A person who possesses knowledge in these fields is not someone who can construct proofs, but rather someone who deliberates well about particular cases (i.e., someone whose deliberation leads to happy results). What can philosophy contribute to a development of the capacity to deliberate well? While philosophy is master in the cognitive realm of pure theory, philosophy has a lesser contribution to make in the fields of ethics and politics. In these fields, experience and skills in deliberation are paramount. Philosophy can provide a vocabulary and a moral grammar that can make deliberation more effective. But knowledge in these fields is ultimately of the particular case, and of the particular case there can be no certain, final, or complete knowledge. The field of practical knowledge is a field in which *pistis* or true belief, as opposed to *episteme,* constitutes the maximum goal. At the conclusion of deliberation—at the moment of ethical and political decision—it is impossible to know with certainty whether the particular case has been judged rightly. Only time can tell that, and never with finality. The final state reached in deliberation is thus a state of being persuaded. Ethical and political deliberation thus calls into play the cognitive categories proper to rhetoric.

Thus, to the extent that classical Greek political philosophy was determined in its content by the totalizing world view of a particularistic ethnic culture, it serves poorly as model for a de-totalized version of liberalism. On the other hand, to the extent that, in its form, classical Greek political philosophy understood itself in terms of rhetorical cognitive categories (i.e., to the extent that it defined itself as belonging to the sphere of practical, as opposed to theoretical, knowledge), then it may indeed offer some guidance for the project of inventing a de-totalized version of liberal political doctrine. Just as it is useful, for present purposes, to categorize modernist liberal political theory into two general types—the

Lockean and Kantian varieties—it is useful to categorize classical political philosophy into three general types. I will call these three types (in honor of their most notable practitioners) the Socratic, Platonic, and Aristotelian varieties. Of these three, the Platonic style of classical political philosophy has the least to offer our contemporary project. Plato, at least the Plato of *The Republic,* seemed bent upon obliterating the distinction between the cognitive domains of theory and practice. However, this is not true of Socratic and Aristotelian versions of Greek political philosophy. These two, if any, types of classical political philosophy might offer models for a de-totalized version of liberal doctrine.

Consider first what we might characterize as the Aristotelian version of classical political philosophy. The role of the Aristotelian political philosopher was to provide a vocabulary and a moral grammar for the language game of political decision making. As we have noted, in the sphere of practical knowledge, the "knower" is the person who has the capacity to deliberate rightly about particular cases. In the case of Greek republican politics, the paradigm of the decision maker was the statesman, the citizen-ruler. Aristotelian political philosophy therefore adopted the standpoint of the citizen-ruler, and sought to provide the moral perspectives and the linguistic resources that could generate prudential insight and sharpen those skills required for political deliberation. Its characteristic task was the classification and evaluation of constitutions. The standard applied in the evaluation of constitutions and laws was the standard that a wise citizen-ruler would naturally adopt—that is, the best possible constitution for a particular people, living under specific conditions, with a particular history, culture, population mix, temperament, and so on. It was the task of the insightful citizen-ruler to assess these traits in any specific case and to construct the constitution dictated by that assessment. If the citizen-ruler (or assembly of citizen-rulers) judged rightly in assessing these traits and selected the appropriate laws, then the people subject to those laws would prosper in the long run (as measured by Greek ethnic standards of prosperity and happiness ideals). The political philosopher as philosopher could not take credit for the prudential insight exercised by wise citizen-rulers. The role of the political philosopher was to provide a scheme of constitutional categories, to clarify the criteria to be applied in the process of assessing particular cases, and perhaps to examine particular cases of political decision making considered by most to have been successful.

Thus, while Aristotelian political philosophy, in its vocabulary and moral grammar, did indeed reflect the particularistic global life ideals proper to the totalizing ethnic world view of the Greeks, it did not define its cognitive task as the formulation of a totalizing theory demonstrating that those life ideals are mandated by the universal nature of human political association. While Aristotelian political philosophy was definitely a component of a totalizing cultural world view, it defined its own function in practical political terms. Its task was not to provide a body of truths that would perhaps render the prudential insight and deliberative skills of the citizen-ruler superfluous, but rather to offer resources for sharpening that insight and making those skills more effective. Thus, Aristotelian political philosophy, in identifying itself strictly as a form of practical reflection as opposed to theoretical cognition (i.e., as belonging to the cognitive domain of *pistis* as opposed to *episteme)*, viewed itself more or less self-consciously as a component of what I would call Greek republican civic culture. The doctrine identified with Aristotelian political philosophy was a doctrine shaped by a clear definition of the rhetorical situation it addressed, the rhetorical standpoint it assumed, and the rhetorical effects it sought to achieve. Understood in this way, the Aristotelian political philosophy might serve as one model for a de-totalized and de-totalizing concept of liberal doctrine.

The Socratic style of classical Greek political philosophy might offer a second model. The Aristotelian model of political philosophy took as its defining task the working out of a vocabulary for the classification and evaluation of constitutions. In performing this function, it adopted the standpoint of the citizen-ruler and regarded the field of political decision making, as it were, from above (i.e., it presupposed in its audience a capacity to adopt the standpoint of the citizen-ruler, a capacity to adopt the normative standpoint of republican citizenship). The Socratic style of classical political philosophy regarded the field of political decision making, the republican public sphere, from a different point of view. It offered, so to speak, a view from below. It began with the assumption that its audience was still in the process of developing the linguistic and moral capacities proper to republican citizenship. The Socratic style of political philosophy took as its defining task the design and practice of a set of educational procedures that could promote the development of civic capacities. The Socratic style of political philosophy, in short, characteristically sought to provide resources for a certain form of civic education.

Socrates himself, it seems, simply pursued the practice of civic education and left it to others to reflect on it and codify its procedures. His practice was to model for his students a certain kind of dialectical self-examination. That practice consisted of the public interrogation of his fellow citizens regarding the standards that they actually applied in making moral and political judgments. The assumption underlying this practice was that citizens typically are inadequately reflective and self-critical about the criteria they bring to bear in political decision making. Without examination, those criteria may well often turn out to be derived from ranking systems and virtue concepts inappropriate to the public sphere. Even in a relatively homogeneous cultural environment such as fifth-century Athens, the most basic and immediate loyalties of citizens were determined by membership in particularistic tribal, village, and religious communities. These communities provided Athenians with their primary moral vocabularies. Athenian citizens, given their linguistic and cultural homogeneity, used the same set of evaluative terms, the same words of moral attribution, in both private and public life. It was to be expected, therefore, that most citizens, when they entered the public sphere, brought with them their usual criteria for applying those evaluative terms—criteria shaped by family and village contexts, and therefore inappropriate to the field of political decision making.

The Socratic versions of Greek political philosophy

addressed the issues raised by this linguistic or terminological importation into the public sphere of moral criteria drawn particularistic cultural contexts. The Socratic antidote to this misapplication of moral criteria was to teach citizens to distinguish clearly between evaluative words they used in making moral judgments, and the actual standards they were applying in using those words. His procedure of civic education was to ask citizens to define the words they used in the attribution of virtue and vice, and in the expression of praise and blame. A primary moral vocabulary in family and village contexts is typically used as a means of generating local solidarity and shaping the behavior of others. In those contexts, the use of moral terms is taught by example, by reference to standard behaviors and model actions that embody local ranking systems. Accordingly, a citizen's usual response to a Socratic request for a definition of concepts such as justice, courage, or piety was to give an example of a just, courageous, or pious action. The examples offered usually reflected the specialized concerns and characteristic perspectives of one or another particular tribal or occupational group.

Thus, the businessman Cephalus, in *The Republic,* defines justice in terms of honest dealings and paying one's debts. Cephalus, of course, was not wrong in believing that it is just to deal honestly and to pay one's debts. He was wrong only in defining the general term "justice" in terms of a standard drawn from commerce. The educational practice of Socrates was to refute all definitions that merely pointed to particular examples of moral conduct or that reflected the restricted moral vocabularies of particular cultural communities. In the ₁ublic sphere, when moral terms are understood and applied in accordance with criteria reflective of particularistic cultural ranking systems, they are misapplied. Moral judgment then becomes a means for imposing the particularistic interests and perspectives of one group or faction on the civic community as a whole. In civic discourse, a more capacious moral language is required, one that allows for the application of moral criteria consistent with a recognition of the equality of fellow citizens who have otherwise conflicting family, tribal, and religious affiliations. The intended effect of Socratic refutation was to move citizens toward an awareness of the distinction between the moral criteria appropriate for public life, and the particularistic moral criteria applied in family and tribal contexts. In learning to make this distinction, citizens learned to use their primary moral vocabularies with a certain ironic or critical distance. Socrates, as teacher, dialogically embodied this ironic distance. His rhetorical posture in the interrogation was that of a person who knew only that he did not know the answer to the question he posed to others—that he did not possess a set of moral criteria perfectly untainted by particularistic cultural content. As we noted earlier, a capacity to speak the secondary moral language of citizenship actually consists of the capacity to apply the descriptions licensed by a primary moral language with a certain tropological detachment. Socratic refutation, as a form of civic education, was a procedure designed to produce that capacity.

As in the case of Aristotelian political philosophy, we must keep in mind that Socratic political philosophy, too, reflected the totalizing cultural project of Greek philosophy in general. That project aimed at the cultural consolidation and the political unification of all Hellenic peoples. It required the criticism of all the cultural sources of political conflict and division—above all, the local religious cults that intensified divisive tribal and territorial allegiances. Greek philosophy, like its main rival, rhetorical education, sought to provide a cultural common ground supportive of pan-Hellenic ethnic identity. Socratic political philosophy, as one expression of this general cultural project, worked with a concept of republican citizenship that conceived of citizenship as an element of a comprehensive ethnic way of life. The Socratic practice of civic education reflected this global concept of citizenship. The Socratic procedure of asking for universal definitions of moral terms could serve the ends of civic education only as long as Greek audiences found it plausible to believe that a right answer was possible (i.e., that ethnic Greek culture was sufficiently homogeneous to allow achievement of a consensus regarding the definition of basic moral terms). Rhetorical education tended to generate a skepticism about the possibility of giving right answers to the sort of questions posed by

Socrates and his followers, a skepticism that undermined completely the effectiveness of Socratic refutation as a form of civic education.

While it may be true that Socratic political philosophy, like Greek philosophy in general, reflected in this way a totalizing cultural world view, it is nevertheless also true that Socratic political philosophy defined its own cognitive tasks independently of that world view. The Socratic practice of refutation as a form of civic education may indeed have gotten its credibility from the larger project of Greek philosophy, and presupposed in its audience the belief that, through inquiry, all Greeks could indeed arrive at agreement about the definitions of basic moral terms. But Socrates himself offered no answers to the questions he asked others. In practice, Socratic refutation was a form of civic therapy. He embodied in his own rhetorical stance the standpoint he wanted his audience to reach—the civic standpoint of tropological detachment from all particularistic moral vocabularies and a sensitivity to the restricted scope of those vocabularies when used in civic discourse. The goal of Socratic political philosophy was not to arrive at a theoretical knowledge of the nature of civic justice, but rather to produce in citizens the moral insight necessary to act justly. In this respect, Socrates had more in common with Protagoras than he did with Plato. The specifically cognitive task of Socratic political philosophy fit comfortably within the cognitive domain of Aristotelian practical reflection and within the de-totalized perspectives of rhetoric. To the extent that this is true, Socratic political philosophy might provide a second model for a de-totalized and de-totalizing concept of liberal doctrine.

What sort of use could be made of Aristotelian and Socratic models of political philosophy in the postmodern reconstruction of liberal political philosophy? As we have seen, this reconstruction involves a shift from a metaphysical to a political or rhetorical concept of liberal doctrine. A rhetorical concept of liberal doctrine defines liberal doctrine explicitly as a component of liberal democratic civic culture. As a component of civic culture, liberal doctrine must define its cognitive task in rhetorical categories. Civic culture is always a countervailing culture. It is addressed to citizens who are adherents of comprehensive doctrines or totalizing cultural world views. The doctrinal, narrative, and representational resources of any civic culture serve to render intelligible to citizens the norms proper to liberal democratic citizenship, and to motivate them to internalize those norms. As a component of civic culture, liberal doctrine must define its cognitive tasks in terms of this basic rhetorical situation. Our initial question was how specifically these cognitive tasks of a political or rhetorical liberalism might be defined. It is in answer to this question that I briefly considered the Aristotelian and Socratic models of classical political philosophy. To the extent that each of these forms of political philosophy identified as its cognitive domain the realm of practice, as opposed to theory (*pistis,* as opposed to *episteme),* both can usefully be represented as components of Greek republican civic culture. Aristotelian and Socratic forms of political philosophy performed different tasks within that civic culture. Aristotelian political philosophy addressed citizen-rulers and provided concepts and vocabulary for the evaluation of constitutions and laws. Socratic political philosophy offered vocabulary and procedures for civic education. It is in the definitions of their respective cognitive tasks that these two forms of classical political philosophy might serve as models in the postmodern reconstruction of liberalism.

Our need for models is great. As we have seen, modernist liberal political theory departed radically from Aristotelian and Socratic political philosophy in the definition of its cognitive tasks. In the first place, modernist liberalism abandoned the very idea that the domain of moral and political practice, in the Aristotelian sense, could be a cognitive domain. In order to be regarded as a seriously cognitive discourse, political philosophy had to meet the strict standards of "objective" and theoretical truth laid down by foundationalist epistemology. Following classical concepts of theoretical knowledge, modernist liberal political theory assigned itself the task of deducing, from indubitable first principles, universal truths about the essence of human political association. The subject matter of Aristotelian practical reflection was thereby reconstituted as a field of theoretical inquiry—as a new cognitive territory covered by a new political science.

The specifically Aristotelian enterprise, of providing a vocabulary for the classification and evaluation of constitutions, was transformed accordingly. Aristotelian political philosophy addressed and adopted the standpoint of the citizen-ruler engaged in actual political decision making. Modernist liberalism, in accordance with the imperatives of the rhetoric of pure theory, adopted the rhetorical posture of an absolutely detached spectator regarding a field of audience-independent "political" facts. Where the cognitive task of the Aristotelian political philosopher was to provide resources for the evaluation of constitutions with respect to a specific set of circumstances, the cognitive task assumed by modernist liberal political theory was the legitimation or justification of political institutions by a quasi-metaphysical deduction, proving their conformity with first principles (i.e., the natural human condition, the autonomous faculty of reason, etc.). A theoretically legitimated set of political arrangements was presumed to be universally valid and normative—the set of political arrangements that all nations should, or eventually will, adopt. Only this sort of modernist concept of the cognitive task of political philosophy could have produced the bizarre intellectual phenomena of the Cold War—a struggle between two totalizing social and political systems, systems whose claims to legitimacy rested on conflicting philosophical demonstrations of the conformity of those systems with the objective nature of things.

Thus, the abandonment by modernist liberalism of classical concepts of practical knowledge forced liberal doctrine to assume the form of a logically compelling philosophical justification of liberal political institutions. This remains, to this day, the form that serious presentations of liberal doctrine are required to take. This requirement even haunts Rawls's *Political Liberalism*, where it is assumed that a quasi-demonstrative procedure of conceptual construction is needed to generate the concept of justice as fairness. What has always been particularly bizarre about this definition of the cognitive task of liberal political philosophy is the very belief that a theoretical

justification of liberal political institutions actually had some
kind of intrinsic value. What possible value could a theoretical
justification of liberal democracy have in the absence of an
effective civic culture? Where a liberal democracy lacks the
cultural resources to make citizenship intelligible to citizens
and to motivate them to achieve liberal moral ideals, there
will be no citizens and, eventually, no liberal democracy—
even if political philosophers finally come up with a knock-
down proof that liberal ideals of civic freedom and equality
are written into the foundation of the world. By forcing liberal doctrine into the mold of a metaphysical deduction, modernist liberal political theory thus cast into oblivion the entire
Aristotelian cognitive domain of practical knowledge, which is
also the sphere of civic culture—that cognitive domain where
the only real foundations of liberal democracy are laid.

If it is true that modernist liberal theory defined its cognitive tasks in ways that promoted neglect of civic culture, it also
had potentially an even more damaging effect. It promoted
universalist and essentialist misconceptions of liberal moral
ideals that today actually have the effect of positively weakening civic culture. Modernist liberal political philosophy presented liberal doctrine as an integral element of a totalizing
cultural perspective—the "scientific" or naturalist world view.
As we have noted, Greek political philosophy was also a component of a totalizing world view. The concept of republican
citizenship found in Greek political philosophy was shaped by
the pan-Hellenic ethnic project sponsored by Greek philosophy in general. However, the classical distinction between
practical and theoretical knowledge gave the sphere of moral
and political practice a relative independence from the universalist and essentialist cognitive claims made by Greek metaphysics. This relative independence allowed for the development of de-totalizing forms of practical reflection that could
support the development of civic attitudes and values. Both
Aristotelian and Socratic modes of political philosophy oper-
ated in this cognitive domain of moral and political practice,
the cognitive domain of civic culture. But the abandonment
of this cognitive domain by modernist liberal political theory
also eliminated a buffer zone that separated politics from

metaphysics in Greek philosophy. Modernist liberal concepts of citizenship thus became swallowed up by totalizing metaphysical theories about the nature of things. Liberal moral ideals became identified with a cultural perspective that claimed to embrace all humanity.

The most visible, and perhaps significant, consequence of this modernist identification of the political with the metaphysical is that modernist liberal political theory failed to generate forms of civic education that could be clearly labeled as such. As I observed earlier, Socratic political philosophy was, in practice, a form of civic education, a procedure for developing in citizens the capacity to adopt a standpoint of reflective distance from the descriptions of the world licensed by their primary moral vocabularies. Socrates invented a form of civic education that allowed him to embody dramatically the normative standpoint of republican citizenship. In his rhetorical posture of an inquirer whose only knowledge was his ignorance of the answers to the questions he asked, Socrates was able to express both love and complete loyalty to a particularistic community—family, friends, city—while at the same time acknowledging that the particularistic moral vocabulary employed by that community do not define criteria for moral judgment that can claim absolutely universal scope. In other words, Socrates embodied awareness of the distinction between competence in applying particularistic communitarian standards of justice, and a knowledge of justice in itself. Socratic political philosophy defined its cognitive task as reflection on the issues raised and the procedures employed by the form of civic education Socrates invented.

Modernist liberal political theory, on the other hand, invented nothing corresponding to this form of Socratic civic education. As I noted in chapter 1, modernist liberal political theory constructed its concept of the normative standpoint of citizenship by drawing an analogy between the reflective distance from particularistic moral languages required for citizenship, and the absolutely objective standpoint of the pure theoretical knower of foundationalist epistemology. The concept of citizenship based on this analogy produced a new concept of the secondary moral vocabulary proper to civic discourse, and a new concept of the way in which citizens develop the capacity to use that secondary moral vocabulary. Because modernist liberalism identified the normative standpoint of citizenship with the standpoint of autonomous reason, the secondary moral vocabulary proper to civic discourse was equated with the radically objective or culture-neutral vocabulary of science. The function of civic education in a liberal democracy is to help citizens develop the capacity to use the secondary moral vocabulary proper to civic discourse. To the extent that this secondary moral vocabulary was equated with the culture- or value-neutral vocabulary of science, so-called scientific education (i.e., what was conceived as scientific education in accordance with foundationalist epistemological theories) became a de facto form of civic education. The move from the exclusive use of a primary moral language shaped by particularistic cultural values, to the more capacious secondary moral language of citizenship, was thereby conceived of by modernist liberalism as a move from a language where subjective value judgments predominate, to a language that permits only objective cognitive judgments.

Thus, modernist liberal political theory produced no form of civic education that could be clearly labeled as such. The role of civic education was played by "scientific" education—or, more accurately, by a form of education governed by a curriculum that presented all subject matter in terms of a dogmatically asserted and radical distinction between fact and value, between objective, value-neutral scientific knowledge of reality, and subjective value-laden cultural and personal perspectives. By now we have learned that, whatever the merits or demerits of this so-called "scientific" education as a form of technical education, as a form of civic education it is a disaster. The goal of civic education is to teach citizens to use their primary moral vocabulary in a different way, with an internalized sense of its restricted scope or with a certain ironic distance. To speak a primary moral language in this way introduces a certain tension and ambiguity into its use. The secondary moral language proper to civic discourse is just such a primary moral language, spoken in this way. But the "scientific" education licensed by modernist liberalism as a form of civic education does not and cannot have this effect.

To the extent that this "scientific" education was viewed as a surrogate for civic education, the secondary moral language of citizenship was tacitly conceived of as analogous to the supposedly value-neutral cognitive language of science. But the supposedly value-neutral language of science is not a moral language at all. The radical distinction between fact and value on which "scientific" education was based in effect banished all moral language to the realm of the culturally arbitrary and the ontologically irrelevant. If all moral language is culturally arbitrary and ontologically irrelevant, however, then each particularistic primary moral vocabulary shares that status with every other. All are equal in their cognitive deficiencies and, therefore, any choice between conflicting primary moral vocabularies is a purely arbitrary one. But this view that all primary moral vocabularies are equal in their arbitrary status effectively absolutizes each one, making it immune to any sort of critical reflection. Critical reflection on one's primary moral vocabulary, however, is the heart and soul of civic education. Modernist "scientific" education, therefore, to the extent that it eliminated any motive for the critical examination of primary moral vocabularies, eliminated the necessary condition for the development of a capacity to speak a primary moral language with critical detachment—which is the very capacity for civic discourse itself. It is modernist "scientific" education, functioning as a surrogate for civic education, that during the last 100 years in America has brought forth that peculiar educational product, the closed open mind. This phenomenon, whose dialectic was described by Allan Bloom in his book, *The Closing of the American Mind*,[28] occurs when students effectively internalize the message of the "scientific" curriculum and become "open-minded" (i.e., learn to see the arbitrary nature and merely relative validity of all particularistic moral values). As a result, they conclude that because all primary moral vocabularies are equal in their arbitrariness

---

[28] Allan Bloom, *The Closing of the American Mind* (New York: Simon and Schuster, 1987).

and cognitive deficiency, there is no real point in seriously investigating other cultural world views or in critically examining their own.

Thus, the cognitive tasks identified with both Aristotelian and Socratic varieties of classical political philosophy were abandoned by modernist liberal political theory, and replaced with a very different set of cognitive tasks. Aristotelian practical reflection on the norms proper to political decision making was replaced by the theoretical legitimation or justification of regimes. Socratic civic education was replaced by a form of education aimed at promoting adherence to the totalizing world view of modernist science. The common intellectual ground shared by both of these developments was the abandonment of the classical distinction between practical and theoretical knowledge. Modernist liberal political theorists took up the anti-rhetorical rhetoric of pure theory invented by foundationalist epistemologists and, following them, collapsed the three different cognitive domains of classical philosophy (those of theoretical, practical and technical knowledge) into one: the cognitive domain of pure theory.

We are today paying the price for this modernist redrawing of the cognitive map. Notice, for example, the difficulty we have in classifying the subject matter of a book like Rawls's *Political Liberalism.* Is the book a contribution to political theory—that is, to the enterprise of discovering the objective truth about the essence of political morality or the invariable laws governing human political association? Emphatically not. The book presents a concept of liberalism as a political doctrine, a type of political morality restricted in scope, both with respect to those who practice it (i.e., citizens of modern constitutional democracies), and with respect to the range of human issues it addresses. Well, is the book then to be understood as an application of theory (the modernist sense of "practical")? Is it a book on social or political policy? Or does Rawls make an argument for his concept of justice as fairness that is designed to win adherents for a particular political program? Hardly. The book's argument is far too abstract for that. It presents itself as a philosophical reflection about the basis and limits of liberal democratic political morality, as a concept of the norms proper to a particular form of political association. But what do we call this sort of exercise? Is it speaking of anything that we, applying modernist standards, would call a concept of morality at all? It comes with no metaphysical pedigree. It finds its only foundations in a particular contingent way of life. Seen with modernist eyes, an arbitrary and groundless morality such as this would be devoid of universally binding normative force.

Even Rawls seems to be uncertain about how to classify in general terms the subject matter and goals of *Political Liberalism*. He presents his concept of liberal morality as validated by a constructivist procedure almost, but not quite, like a Kantian one. It seems that his careful observance of all the rhetorical conventions of modernist liberal political theory functions almost as a strategy for avoiding the question. But this question cannot be avoided. Nothing can hide the fact that *Political Liberalism* stands on what is, for us at least, new cognitive ground. It is the cognitive ground of Aristotelian practical philosophy. It remains to be seen how far classical concepts of practical knowledge can advance our project of inventing a postmodern political or rhetorical concept of liberal doctrine. It seems to me, however, that we will make no sense at all of this project until we have succeeded in recovering the basic perspectives underlying Aristotelian practical philosophy and Socratic civic education.

The de-totalization of the liberal democratic public sphere

The rhetorical turn in the reconstruction of liberal political philosophy addresses the issue of the intelligibility of liberal doctrine and of liberal democratic citizenship itself. Thus far in this exploration of some of the implications of the shift from a metaphysical to a political or rhetorical concept of liberal doctrine, we have been trying to get some idea of what a thoroughly non-metaphysical or de-totalized form of liberal doctrine would look like, or how a postmodern version of liberal political philosophy would define its cognitive tasks. Now, I want to look at the scene from a different angle—turning away from the question of doctrinal form or cognitive status, and focusing on the question of doctrinal content or subject matter.

The particular question of doctrinal content or subject matter I want to consider deals with a certain reversal in our understanding of the relationship between the public sphere and the private sphere that a political or rhetorical version of liberal doctrine must accomplish. A political or rhetorical version of liberal doctrine presents liberalism as a doctrine that is partial, rather than comprehensive, in scope. This is what Rawls tells us. But, as I indicated earlier, I think we must take this concept of the partial character of liberal doctrine one step further. To conceive of liberalism now as a doctrine pertaining only to the part rather than to the whole of life is to do more than merely introduce into our view of liberalism the idea of its limitation in scope. Rather, and far more, it is to assign to liberal doctrine, within the context of a postmodern civic culture, a new rhetorical function. To the extent that modernist liberal political theory represented liberalism as a comprehensive or totalizing doctrine, a political or rhetorical concept of liberal doctrine must actively undo this totalization. It must reverse the effects of the modernist representation of liberal moral and political ideals as elements of a totalizing world view.

One particular area in which this reversal must be accomplished concerns our understanding of the relative cultural standing and significance of the public and private spheres. The direction of this reversal is indicated in Rawls's concept of an overlapping consensus. According to Rawls, a political concept of justice (i.e., one that fully acknowledges and affirms it own restricted scope) cannot provide a basis for social unity and stability. Social unity and stability can be provided only by an overlapping consensus in support of liberal moral ideals and political arrangements[29] among members of diverse cultural communities. This means that the liberal concept of justice that governs political arrangements and provides order to the public sphere must be defined and present-

---

[29] Rawls, *PL*, p. 134.

ed in such a way that it is capable of gaining the support of the diverse cultural communities subject to it. Rawls himself does not emphasize it, but this view of the role of an overlapping consensus definitely constitutes a reversal in our understanding of a certain aspect of the relationship between the public and private spheres in a liberal democracy.

It is this reversal that must not only be observed, but also pursued actively as one piece of the postmodern reconstruction of liberalism. This reversal concerns the relative dependence and independence of the cultural perspectives proper to the public and private spheres. The reversal is due to the demise of modernist liberal concepts of liberalism as a comprehensive doctrine. When conceived as a comprehensive doctrine or totalizing world view, liberalism seemed capable of providing the basis of social unity and stability. For modernist liberalism, the totalizing cultural standpoint proper to the liberal democratic public sphere was capable by itself of providing norms and justifying political arrangements, independently of the diverse cultural world views proper to particular ethnic, class, and religious communities. But now, with the abandonment of totalizing modernist concepts of liberal doctrine, the tables must be turned. The relationship of dependence must be reversed. Liberalism, as a doctrine pertaining only to the part and not to the whole of life, can no longer, using its own resources alone, provide a cultural basis for social stability and unity. That cultural basis must be supplied by a consensus among members of the diverse cultural communities that make up any particular liberal democracy. It is this reversal that I have in mind when I speak of the "detotalization of the public sphere."

What I want to do here is to explore briefly a few of the implications of this reversal. But first let us make sure that we clearly understand the nature of the reversal itself. The detotalization of the public sphere is a project that is part of a general reorientation of liberal political philosophy. This project aims at replacing the modernist concept of liberal doctrine, as one sufficient by itself to provide the cultural basis of the unity and stability of society, with a political or rhetorical concept of liberal doctrine that views the stability and unity of society as dependent upon the development of an overlapping cultural consensus supportive of liberal moral ideals and political arrangements. Liberal moral ideals and political arrangements define the public sphere of a liberal democracy. The public sphere is the realm of speech and action in which the issues pertaining to the basic institutional structure of society are addressed and in which citizens address and behave toward one another explicitly as citizens (i.e., as free and equal individuals). Modernist liberal political theory conceived of the public sphere in a way that represented it as culturally self-sufficient, as sufficient to provide a cultural basis for the unity and stability of society. It interpreted those ideas and ideals as components of a comprehensive or totalizing world view, a world view capable of addressing satisfactorily all the basic issues of human life.

Let us recall briefly how this cultural totalization of the public sphere was represented by modernist liberal civic culture. As we noted earlier, modernist liberal political theory identified the normative standpoint of citizenship—the standpoint of free and equal individuality—as the universal and essential standpoint of humanity as such. If the public sphere of a liberal democracy is the field of activity wherein citizens assume the standpoint of free and equal individuality, and if the standpoint of free and equal individuality is identified as the universal and essential standpoint of humanity as such, then, in this interpretation, the liberal democratic public sphere assumes a profound moral and metaphysical significance. It becomes the primary locus or encompassing setting within which the metaphysical drama of human life is played out. It is in the liberal democratic public sphere that the metaphysically defining traits of human beings—the basis for concepts of universal human rights—are either given their full weight or denied.

Interpreted in this way, the public sphere could not be viewed simply as one contingent field of activity and aspiration among others. The properties attributed to human beings as members of particularistic cultural communities are not metaphysically indelible. As persons alter their ethnic, class, and religious identifications and affiliations, old descriptions are replaced by new. But, through all such changes, a person's underlying, metaphysically permanent identity—that of a free and equal individual—remains. This way of representing the relationship between civic identity and communitarian identity was the basis for the modernist liberal interpretation of the public sphere as the culturally basic and all-encompassing field of activity and aspiration. Thus interpreted, the public sphere could easily be represented as culturally self-sufficient—that is, as containing within itself all the cultural resources necessary to provide a cultural basis for the unity and stability of society.

We must keep in mind, of course, that we are now speaking only of the way in which the public sphere was represented by the form of civic culture shaped in its content specifically by the ideas of modernist liberal political theory. Further, we must keep in mind that this attribution of metaphysical significance and priority to the public sphere affected only the beliefs of those citizens actually influenced by modernist civic culture (i.e., the citizens most politically active and self-consciously liberal). Needless to say, large numbers of nominal citizens in every liberal democracy develop the moral and linguistic capacities of citizenship either only partially or not at all. Such nominal citizens either marginalize themselves to some degree politically and culturally—at the extreme, for example, think of the Amish in Pennsylvania or the Lubavitcher sect in Brooklyn—or participate in reactionary cultural and political movements that are actively hostile to the values of the liberal democratic public sphere. Among such nominal citizens, the totalizing culture of the public sphere generally had little positive impact. But where modernist liberal civic culture did take hold and create citizens, the totalizing culture of the public sphere did influence beliefs. From the standpoint of this totalizing culture, there was no question as to the proper rank and cultural significance to be assigned to the public sphere. The cultural worlds inhabited by particularistic ethnic, class, and religious communities were seen as having a clearly secondary and subordinate status. In the norms proper to those cultural worlds, the metaphysically defining traits of humanity at large are not at issue. At issue in those particularistic cultural worlds are merely the arbitrary projects fostered by the accidental historical conditions of local community life. Thus, among citizens actually influenced by the totalizing culture of the modernist liberal public sphere, the consequence of affirming the cultural self-sufficiency of the public sphere was a certain diminution of the cognitive and moral authority of particularistic cultural beliefs and life ideals.

Since it was above all the particularistic cultural beliefs and life ideals of religious communities that were diminished in moral authority by the modernist liberal totalization of the public sphere, let us refer to this general consequence as the process of secularization. Modernist liberal political theory represented the liberal democratic public sphere as containing within itself the cultural resources necessary to provide a cultural basis for the unity and stability of society. The unity and stability of society was an interest common to all citizens. A good citizen is one whose beliefs as well as actions are consistent with the goal of maintaining a united and stable society. When the public sphere is represented as containing within itself the cultural resources necessary for social unity and stability, the natural presumption is that the cultural resources offered by the public sphere are alone consistent with good citizenship. To the extent that this sort of presumption made itself felt, the cognitive and moral requirements of good citizenship seemed to be in direct conflict with the cognitive and moral requirements imposed by adherence to particularistic cultural world views, especially religious world views. The totalizing culture of the liberal public sphere offered moral ideals that were incompatible with those identified with particular ethnic, class, and religious communities. Two of these liberal moral ideals, what I have called the civic ethics of authenticity and the civic ethics of autonomy, were particularly hostile to religious values and beliefs. Yet, from the standpoint of modernist liberal civic culture, it seemed that the unity and stability of society could be guaranteed only by widespread, if not exclusive, adherence to these liberal moral ideals.

Thus, the totalization of the public sphere by modernist liberalism seemed to impose on society as a whole a process of cultural secularization—that is, a process mandating, in the name of good citizenship and the unity and stability of society, acceptance of a totalizing cultural world view that diminished the authority of beliefs and values held by particular ethnic, class, and religious communities. The totalization of the public sphere in modernist liberal civic culture produced, in this way, something like an informally established, state-sponsored secular "religion"—a totalizing cultural world view whose acceptance was tacitly required as a condition for full cultural citizenship. Fundamentalist Christian critics of liberalism—critics whose entire point of view has been largely determined by their reaction against this secular "religion"—have given it the name of "secular humanism." If nothing else, their campaign against what they call secular humanism demonstrates their acute awareness of the cultural forces arrayed against them (and against all other religious persons inclined toward orthodoxy) in modernist civic culture. It also points to a problem that any political or rhetorical concept of liberal doctrine must address. Metaphysical liberalism asserted the cultural independence and self-sufficiency of the public realm in a way that set it in opposition to the moral ideals and world views of particularistic cultural communities. The totalizing culture of the modernist liberal public sphere defined the public sphere in a way that was in principle, and always potentially, totalitarian—by joining the liberal democratic public sphere with a cultural world view claiming inclusive and exclusive dominion.

Rawls's concept of an overlapping cultural consensus addresses this problem. With the demise of Enlightenment concepts of reason and knowledge, the world view that provided the cultural resources supporting the cultural independence of the public sphere has collapsed. This fact alone renders obsolete the modernist liberal representation of the political sphere as culturally self-sufficient. A post-Enlightenment political or rhetorical concept of liberal doctrine is one that acknowledges and embraces its restricted cognitive and moral scope. For such a concept of liberal doctrine, the public sphere cannot supply the cultural resources necessary to provide a cultural basis for the unity and stability of society. This cultural basis must be supplied by an overlapping consensus among the particularistic cultural communities that make up any given liberal democracy. This does not mean that the public sphere, by itself, cannot offer some cultural perspectives supportive of social unity and stability. The resources that it can provide I will describe in chapter 4. What it means is that the liberal moral ideals and political arrangements defining the public sphere must be supported primarily by cultural resources drawn from particularistic ethnic, class, and religious world views. It also means that, in order to secure this support, liberal doctrine must not be formulated or understood in such a way as to conflict gratuitously with beliefs and moral ideals sponsored by particularistic cultural communities—rather, it must be conceived explicitly as a doctrine pertaining only to a part and not to the whole of life, one that leaves plenty of room for orthodoxies of all kinds.

The nature of that reversal in our understanding of the relationship between the public and private spheres is announced in Rawls's concept of an overlapping cultural consensus. The philosophical project of carrying through this reversal systematically I have called the de-totalization of the public sphere. Once the nature and goals of this project have been roughly defined, the next step is to begin the process of rethinking liberalism in a way that no longer represents the liberal democratic public sphere as culturally self-sufficient. One of the primary tasks of a political or rhetorical concept of liberalism is to establish clearly the cultural limits of the public sphere. If liberalism is a moral doctrine pertaining only to the part and not to the whole of life, the next task must be to define that part. If liberal moral ideals and political arrangements apply only to a limited range of life issues, then just what is their specific range of application?

Getting a handle on this question has its difficulties—for there is a definite sense in which liberal moral ideals and political arrangements are encompassing in scope. According to Rawls, liberalism as a political doctrine takes as its subject the basic institutional structure of society. A particular concept of civic justice defines a specific way of ordering that basic structure. Needless to say, the way in which this question is answered by citizens of any particular liberal democracy has an impact on every aspect of their lives. The basic institutional structure of a liberal democracy shapes an entire way of life. It define rights, liberties, and protections. It assigns duties and responsibilities. From the basic structure of society are derived rules that govern the relationships between employer and employee, husband and wife, parent and child, merchant and customer. To determine the basic institutional structure of a society is to structure these relationships. Because questions about the basic structure of society involve every aspect of life and affect every citizen, the perspective that must be adopted in answering those questions (i.e., the perspective proper to the liberal democratic public sphere) is a perspective on the whole society. The legislator, the elected official, the civil administrator, the judge—these roles above all require that the individuals assuming them adopt this perspective on the whole.

This perspective "on the whole," however, encompasses the whole of society only with respect to one issue—the issue of civic justice. The basic structure of society structures the relationships between employer and employee, husband and wife, parent and child, merchant and customer—but only with respect to the question of whether the definition and the functioning of these relationships are just (i.e., are in accordance with the fundamental concept of civic justice embodied in the basic political arrangements of society). On the other hand, each one of these relationships has its primary setting within a more encompassing context of life issues—the general life issues of sex, friendship, work, suffering, sin, death, and salvation—a context in which civic justice is but one issue among others. Thus, while it is true that the cultural and political perspective proper to the public sphere is a perspective on the whole of society (i.e., encompasses all citizens and affects all their relationships and activities), it nevertheless encompasses the whole only with respect to one issue in the universe of human concerns. A political or rhetorical concept of liberal doctrine addresses only this one issue. Comprehensive doctrines or totalizing world views, on the other hand, speak to them all.

Liberal democracy is distinguished from other forms of

political association by the way it makes questions of civic justice answerable independently of the global answers given to
other life issues. The citizens of a liberal democracy, in a con-
tinuous process of public deliberation, decide how they will
organize their cooperation. Whatever decisions they may
make in any particular case, the point of agreement from
which they begin their deliberation is the principle that political or civic justice is not to be determined by the criteria established by one or another global response to the entire context
of human life issues. This relative independence of the issue
of civic justice finds its expression in the liberal doctrine of
the priority of the right over the good. Within the entire context of human life issues, only civic justice, as conceived by liberal doctrine, can be given this kind of independence.

In decisions involving judgments about sex, friendship,
work, suffering, sin, death, and salvation, human beings apply
criteria drawn from one or another comprehensive concept
of the good life. Decisions about these questions normally
require reference to ultimate purposes and goals—some concept of what life is finally all about, some concept of what is
of lasting importance, some more or less clear specification of
priorities. Particular decisions by individuals about these questions determine and reflect their membership in particularistic cultural communities. The criteria applied in such decisions are normally drawn from and guided by shared
traditions of coherent and comprehensive belief—traditions
that attempt to provide a coherent set of responses to the full
range of human life issues, so that responses to the issue of
sex or reproduction cohere with responses to the issue
of friendship or companionship, with responses to the issue of
work, and so on. In questions of political or civic justice, however, liberalism requires citizens to apply criteria drawn from
a source that lies external to any particularistic cultural tradition or community. They must measure the justice of their
relationships and their actions not by reference to criteria
drawn from one or another shared concept of the good, but
rather by reference to criteria drawn from a set of agreed-
upon principles of civic justice that govern their cooperation.

Liberal doctrine pertains to the part rather than the whole

of life, then, in the sense that it concerns only that sphere defined by the principles of civic justice. It is important to note that, more strictly, liberal doctrine pertains not just to a part of life, but to a part of a part. The issue of civic justice is only one aspect of the general life issue of justice. The general life issue of justice arises from the human need for a socially confirmed sense of dignity or self-respect. The rule of justice is "equals to equals." This means that persons who are considered equal (in some respect and in accordance with some measure) should be treated equally. To be socially confirmed in one's self-respect (i.e., to be treated justly), one must be treated in ways that are perceived to be equal to the treatment of other persons who are considered to be of the same status and rank. In defining status and rank, criteria must be applied. Some criteria that define differentials of status and rank are drawn from intrinsic features of particular life activities or life issues. Thus, with respect to the life issue of sex or reproduction, rank and relative worth are determined by beauty, strength, fertility, and so on. With respect to the life issue of friendship or companionship, rank and relative worth are determined by family relationship, common interests, and personal compatibility. With respect to the life issue of work, rank and relative worth are determined by talent, economic resources, and industry.

In addition to these criteria of rank and status drawn from intrinsic features of particular life activities and life issues, other criteria are drawn from the ranking systems defined by different concepts of the good or cultural traditions. In different cultural traditions, the various life issues are assigned different degrees of importance for the overall meaning and purpose of life. In some cultural traditions, sin and salvation are accorded supreme importance, while sex and reproduction are ranked lower. In other cultural traditions, work and friendship are given primacy over both sex and salvation. These cultural differences determine the culturally defined status and rank of any particular individual with respect to any particular life issue and life activity. General features of human life—such as age, health, gender, and race or birth—will affect an individual's rank or status differently, depending on membership in different cultural communities. Accordingly, if the general life issue of justice (i.e., the issue raised by the need for a socially confirmed sense of self-respect) is a matter of securing equal treatment for persons of equal rank or status, then this issue will be decided in most cases by resort to local, culturally determined ranking systems—for it is such local ranking systems that define, with respect to most life issues, what constitutes equal status and rank in any given case.

Let us call issues of justice that are resolved by resort to such local, culturally sensitive ranking systems issues of communitarian justice. In matters of communitarian justice, the reverse of the liberal principle holds—that is, the good has priority over and defines the right. In matters of communitarian justice, the rule of justice ("equals to equals") is given its concrete application and content by reference to one or another local concept of the good. However, with the establishment of liberal political institutions, the issue of justice is defined in a new way. Of course, even in a liberal democracy, most questions of justice remain questions of communitarian justice. But liberal political institutions introduce a new set of criteria for determining rank and relative worth. We have called issues of justice that are resolved by resort to these new criteria issues of civic justice. Liberal doctrine pertains only to that sphere of life defined by the proper application of the criteria of civic justice. Liberal doctrine thus pertains not only to a part of life, to one life issue among many, but more exactly to a part of that part, to the life issue of justice as civic justice. Issues of civic justice are resolved not by resort to ranking systems belonging to one or another particularistic cultural community, but rather by resort to a set of agreed upon principles underlying the institutional structure of a liberal democracy. These principles constitute the criteria of civic justice, the criteria according to which the rule of justice is applied to define the equal status and determine the equal treatment of citizens.

Of course, the specific principles that determine the specific criteria of civic justice will differ from one liberal democracy to another. Those specific principles are always a matter for decision by citizens. They are subject to revision. As we noted earlier, there can be no "theory" of civic justice that could claim to define the principles of civic justice for any particular liberal democracy in advance of the political process through which those principles are actually found acceptable. However, while the principles of civic justice cannot be defined in advance of that political process, if they are to qualify as principles of liberal or civic justice they must be consistent with the concept of equality inherent in the notion of citizenship itself.

A citizen is a human being whose rank or status is determined by reference to the basic structure of a modern constitutional democracy. As citizens, in their relationship to the state and to the basic structure of society, human beings are not distinguished by reference to their membership in particular ethnic, class, or religious communities. They are not distinguished by reference to their race, age, or gender. Thus, in their relationship to the basic structure of a liberal democratic society, human beings are taken simply as individuals. Further, the differentials of status, rank, and relative worth that come into play for various purposes when human beings are viewed as members of ethnic, class, and religious communities have no relevance when they are viewed simply as citizens. Thus, in their relationship to the basic structure of liberal democratic society, human beings are viewed as possessing equal status or rank, whatever may be their rank or status in other contexts. Further, as we have seen, the personal goals and commitments assumed by human beings as members of particularistic ethnic, class, or religious communities define their identities as members of those communities. But when viewed in relation to the basic structure of a liberal democratic society, the identities of human beings are defined only by rights and duties, liberties and constraints applying to all citizens equally as specified by law. In that relationship, human beings are understood as being free—free to alter their purely personal goals, commitments, and identities at will.

In their relationship to the basic structure of a liberal democratic society, then, human beings are viewed as free and equal individuals. When addressing and acting toward one another explicitly in this way (i.e., as free and equal individuals), human beings explicitly assume the attributes and standpoint proper to citizenship. In addressing one another as citizens, human beings adopt standards of relevance that render differences of race, age, gender, ethnicity, social class, and religious belief irrelevant. The specific principles of civic justice adopted at any given time by any particular liberal democracy may vary widely in their content. But, to qualify as principles of liberal or civic justice, they must be consistent with this normative concept of free and equal individuality inherent in the very notion of liberal democratic citizenship.

In any case, it is clear that liberal doctrine, understood in this way as pertaining only to matters of civic justice, pertains only to the part, rather than the whole, of life. In the same way, the liberal democratic public sphere, as the sphere defined by a common interest in civic justice, must also be represented as encompassing issues relevant only to a restricted set of concerns. Conceived of in this way, the public sphere cannot be represented as a sphere providing, on its own, resources sufficient to provide a cultural basis for social stability and unity. The interest in civic justice, however intense, is simply too abstract, too culturally "thin" to generate the deep commitment to civic values and the strong feelings of civic friendship required for social stability and unity. The cultural resources required for the generation of such commitment and feeling must be drawn from the resources of the various cultural communities that make up any particular liberal democracy. But if, conceived in this way, the liberal democratic public sphere cannot be represented as culturally self-sufficient, neither can it be represented as mandating acceptance of a totalizing cultural world view as a condition for full cultural citizenship, a totalizing world view that is competitive with or hostile to the cultural world views and life ideals of particularistic cultural communities. Conceived of in this way, the cultural perspectives proper to the public sphere cannot present an obstacle to the formation of the overlapping cultural consensus necessary for the survival of any postmodern liberal democracy.

The de-totalization of the cultural perspectives proper to

the public sphere thus can make an important contribution to the intelligibility of postmodern liberal democratic citizenship. Rawls's concept of the overlapping cultural consensus that must provide the cultural basis for social unity and stability effectively reverses the relationship of dependence between the public and private spheres. Speech and action within the public sphere must be modified accordingly. If the cultural perspectives proper to the public sphere encompass only matters relevant to the issue of civic justice, then the public sphere can no longer be understood as a secularized and secularizing setting within which the drama of human life as a whole is played out—a totalizing cultural domain demanding acceptance of its moral and cognitive ideals in the name of social stability and unity. Rather, the liberal democratic public sphere must find its cultural foundations beyond itself, by an appeal to beliefs and values that have their home outside the domain of political life. Liberal doctrine in the future must be understood and formulated in such a way as to make that appeal successful.

This is not to say, however, that, with the de-totalization of the public sphere and of liberal doctrine in general, all tension is removed between civic and communitarian moral ideals. But the tensions that remain have more to do with questions of motivation than with questions of intelligibility. Civic and communitarian moral ideals, after all, serve very different life functions. The ideal of civic justice, for example, will always in some measure conflict with ideals of communitarian justice. The criteria proper to communitarian justice are specified by the totalizing world views of particularistic cultural communities. These cultural communities are communities of shared aspiration and interest. Such communities are ultimately rooted in the soil of biological life. They develop distinctive styles of reproduction, nourishment, labor, speech, and mutual care that are at the same time styles and modalities of human desire. These totalizing world views or concepts of the good have as their function the nurturing, direction, and support of that desire. Wherever human desire and aspiration must be nurtured, there also must hierarchy and rank exist. Characteristic of communities of aspiration and common interest are relations of command and submission, dependence and domination. In such communities, various forms of servitude, hierarchical social organization, and segregation based on age and gender are typical. The moral ideals sponsored by such communities are designed to give form and direction to the lives of individuals by shaping desire in specific ways. Those ideals define hierarchies of excellence and achievement that determine the rank order of the individuals subject to them. Nothing could be more foreign to such communities than the civic moral ideals of freedom and equality.

Here the issue of motivation arises. Properly understood, civic culture is always a partial and a countervailing culture. Civic culture is the culture proper to the public sphere. It is a "thin" culture, addressed to only one general life issue (i.e., the issue of civic justice). Civic culture differs radically in purpose from communitarian cultures. It does not provide an interpretative framework for life as a whole. It does not define a standard reproductive style, an ideal of family life, or a set of answers to life's deepest questions. It does not provide hierarchies of excellence and achievement designed to nurture and direct human desire and aspiration. Rather, civic culture has but one function. It must provide the cultural resources sufficient to render intelligible the liberal democratic moral ideals of individual freedom and equality, and to motivate citizens to pursue those ideals. When a civic culture successfully carries out this function, it does not create a new particularistic community of aspiration and common interest that stands opposed to other particularistic cultural communities. It does not create a new totalizing communitarian culture that provides a global concept of a complete and flourishing human life. Rather, when civic culture functions effectively, it provides citizens with the linguistic and moral capacities to meet the requirements of civic justice—that is, to treat one another as free and equal individuals in accordance with a set of agreed-upon principles or rules. These civic capacities do not exist apart from the capacities required for the successful pursuit of goals defined by communitarian culture. They exist only as a modification of those capacities.

Civic culture, then, as a partial and countervailing culture, presupposes and remains dependent upon communitarian culture. It cannot stand by itself. The modernist liberal project, of constructing a civic culture that could be misunderstood as something like a communitarian culture, resembles a project of making the tail wag the dog. This is what Rawls's doctrine of the overlapping cultural consensus tells us. It tells us that the relationship of dependence between civic and communitarian culture established by modernist liberal political theory must be reversed. A civic culture, to carry out its function successfully, must draw upon the traditions and moral ideals of the particularistic cultural communities it addresses. What the notion of an overlapping cultural consensus does not do is tell us how this can be done. The civic moral ideals of individual freedom and equality are not only partial and "thin" as moral ideals. They also can be unsettling to adherents of communitarian cultures. Civic moral ideals can be dangerous. Citizens in the full cultural sense are those who have developed the capacity to put aside the ranking systems and hierarchies proper to their communitarian cultures, and to address other citizens within the public sphere as free and equal individuals. But to put aside communitarian ranking systems and hierarchies is at least to place limits on their otherwise all-encompassing claims to authority. Liberal civic culture can often appear, to adherents of communitarian cultures, as a culture that requires the abandonment of all ranking systems and the overturning of all hierarchies.

Whereas the specific conflict between civic and communitarian cultures produced by modernist liberalism can be overcome by the de-totalization of the public sphere, this other conflict—the conflict between civic and communitarian ideals of justice—is intrinsic to the relationship between civic and communitarian cultures. Civic culture is a countervailing culture. It seeks to modify the speech, the actions, and the very identities of adherents of particularistic communitarian cultures in ways that can be unsettling. If civic culture is to be effective in producing these modifications, it must be persuasive. But what means of persuasion are available to it? If civic culture seems to threaten the abandonment of all ranking systems and the overturning of all hierarchies—ranking systems and hierarchies that are required for the nurturing and direction of human desire—how can adherents of particularistic communitarian cultures be convinced that it is worthwhile to undertake the considerable moral and intellectual task of becoming citizens in the full cultural sense? Once we have understood the partial and dependent nature of civic culture, we must turn to this next issue—the issue of motivation. Let us now address one aspect of that issue.

4 The Liberation of Desire

Motivating full cultural citizenship

What I have called the rhetorical turn in contemporary liberal political philosophy addresses the issue of the intelligibility of liberal doctrine and of liberal democratic citizenship itself. There is such a thing as an "intelligibility issue" for a post-Enlightenment civic culture because modernist liberal political theory interpreted liberalism as a comprehensive doctrine or totalizing world view. Such a concept of liberal doctrine misrepresents both its scope (i.e., the range of life issues it encompasses) and its rhetorical function. A political or rhetorical concept of liberal doctrine corrects both of these misrepresentations and therefore, as a component of a postmodern civic culture, can clear away some of the purely conceptual obstacles to the realization of full cultural citizenship. In the same way, there is such a thing as a "motivational issue" for a post-Enlightenment civic culture because the motivational resources provided by modernist liberal political theory depended on viewing liberal moral ideals in universalist and essentialist terms. Such a concept of liberal moral ideals mis-

159

represents the real grounds for the desirability of their realization. Moreover, this universalist and essentialist misreading of
liberal moral ideals provided motivation by subtly disparaging
the moral ideals of particularistic cultural communities. As we
have seen, this aspect of modernist liberalism is particularly
damaging to the project of forging an overlapping consensus
among those cultural communities in support of liberal
democratic political institutions.

Just as the rhetorical turn in contemporary liberal thought
speaks to the issue of intelligibility, so what I have called the
teleological turn addresses the issue of motivation. The issue
of motivation has to do with the persuasive power of any form
of liberal democratic civic culture. It is one thing to understand the nature of citizenship, but it is quite another to perceive as something desirable the development and exercise of
the moral and intellectual capacities proper to citizenship. As
we have seen, modernist liberal concepts of civic moral ideals
did not represent them in terms of their desirability at all.
The civic ethics of authenticity and autonomy were expressions of the general principle of the priority of the right over
the good. The modernist liberal concept of this principle
specified that the criterion of moral rightness (i.e., the conformity of action to law) must not be drawn from any particularistic cultural concept of the good life. The criterion proper to
civic justice, in other words, must not have any particularistic
cultural content. Moral rightness cannot be based upon the
mere desirability of a particular way of life. Moral rightness
had to be defined, therefore, in absolutely universal terms, as
a matter of conformity to universal law—law applicable to all
persons everywhere and at all times. This modernist concept
of moral rightness produced an interpretation of liberal
moral ideals that was excessively formalist in character. The
civic ethics of authenticity and autonomy mandated not the
attainment of a particular object of desire, but rather the
practice of a certain way of pursuing any particular object of
desire whatever. The moral ideals of authenticity and autonomy mandated a certain "how" of action, and not a particular
"what" of desire.

These modernist liberal moral ideals have lost their persuasive power. That persuasive power was derived from the belief that it was indeed possible to specify a criterion for moral rightness that was free of all contamination from any particularistic concept of the good, a criterion for civic justice that was applicable to all times and places. But with the discrediting of this belief, the liberal moral ideals of authenticity and autonomy also lose their normative and persuasive power. If every criterion of moral rightness is contaminated by particularistic historical and cultural conditions, then so also is the liberal democratic moral criterion of rightness. The criterion of civic justice, too, must be derived from some particularistic concept of the good, from affirmation of the desirability of some particularistic way of life. The teleological turn in contemporary liberal thought takes this recognition as its point of departure. The liberal doctrine of the priority of the right over the good must be interpreted in teleological terms. It must no longer be read as a doctrine establishing a set of universally obligatory laws or principles as constraints on the pursuit of happiness. Rather, it must be recast as a doctrine asserting the priority, under certain circumstances, of a particularistic object of desire, a particularistic happiness ideal, over other equally particularistic objects of desire and happiness ideals. This means that we must learn to see liberal democracies as perfectionist regimes of a very special type. A liberal democracy, that is to say, is a form of political association aimed at the realization of a substantive, particularistic concept of the good, and the success of any particular liberal democracy is to be measured by the degree of its success in providing conditions for the attainment of that good. The liberal state thus cannot, in principle, be properly conceived as occupying a standpoint that is culturally and morally neutralist.

The persuasive power of a postmodern form of liberal democratic civic culture will depend on the clarity and insight of its definition of the nature of this civic good. A teleological concept of liberal doctrine must provide that definition. What is the unique good that can be achieved only through the attainment of full cultural citizenship? Why is the attainment of full cultural citizenship desirable? What sort of case could be made to any nominal citizen that could succeed in persuading him or her to undertake the difficult moral and intellectual work involved in developing and exercising the capacities proper to liberal democratic citizenship? Before we take a first cut at providing an answer to this question, two further points must be noted.

First, a concept of the civic good, to be effective as a component of civic culture, must be represented as a final, and not merely as an instrumental, good. One readily available and familiar type of answer to the question as to why liberal political arrangements are desirable—the answer offered by so-called *modus vivendi* versions of liberal doctrine—conceives of that desirability in purely instrumental terms. According to *modus vivendi* liberalism, the benefit offered by the liberal form of political association becomes apparent above all in situations of protracted political and cultural conflict. That benefit is civil peace. Faced with the threat of unremitting civil war, it is in the mutual interest of all the opposing parties to find some way to live and let live. When no single community is strong enough to impose its cultural and political will on all others, then a prudent political compromise, some institutional means of sharing political power more or less equitably, will be the best outcome any group can hope for.

This kind of answer, basic to all forms of *modus vivendi* liberalism, is perhaps less a philosophical response to the question of motivation than an instinctive political strategy triggered by conditions of chronic cultural and civil strife. For *modus vivendi* liberalism, citizenship is indeed a good, but merely an instrumental, and not a substantive or final, good. Citizenship defines a relationship between members of different particularistic cultural communities that establishes a regime permitting peaceful coexistence among those communities. For *modus vivendi* liberalism, liberal political institutions have as their cultural basis a compromise among antagonistic cultural communities, a compromise that places certain limits on the public conduct of their members in exchange for a guarantee of noninterference by outsiders on questions of how those communities handle their internal affairs. For *modus vivendi* liberalism, then, citizenship is a good only as a means to an end—the pursuit of a particularistic way of life in peace. The interest any citizen would have in that status would be basically similar to the interest a person would have in securing any other resource necessary for the realization of his or her concept of the good life.

As a sort of minimalist case for the establishment of liberal political arrangements, of course, *modus vivendi* liberalism can be a conceptually coherent and effective persuasive strategy, particularly in times of great civil conflict. But the problem with *modus vivendi* liberalism is that it is far too minimalist to provide the basis for an effective civic culture and a program of civic education. *Modus vivendi* liberalism sees the standpoint of citizenship as qualitatively indistinguishable from the standpoint of membership in a particularistic cultural community. To be a citizen means simply to observe certain behavioral constraints—the behavioral constraints specified by the law (i.e., by the liberal state)—over and beyond the behavioral constraints imposed by any membership in a particularistic cultural community. Those additional constraints are observed in the interest of maintaining social conditions conducive to the peaceful pursuit of private happiness. Thus, for *modus vivendi* liberalism, the standpoint of citizenship represents a merely external and accidental modification of the standpoint of membership in a particular cultural community. But the standpoint of citizenship can never be properly understood in this minimalist way. Active and effective citizens can never be produced and supported by a civic culture appealing to such a minimalist concept of citizenship. In fact, because this minimalist concept of citizenship requires no internalization of the perspectives and principles that make legal constraints on behavior intelligible, it cannot even produce citizens dependably obedient to the law.

Adoption of the standpoint of citizenship requires, at the very least, the capacity to comprehend the most general principles on which the laws of a liberal democracy are based. Those principles, whatever their specific content in any given liberal democracy, affirm that all citizens are to be treated as free and equal individuals. The capacity to comprehend those principles requires more than the mere readiness to submit to the law as part of a compromise aimed at achieving private goals—it requires some internalized understanding of the perspective articulated by the principles, the perspective within which citizens are indeed viewed as free and equal individuals. An internalized understanding of this perspective involves the learning of skills and the development of attitudes and dispositions that are new—that cannot be reduced to merely external and accidental modifications of attitudes and dispositions proper to members of particularistic cultural communities. In short, liberal democratic principles of justice and political arrangements cannot really be understood where no cultural basis exists for the development of a bond of civic friendship among all citizens. *Modus vivendi* concepts of liberalism cannot provide such a cultural basis. While it is certainly better for warring groups to stop killing each other and find some basis for mutual accommodation, a peaceful society composed of groups living at peace together in a state of mutual isolation, suspicion, and incomprehension would bear little resemblance to an ideal liberal democracy.

With the waning of the normative and persuasive force of the modernist liberal moral ideals of authenticity and autonomy, *modus vivendi* liberalism has emerged as one of the few motivational resources left to modernist civic culture. But the meager resources of this impoverished and minimalist form of liberalism cannot contribute much to the reconstruction of liberalism and the invention a viable postmodern civic culture. What we need is a new and far more positive way of addressing the issue of motivation, of answering the question of the value of citizenship—a new way of understanding the sense in which citizenship is not merely an instrumental good, useful insofar as it furthers the pursuit of private happiness, but also a final and substantive good desirable in itself.

A second point we must keep in mind, as we explore the ramifications of the teleological turn in contemporary liberal political philosophy, is that the motivational resources proper to the liberal democratic public sphere are necessarily limited. Civic culture is a "thin" culture. The concept of the civic good that depends on the cultural resources available only within the public sphere (i.e., within the perspectives shaped by the basic political arrangements of any liberal democracy) is bound to be insufficient by itself to provide the sort of motivation required to support large numbers of citizens in their pursuit of full cultural citizenship. The motivational resources that cannot be provided from the cultural perspectives proper to the public sphere alone must be provided from the cultural perspectives of particularistic cultural communities.

This is the import of the concept of an overlapping cultural consensus. In any liberal democracy, most of the motivational cards are held by the particularistic cultural communities that comprise it. Members of those communities are also citizens, some of them citizens in the full cultural sense—that is, citizens who have a clear understanding of the nature of the civic good. It is the civic responsibility of such citizens to shape their local cultural traditions in ways that support the development of civic moral and linguistic capacities. In addition to whatever motivational resources are provided by the general civic culture, these citizens must identify and strengthen the doctrines, themes and practices within their local cultural traditions that can provide additional normative and persuasive resources in support of liberal moral ideals. Different cultural traditions possess such resources in different degrees. But where such resources are weak or absent, they can always be strengthened or invented. This is the sort of cultural work that must be carried out by citizens if an overlapping consensus supportive of liberal political arrangements is to be realized and maintained.

In chapter 5, I will offer a model for this sort of project, by suggesting a way in which a postmodern understanding of the doctrines of one particular, but numerically very significant, cultural community—the Christian community—might be shaped to offer motivation for the pursuit of civic moral ideals. In this chapter, however, I want to focus on the motivational resources that might be drawn from the cultural perspectives proper to the liberal democratic public sphere alone. The motivational resources offered by the public sphere (i.e., by the perspectives shaped by participation in civic life) address all citizens in a moral language that all citizens can speak and understand. These motivational resources are "non-denominational." They make a case for the civic good that presupposes only adherence to the ideals of one particular form of political association—liberal democracy—and are otherwise independent of all reference to particularistic cultural belief. Even if such a case for the civic good can never be motivationally sufficient, it must be the starting point for the project of constructing an overlapping consensus—for the work of shaping particularistic cultural traditions in ways that support liberal moral ideals presupposes an understanding of the good ultimately served by such work. What, then, is the nature of the civic good that can be expressed in moral language that all citizens, regardless of their other beliefs and moral ideals, can equally embrace?

As we noted in chapter 2, Rawls's teleological concept of moral personality provides a basis for an answer to this question. This concept of moral personality defines the traits that every citizen must assume to be possessed by other citizens when engaging in civic discourse. Rawls distinguishes two such traits, which he calls moral powers: (1) the capacity to pursue rationally a concept of the good, and (2) the capacity for an effective sense of justice. Conceptually inseparable from these two moral powers, according to Rawls, are two highest-order interests in exercising and fully developing those powers. A highest-order interest is one that is given priority over all other interests. In any ranking of interests, it is given the highest ranking. This means that a citizen (i.e., one who must be expected to possess the traits proper to moral personality) is one who in fact ranks his or her interests in this way, identifying as his or her highest interest the full development and exercise of the moral powers proper to citizenship—even if the pursuit of that interest requires the sacrifice of interests or desires generated by membership in one particularistic cultural community or another.

Rawls's answer to the question of the value of citizenship thus would be given in terms of this concept of the highest-order interests proper to moral personality or full cultural citizenship. The status or role of citizen is good not merely instrumentally, as in *modus vivendi* liberalism—that is, not merely because it is useful for the realization of a particular, non-civic concept of the good life. Rather, for those who are citizens, for those who have adopted the standpoint of citizenship and have acquired the traits of moral personality, full cultural citizenship is a substantive, final, or intrinsic good. Once a human being has acquired the traits and developed the highest-order interests belonging to moral personality, then, for that person the legal status of citizenship is good in itself, because only through the possession of that status can the highest order interests proper to that status be achieved.

However, to the extent that Rawls's concept of moral personality addresses the question of the value of citizenship, it addresses that question only from the standpoint of those who have already developed the moral powers proper to that status. Citizenship is a final good only for citizens who are citizens in the full cultural sense. But what about those who have not yet fully realized the ideals proper to the status of formal citizenship—that is, who have not yet acquired the moral powers and highest-order interests specified by the concept of moral personality? What sort of case for the value of citizenship could be made to those who still regard it externally, from the standpoint of membership in one or another particularistic cultural community? It is above all such citizens that a civic culture must effectively address. *Modus vivendi* liberalism carries considerable persuasive power when viewed as an argument addressed to an audience with this pre-civic or external standpoint. But it is precisely this external way of raising the question of the value of citizenship that is relevant when considering the issue of motivation.

Civic education is a persuasive enterprise. It is addressed to those who have not yet fully developed the moral powers proper to citizenship. It is addressed to those whose self-understanding continues to be shaped primarily by the ranking systems of particularistic cultural communities. This means, of course, that the motivational resources of civic culture are addressed at every moment to every citizen, because no citizen can ever claim to have fully developed or to have exercised unfailingly the moral powers proper to citizenship. Civic education is aimed at motivating nominal citizens to acquire the moral powers and highest-order interests that define citizenship in the full cultural sense. From this point of view, the question of the value of citizenship becomes the question of why any member of a particularistic cultural community, any adherent of an exclusivist, totalizing world view, would want to embrace the status of citizenship and develop its appropriate powers, interests, and perspectives. Rawls's concept of moral personality supplies an adequate provisional concept of the civic good. But it remains much too abstract to make clear its attractive power. Why would any human being desire to develop fully a sense of civic justice and a capacity to pursue rationally a concept of the good? Assuming the provisional acceptance of Rawls's concept of moral personality as an adequate concept of the civic good, what is at stake for anyone in the question of whether or not that civic good is actually attained? This is the question that the teleological turn in postmodern liberal political philosophy requires us to answer.

The counter-narrative force of civic freedom

Let us observe once again that answering this question about the intrinsic value of citizenship is no easy task. Citizenship is in many ways a difficult and peculiar way of life. Even the minimalist citizenship called for by *modus vivendi* liberalism—the citizenship that requires no more than the cultivation of an attitude of "live and let live," a posture of benign mutual indifference in the name of civil peace—can be difficult for many who have strong commitments to totalizing life ideals. Such people often find intolerable the experience of being surrounded by people of alien belief and behavior, even when the political arrangements producing that experience otherwise hold important advantages. If such minimalist citizenship can be burdensome to many, then even more difficult is practice of the full cultural citizenship that alone insures the success of liberal political institutions. As we have often noted, the most complete development of the two moral powers defining full cultural citizenship introduces tensions and complexities that far exceed those produced by the requirements of simple *modus vivendi* tolerance. To answer the question of the intrinsic value of citizenship, we must understand anew how the inherent benefits of full cultural citizenship outweigh the burdens that come with it. The abstract question of the nature of the civic good can thus be reduced effectively to the question of what sort of case can be made for the desirability of full cultural citizenship, in the light of the unsettling and even dangerous process involved in its attainment. Before attempting to lay out such a case, let us make sure we understand clearly the sort of burdens and dangers that attend the pursuit of civic moral ideals.

At first glance, the discontents of citizenship seem painfully obvious. Viewed from the standpoint of a citizen of a modern constitutional democracy, a life passed within the cultural framework of a single ethnic, class, or religious community—say, a peasant village—seems to have an enviable sort of simplicity and tranquillity. Life within such a community is passed among people with the same general view of the world, people who share the same set of values and who agree in principle about the proper way to address the general human life issues of sex, friendship, work, suffering, sin, death, and salvation. Identities in such communities are shaped by stable and well-known assignments of duties and responsibilities. Conduct is evaluated by ranking systems, by virtue concepts, by standards of excellence and achievement, that are relatively unambiguous and unquestioned. Human desire is nurtured and given definite direction toward a clear and generally attainable set of goals. In such monocultural communities, the everyday speech addressed to others from this standpoint gains a special intelligibility, effectiveness, and even profundity through its constant implicit appeal to and dependence upon a host of shared and unspoken background assumptions. Within such communities, whatever other problems arise to disrupt life and cause suffering—plague, invasion, oppression, famine—this monoculturalism generally prevents the emergence of problems focusing on questions of meaning and purpose, value and responsibility.

This fact alone makes it easy to understand why, among citizens of liberal democracies, there is never a shortage of communitarian nostalgia for this monocultural way of life. The establishment of a liberal form of political association breaks open irreparably the tranquil world of monocultural solidarity, and exposes its former inhabitants to a whole new range of problems focusing precisely on questions of meaning, purpose, and value—what I will call "problems of narrative coherence and intelligibility." To understand how these problems arise with the transition from membership in a closed monocultural community to citizenship in a liberal democracy, let us briefly examine the educational process necessary to make that transition. I want to consider first one aspect of the process in particular: the process through which a capacity for civic freedom is developed. What sort of transformation in outlook, character, and self-understanding is necessary if a capacity for civic freedom is to be acquired?

What I call a capacity for civic freedom is linked to one of the two powers of moral personality distinguished by Rawls— the power to pursue rationally a particular concept of the good. We must note carefully the full significance of two of the terms central to the definition of this moral power. First, the power in question is the capacity to pursue a particular concept of the good *rationally*. Second, the power in question is the capacity to pursue a *particular* concept of the good. Properly understood, these two terms together define what makes this capacity specifically a capacity proper to citizenship in a liberal democracy. To pursue a particular concept of the good rationally is to pursue a life plan or life ideal critically, rather than blindly or obsessively. This means not only that the methods selected for the attainment of the life ideal are subject to critical scrutiny, but also that reasons for the pursuit of the life ideal itself also require examination. Further, to pursue a particular concept of the good *as* a *particular* concept of the good is to pursue a life plan explicitly, as one among many other possible life plans, rather than as an inescapable fate or a divinely ordained mission. This means that the life ideal being pursued is explicitly understood as an option, as an object of choice. To pursue a life plan either obsessively or as an inescapable fate is not to pursue it freely. Thus, the moral power to pursue rationally a particular concept of the good can be described as the capacity for civic freedom. Rawls tells us that:

...citizens are free in that they conceive of themselves and of one another as having the moral power to have a concept of the good. This is not to say that...they view themselves as inevitably tied to the pursuit of the particular concept of the good which they affirm at any given time. Instead, as citizens, they are regarded as capable of revising and changing this concept on reasonable and rational grounds, and they may do this if they so desire. Thus, as free persons, citizens claim the right to view their persons as independent from and as not identified with any particular concepts of the good, or scheme of final ends.[30]

Thus, in order to move from the standpoint of a member of a monocultural community to the standpoint of liberal democratic citizenship, a person must acquire the capacity for freedom, the capacity effectively to define himself or herself independently of any single life plan or life ideal. Developing this kind of independence is far easier said than done. Its basic requirement is that persons make the Socratic distinction between the good, by itself, and any particular concept of the good to which they might adhere at one time or another. As we have noted, this distinction is generally absent in monocultural communities. Its absence, in fact, defines monocultural community. The particular concept of the good life pursued by members of such communities is indistinguishable from the good itself. It is not *a* concept of the good life that they pursue—it is simply the good life. The members of a monocultural community bear identities that are wholly defined by the particularistic standards of excellence, the virtue concepts, the ranking system, and the ascriptions of rights and duties grounded in the totalizing world view of their community. Those who have been shaped by a single monocultural life ideal typically cannot conceive of themselves or imagine their lives apart from it. They typically understand the local cultural vocabulary they use to describe self and world not as one cultural vocabulary among others,

---

[30] Rawls, "Political not Metaphysical," pp. 240–241.

but rather as the vocabulary that alone expresses the very nature of things. Members of other communities, to the extent that their ideals and behavior cannot be comprehended by this vocabulary, seem hopelessly alien.

Full cultural citizenship requires a break with this sort of monoculturalism. Citizens must acquire the moral power to pursue a particular concept of the good *as* a particular concept (i.e., as one among others). They must learn to distinguish the good, as defined by their current particularistic life ideal, from the good as such. The first step in the process of developing this power, the first step in the process of civic education, is learning how to address properly the Socratic question, "What is the good as such?" The capacity for freedom, the realization of full cultural citizenship, grows as the experienced distance grows between the good as such and one or another local concept of the good. As the experienced space between local good and the good as such increases, the citizen grows in the capacity to separate his or her own identity as a citizen from attributions based on the ranking system, virtue concepts, and standards of excellence defined by any one particularistic concept of the good. This space is the space of civic freedom, the space of civic discourse. Within this space, citizens grow in their capacity to describe and address one another in terms of categories that do not give precedence to any one particularistic life ideal over others. They learn to address one another as free and equal individuals. Adherents of incommensurable world views or life ideals often find one another's speech and behavior alien and unintelligible. However, as they learn to meet and address one another within the space of civic freedom and civic discourse, a special sort of mutual understanding and even friendship becomes possible, even though full mutual understanding beyond that space may remain impossible.

Attainment of this capacity for civic freedom is always a matter of degree. The difficulty involved in acquiring this capacity for freedom is that it involves, at the same time, both independence from and adherence to a particular concept of the good. The capacity for civic freedom does not imply an absence of wholehearted commitment to a particular concept of the good or a renunciation of membership in a particular ethnic, class, or religious community. On the contrary, the practice of civic freedom assumes such commitment and presupposes such membership. We must remember that the perspective proper to the practice of civic freedom does not contain in itself cultural resources rich enough to provide the basis for a comprehensive life ideal. Civic freedom, as a component of the civic good, applies to the part and not to the whole of life. Accordingly, attainment of a capacity for freedom cannot be taken as the sort of good that could ever rival the totalizing concepts of the good proper to particularistic cultural traditions. Even less can it be identified with the good as such. The function of totalizing world views is to nurture human desire as a whole and to direct it toward some achievable set of goals. This sort of direction cannot come from the practice of civic freedom. Civic freedom, as a component of the civic good, exists only through its difference from every particularistic happiness ideal. To move from the standpoint of a member of a particularistic cultural community to the normative standpoint of citizenship, a person must both retain his or her adherence to one or another particular concept of the good, while at the same time adopting an attitude of critical independence toward all such adherence, viewing such adherence in all cases as subject to revision and revocation.

A capacity for civic freedom thus requires an almost self-contradictory attitude in the pursuit of a particularistic concept of the good. It requires both a continuing commitment to a particularistic life ideal and, at the same time, an affirmation of its revocability, an affirmation of the purely voluntary nature of that commitment. What makes this stance difficult is the central role played by totalizing life ideals in the nurturing and direction of human desire. Human desire flourishes most completely not by being satisfied, but rather in the anticipation of its satisfaction. Human desire is a form of animal desire that is intensified by the expectation of fulfillment and diminished by the expectation of frustration. In despair, for example, a sense of the futility of all desire diminishes desire itself, engendering apathy and self-destructive impulses. On the other hand, a sense of promised future satisfaction has the

opposite effect, enlivening the senses and making the experience of desire itself ever more desirable. All this is to say that
human desire is a form of animal desire that is bound up with
a representation of time—with primacy given to the representation of the future. Human desire, for this reason, flourishes
most completely when the objects of desire are clearly identified, attainable, and unquestioned in their desirability. It is
the biological function, so to speak, of comprehensive doctrines or totalizing life ideals to provide this identification of
the objects of desire and to represent those objects as attainable.

The development of a capacity for civic freedom, however,
runs counter to the central role played by totalizing world
views in the fostering and direction of human desire. This is
because the capacity for civic freedom is the capacity to adopt
a standpoint that is independent of any specific totalizing
world view or life ideal. But this attainment of this sort of
independence requires a certain externalization of the standpoints and attitudes defined by one or another particularistic
life ideal—an externalization, therefore, of the cultural perspectives that nurture and direct desire. Development of a
capacity for civic freedom is thus bound, at the very least, to
introduce into the quest for the good life a certain ambiguity
and complexity. This complexity and ambiguity affects the
very intelligibility of desire itself.

To the extent that human desire is a form of animal desire
that is bound up with the representation of time, the intelligibility of human desire (i.e., the way in which human beings
achieve self-understanding as desiring, living beings) is
embodied linguistically through narration, in the form of the
life story. Life stories are narratives of desire in both the subjective and objective senses of the genitive. Life stories are
narratives of desire in the sense that they provide a linguistic
representation of the quest for the good, the quest for the
object of desire. But life stories are narratives of desire, also,
in the sense that they constitute the way in which desire itself
becomes intelligible to itself as human desire. The story of his
or her life that a particular person relates to others (including
self as other) is a construction of hope, ordered by a plot that

anticipates, as the narrative closure or conclusion, the eventual possession of the object of desire, the eventual realization of some particular concept of the good life. But if human desire gets its intelligibility in this way through narrative interpretation, we must attempt to understand in narrative terms also the alteration of desire brought about by the development of a capacity for civic freedom.

The capacity for civic freedom is the capacity to achieve an identity independent of the interpretive framework defined by any particular concept of the good. It is therefore a capacity to achieve and maintain an identity that is independent of any narrative representation of the pursuit of a particularistic happiness ideal. An identity whose standpoint is defined simply by its independence of or its externality to any particular narrative representation of desire is one that cannot itself become the subject of such a narrative representation. The capacity for civic freedom is thus the capacity to achieve and maintain an identity that cannot itself be represented in narrative terms, that cannot be rendered intelligible by a narrative of desire. To the degree that this capacity is developed and exercised, this unnarrated and unnarratable identity or standpoint emerges in explicit contrast to the identity whose standpoint gains its intelligibility through narrative representation. The capacity for civic freedom is measured by the degree to which this contrast is incorporated into the narrative representation of desire itself. Development of a capacity for civic freedom, then, is to be understood in narrative terms as the incorporation of a certain counter-narrative principle of intelligibility into the narrative representation of desire itself.

It is this counter-narrative force that gives civic freedom its difficult and even paradoxical character. Full cultural citizenship requires that persons develop a capacity for civic freedom. They must come to consider the development of this capacity a highest-order interest, giving its full realization the highest priority. Citizens must learn, in other words, to desire civic freedom as a good, as a component of the civic good. Yet what is being desired in the desire for civic freedom is the development of an identity whose defining standpoint cannot be rendered intelligible in narrative terms. This civic identity, as we have seen, exists as a modification of the primary identity that is defined through a particular life narrative. A particular life narrative defines an identity, a self—the subject or leading character of the life story—in terms of a quest for realization of a particularistic concept of the good. This self or identity is the subject of a life narrative encompassing the whole of life, from birth to death. This narratively constructed self or identity is one that adopts one or another totalizing perspective upon the general life issues of sex, friendship, work, justice, suffering, sin, death, and salvation.

The capacity for civic freedom, however, requires a modification of this narratively constructed identity, a modification consisting in the incorporation of what we might call an authorial perspective on every particular life-narrative employment—an external perspective that itself escapes definition through any particular narrative representation, and from which every particular narrative representation of desire is viewed as constructed or invented. This extra-narrational or authorial standpoint obviously cannot itself provide the basis for a narratively represented identity or self. The author of a fictional narrative can represent his or her own life in a narrative that gives narrative significance to the creation of that fictional narrative. The extra-narrational authorial standpoint proper to civic freedom, however, cannot itself be comprehended this way in narrative terms, for that would in effect incorporate that extra-narrational standpoint into a particularistic narrative of desire. As we have seen, the standpoint proper to civic freedom is one that is external to all particularistic narratives of desire. A highest-order interest in the adoption of this extra-narrational authorial standpoint (i.e., in the development of a capacity for civic freedom) can therefore never be an attribute of a narratively constructed identity or self. Rather, this highest-order interest in the practice of civic freedom must be conceived of as an interest in the incorporation into every narratively constructed identity or self of a recognition and affirmation of its own narrative construction—a recognition and affirmation that every narratively constructed identity or self can be constructed differently, and therefore exists only through a responsible authorial choice.

If this authorial standpoint proper to civic freedom is one that cannot itself be represented in narrative terms, it is nevertheless a standpoint that can be acquired and maintained only through the cultivation of a special kind of narrative imagination. It is the task of civic education to cultivate this kind of narrative imagination. To understand the nature of this sort of narrative imagination, we must keep in mind once again that life narratives, or narratives of desire, have a rhetorical function different from other sorts of narratives. In general, to tell a story is to define a pattern of relationships between events in the light of a narrative closure (i.e., in the light of an anticipated end of the story). An event taken as a mere brute fact and in isolation from other events, if such a thing can even be conceived of at all, is one that would have no narrative significance whatsoever. Events gain narrative significance only by being incorporated into a coherent story. The closest approximation possible to a linguistic representation of events taken as brute facts (i.e., with all narrative significance stripped away) is the chronicle. But even a chronicle, no matter how bare of narrative interpretation, in its selection of detail describing the events chronicled already suggests, at the very least, an anticipation of the narrative significance that the chronicled events might have for a specific audience.

A narration is thus a human reading of events, a representation of events that first invents and defines their specific narrative significance and connection. The narrative significance of a series of events is invented when those events are incorporated into a story that refers them to an outcome, a narrative closure, to which events "in themselves" (i.e., as merely listed or chronicled) do not intrinsically refer. Thus, when a witness during a criminal trial casts his or her observations in narrative form, the events themselves and the narrative connections between them are defined by their relationship to and relevance for a specific narrative closure—one that consists in the judgment of guilt or innocence. Trial witnesses are asked to construct a coherent story out of the events they have witnessed, incorporating into that story only details that are or may be relevant to the proceedings at hand. In the same way, when a military historian tells the story of a particular battle, the events depicted in the story are defined in their narrative significance by reference to a specific narrative closure—typically, the outcome of the battle and the final outcome of the war.

Life narratives or narratives of desire, on the other hand, differ in their rhetorical function from narratives such as witness testimonies or military histories. Witness testimonies and military histories define the narrative connections between events in accordance with criteria of relevance drawn from socially mandated or conventionally designated narrative closures. Such stories are told for specific socially defined reasons and are, in effect, speech acts that get their function from the more comprehensive language games or patterns of interaction of which they are components. For example, when a military historian tells the story of a particular battle or campaign, the story aims at representing the narrative connection between events by reference to some specific later consequence of interest to the historian's audience as determined by the rhetorical occasion for the narration. The Japanese attack on Pearl Harbor on December 7, 1941, will be defined in its narrative significance (i.e., will be narratively connected to other events) differently, depending on whether the event is viewed in its relevance to the outcome of the Pacific War, to the attainment of Hawaiian statehood, to U.S.-Japanese economic relations in the postwar era, or to the biography of the narrative's author.

In the same way, witness testimonies are stories embedded in a more comprehensive language game governed by criteria of relevance drawn from the judicial process and mandating a specific narrative closure—a judgment of guilt or innocence. The events that occurred before, during and after, say, a convenience store robbery could be represented in their narrative connection in many different ways, depending on the different narrative closures to which they might be referred. For example, those events will be given different narrative readings if they are represented in their relationship to some later event in the biography of the store owner, or in their relationship to the economic decline of a city. In a court of law, however, society mandates that the relevant narrative closure, with a view to which the events are to be described, is the judgment of guilt or innocence. Narrative interpretations of the events surrounding the robbery, which are not relevant to that consequence, are therefore ruled out. Narratives like witness testimonies and military histories, then, characteristically define the narrative significance of events in terms of a narrative closure or criterion of relevance that is, in one way or another, known, fixed, or identified in advance. Let us call narratives like these "closed-criterion narratives."

Life narratives or narratives of desire, on the other hand, are "open-criterion narratives." Life stories embody the intelligibility of human desire. In life stories, desire becomes intelligible to itself as human desire. Human desire is fostered, shaped, and directed by particular concepts of the good, by particular totalizing world views that define a specific way of addressing the general human issues of sex, friendship, work, justice, suffering, sin, death, and salvation. Life stories are narratives of the quest for the attainment of the good life, as conceived of by one or another comprehensive doctrine. The attainment of the good, the attainment of a particular happiness ideal, is the relevant narrative closure in terms of which the events related in a life story are given their narrative significance. When a person relates his or her life story to others (including self as other), the events narrated are defined in their narrative significance and connection by reference to the particular happiness ideal that is the ultimate object of desire. The rhetorical function of a life story is to render intelligible and to represent in narrative terms the status of desire with respect to its object—that is, to represent in narrative terms "how things are going."

Thus, the life story of a person who has lost hope, or who has become cynical and embittered in the pursuit of his or her life plan, will interpret the narrative significance of past life events accordingly. Such a person will tell a story of defeat, injustice, and ultimate frustration. On the other hand, the life story of a person whose desire flourishes in anticipation of ultimate satisfaction will also give narrative significance to past and present events by reference to the expected future fulfillment. Such a person, however, will tell a story that anticipates victory and the consummation of desire. In the case of life narratives, then, the narrative connections between events are not determined by reference to some previously decided or socially mandated narrative closure or criterion of relevance. Life narratives are not closed-criterion narratives. Rather, life narratives define the narrative connections between life events by reference to a state of affairs that is not already decided or socially mandated, but only willed or desired—the attainment of a particular happiness ideal. The function of a life narrative is not to relate events "as they actually happened" (in terms of one or another predetermined criterion of relevance), but rather to render intelligible the present state of desire in relation to its ultimate object.

It is this characteristic of life narratives that makes them open-criterion narratives. In the case of life narratives, the criterion of relevance for the determination of narrative significance (i.e., the narrative closure to which all events are referred) can never be fixed once and for all. The narrative closure of a life narrative remains forever (at least for the person who tells his or her own life story) in the future, and therefore undetermined. The narrative closure of a life narrative is not a fact, but an object of desire, a wish, a state of affairs that is willed rather than known. Because this is the case, life narratives are uniquely subject to continual reinterpretation and reconstruction. In the case of closed-criterion narratives, this is not the case. In the case of military histories or witness narratives, consensus and even practical certainty can be attained about the narrative order of events—because the criterion that determines their narrative order is undisputed. But in the case of a life narrative, the opposite is true. In the case of a life narrative, the criterion that determines narrative order and significance remains always finally undetermined—even after the completion of the life that is the subject of narration. Thus, the Greek proverb asserting that no one's life should be judged happy until after death does not even go far enough. The life story that is today a story of victory and flourishing desire can, by misfortune, be transformed tomorrow into a story of tragedy and defeat. But even after a life is over, the story of it is not. Those who make judgments about the luck or misfortune of the dead make those judgments in view of their own ongoing and unfinished life narratives. The criterion that they apply to the lives of the dead thus also remains open, and the person judged today to have lived a tragically unhappy life may, with the changing perspectives of those who judge, be judged differently tomorrow.

Life narratives, then, are open-criterion narratives because their rhetorical function is to render intelligible the present state of desire with respect to its ultimate object. Because possession or loss of that ultimate object is forever in the future, the narrative closure—by reference to which the events represented in a life story are given their narrative significance—can never be finally determined. In life stories, the criterion for assigning narrative order and significance to events remains always open or subject to revision. The events in a life story are represented in their narrative significance by their relevance to the attainment of one or another particularistic concept of the good. As a person's concept of the good changes, or as a person's changing life circumstances affect the prospects for attainment of the good, so also will change the narrative significance attributed to life events. Thus, for example, the bankruptcy whose narrative significance is today understood by a businessman as final ruin may tomorrow, following his conversion to Christianity, be interpreted as an act of God's mercy. In such a case, it is not a matter of a false interpretation being replaced by a correct interpretation of the event, but rather a matter of giving a second reading to the event that places it in the narrative context of a different concept of the good, and gives narrative representation and intelligibility to a the pursuit of a new object of desire.

The fact that it is possible for human life narratives to be constructed as open-criterion narratives makes possible the cultural construction of a capacity for civic freedom. A capacity for civic freedom consists of a capacity to incorporate into every narratively constructed identity or self a recognition and affirmation of its own narratively constructed status. This is to say that the capacity for civic freedom is the capacity to construct a human life narrative as an open-criterion narrative. Note that there is no metaphysical issue here about the possibility of human freedom. There can be no doubt that, even though it is difficult and perhaps rare, human life narratives can indeed be constructed as open-criterion narratives. They don't have to be so constructed. Cultural support for their construction in this way is generally found only in liberal democracies. If it were in fact the case that for some reason human life narratives could not be constructed as open-criterion narratives, then there would be no capacity for civic freedom—and liberal democracy as a form of political association would not exist. The narrative closures of life stories would then be viewed as fixed once and for all—whether by fate, biology, or historical circumstances—and it would be impossible to adopt the authorial perspective on human life narratives that permits recognition of the narratively constructed nature of human identity.

Once again, with regard to the question of the possibility of civic freedom, the battle between opposing metaphysical theories of freedom and determinism is simply irrelevant. The question of the possibility of civic freedom is a cultural and political one: do we want to teach citizens to construct their life narratives as open-criterion narratives, or not? The political health of any liberal democracy, of course, depends on an affirmative answer to that question. Persons who construct their life narratives as closed-criterion narratives (i.e., who represent their destinies as determined by fate, biology, or historical circumstances) have not learned to adopt the extra-narrational authorial perspective on their life narratives that would enable them to view the narrative closure of their lives as a matter of their own responsibility. Such persons can never become free and responsible citizens.

The perception that human life narratives are open-criterion narratives accounted for the partial truth of Sartrean existentialism. But the Sartrean concept of freedom misread what is properly understood as a fact about the rhetorical function of human life narratives as a metaphysical property of human consciousness. Civic freedom became, for Sartrean existentialism, a universally defining trait of human beings as such, rather than a linguistic capacity required for the attainment of full cultural citizenship in modern constitutional democracies. In conceiving of civic freedom in metaphysical terms, Sartrean existentialism stripped it of its political function and, therefore, could offer no program of civic education designed to promote its development.

If a capacity for civic freedom is made possible by the fact that human life narratives can be constructed as open-criterion narratives, then liberalism may be understood as a form of political association that, because it requires the practice of civic freedom and responsibility, requires citizens to construct their life narratives in that way. In the case of monocultural communities, the opposite is the case. Monocultural communities—tribal or village communities, in particular—mandate or at least encourage adherence to a single concept of the good, a single way of life. Life narratives in such communities therefore tend to be represented in terms of a limited range of possible narrative closures. Monoculturalism thus supports and even mandates the construction of human life narratives as closed-criterion narratives. Members of such communities tend to see their lives as determined by birth, family, divine command, or fate. Rather than learning to conceive of the events in their lives as open to an indefinite number and range of interpretations, those events seem to express the iron law of necessity. Liberal political communities, on the other hand, are not monocultural but multicultural. Liberal political communities encourage the cultivation of a multiplicity of diverse and conflicting concepts of the good, among which citizens may choose. The exercise of such choice presupposes an interpretation of human life narratives as open-criterion narratives. It requires a capacity to form an identity that is not wholly determined by one or another particular narrative reading of life events. It requires a capacity to adopt different narrative readings of life events by referring them to a variety of diverse and conflicting ideals of happiness. To develop this capacity, citizens must be taught to develop and exercise a very peculiar form of narrative imagination.

It is the task of civic education to cultivate this form of imagination. Cultivation of this form of narrative imagination is designed to generate the extra-narrational authorial perspective required for a recognition and affirmation of human identities, as narratively constructed. In learning how to adopt this authorial perspective, a citizen must learn to imagine himself or herself credibly as pursuing a number of different ways of life while retaining the same identity. As opposed to this sort of narrative imagination, most narrative imagining—most desire-motivated envisioning of narrative possibilities—is monocultural. It has the effect of binding the imaginer's desire and identity more closely to his or her current concept of the good life, and therefore with his or her current narrative representation of life events. Thus an athlete, whose object of desire is athletic glory, dreams of victory; a businessman, whose ideal of happiness is the possession of vast wealth and financial power, dreams of making a killing in the stock market; the fanatical patriot, whose life's project is the realization of unlimited ethnic or national hegemony, dreams of glorious conquest; the scholar, whose life is invested in the goal of shaping the discourse and self-understanding of future generations, dreams of discovery; and so on. In all such cases, the imagination of narrative possibilities serves to bind desire ever more securely to its current object. It serves to increase the imaginer's bodily investment in and attachment to his or her current way of life, wedding both desire and identity ever more completely to the particularistic cultural community, and to the world view that currently determines their shape and direction. This kind of imagining is inevitable, and plays a necessary role in the pursuit of any particularistic concept of the good. It can intensify desire and inspire hope and confidence. Compared to this kind of imagining, however, the special kind of narrative imagination that produces a capacity for civic freedom can seem to be virtually an exercise in self-contradiction.

As we have seen, to learn how to adopt the extra-narrational authorial perspective on all life-narrative representation, which is required for the practice of civic freedom, is to learn how to incorporate into a particular narratively constructed self or identity a recognition of its own narrative construction. Without this recognition, a person cannot pursue a particularistic concept of the good, either freely or rationally—that is, with the readiness to examine critically and dispassionately both means and ends. This sort of rationality can be fully developed only by the practice of a form of narrative imagination that can liberate desire from its narrative identification with its current object. The sort of narrative imagination I have in mind is the sort that can sometimes be generated by exposure to fictional narratives. In reading themselves into a fictional narrative, persons sometimes can learn to imagine credibly the possibility of pursuing different ways of life or the possibility of giving very different narrative readings to the events in their own lives. These possibilities are imagined credibly when they raise the possibility of actually desiring differently, when they imaginatively evoke and nourish a desire for a different set of life goals. The practice of this kind of narrative imagination can serve to loosen, rather than tighten, the bonds that tie identity and desire to the particularistic cultural community and totalizing world view that currently determine their shape and direction. By this kind of imagining, for example, the athlete might come to imagine the possibility of actually desiring the satisfactions proper to the scholarly life; the businessman might come to imagine the possibility of actually desiring the satisfactions proper to the life of religious seclusion; the patriot might come to imagine the possibility of actually desiring the satisfactions proper to the life of the creative artist; and so on.

Let us call this kind of narrative imagination "the practice of life-narrational de-centering," since its function is not so much to lead to the actual choice of a different way of life as it is to cultivate the capacity to give different narrative readings to the "same" life events. The purpose of cultivating this capacity is to liberate desire from total and exclusive narrative investment in its current object. As we have noted, human desire gains its intelligibility and direction from narrative representation. Life stories are narratives of desire in that a particular narrative reading of life events constitutes a particular linguistic embodiment and self-interpretation of desire. But when the narrative investment of desire in its current object becomes total and exclusive, when the force and vitality of human desire become too dependent upon or even identified with a particular narrative reading of life events, desire itself can be threatened.

For example, the birth of a child usually occasions a narrative investment of desire on the part of the child's parents. The bond between parents and child is a bond of desire, a bond forged by shared hopes and common goals. But, as a bond of desire, it is also a narrative bond, a bond whose very life consists in the ongoing construction of a common life story in which the lives of parents and child are narratively interwoven. The death of a child under such circumstances can produce a profound disruption in the narrative self-understanding of the bereaved parents. To the extent that their desire and their identities were heavily invested in narratives of parenthood and child-rearing, a child's death can produce in the bereaved parents something like a state of life-narrative shock. Narratives of parenthood and child-rearing can no longer provide meaning and direction to their desire. They must "put their lives back together" by constructing new life narratives embodying new hopes and goals—life narratives that do not invest desire heavily in narratives of parenthood and child rearing. But what if, in some particular case, this cannot be done? What if, in such a case, the investment of desire in narratives of parenthood and child rearing were so great that no other narrative reading of life events were possible?

Desire that has been narratively captured in this way by its current object is at risk when events occur that threaten the narrative intelligibility and coherence of life. Such exclusive and total investment in a particular narrative reading of life events can produce obsession, apathy, and despair when something happens making that reading no longer tenable. The practice of life-narrational de-centering is designed to prevent this sort of total and exclusive narrative investment of desire in its current object. The practice of this form of narrative imagination can elicit and nurture a sort of desire that is immune to capture by any particular narrative reading of life events. It achieves this by constructing narrative representations of desire that credibly and persuasively render alternative objects of desire (i.e., alternative life plans, happiness ideals and concepts of the good) in their desirability. These representations of alternative desires are credibly and persuasively rendered to the degree that they suggest different possible narrative readings of a particular course of life. Imaginative explorations of alternative narrative readings of life events are also imaginative explorations of different possible identities that could be constructed by those narrative readings. The practice of this form of imagination, then, promotes in this way recognition of the narratively constructed nature of human identity in general.

Here, in the liberating effects of this form of narrative imagination, is revealed the narrative basis of civic rationality, as well as civic freedom. As we have seen, the capacity for civic freedom is the capacity to incorporate into every narratively constructed self or identity a recognition and affirmation of its own narrative construction. The practice of civic freedom is the practice of adopting an extra-narrational authorial perspective on all life narrative construction, viewing the subject of every life narrative (i.e., one's own narrative identity in particular) as tentative, and as subject to responsible narrative reconstruction and redefinition. To the extent that desire gets its primary intelligibility not from some particular narrative reading of life events, but rather from a relationship to this extra-narrational authorial perspective, desire is immune from capture by any particular narrative reading of life events. But this form of desire also constitutes the basis of civic rationality. To pursue a particularistic concept of the good rationally is to pursue it with a readiness to examine that pursuit critically with respect to both means and ends. Critical examination of the pursuit of a particularistic concept of the good is impossible to the extent that desire is narratively invested in that pursuit totally and exclusively. The liberation of desire from narrative capture by its current object, therefore, constitutes the condition for the development of a capacity for civic rationality.

Western philosophy has typically neglected the role of narrative imagination in both its concept of rationality and in its characteristic methods of training others in the use of reason. Since Plato, the faculty of reason has been identified with a capacity for logical inference, and the primary educational means for developing this capacity has been restricted to training in logic, dialectic, or argumentation. However, if we understand rationality as the capacity to examine critically the means and ends involved in the pursuit of a particularistic concept of the good, then we must view logical inference and argument as playing a secondary role in the production and exercise of this capacity. There is no doubt that the critical examination of the means and ends of action requires a capacity for logical inference and the exercise of argumentative skills. But these come in during the process of deliberation, when alternative means and ends are being considered. Before the powers of logical inference and dialectic can have any role to play, alternatives must be identified and affirmed as real possibilities. To the extent that desire has become exclusively and totally invested in its current object of pursuit, however, no other real alternatives can enter the field of decision making, and there will be nothing to deliberate about. Accordingly, in our concept of rationality and in our pedagogical means of cultivating a capacity for reason, the narrative liberation of desire must take priority. One way that this narrative liberation of desire can be achieved is through the practice of life-narrational de-centering. This means that the postmodern reconstruction of civic education must place no less an emphasis on the cultivation of this form of narrative imagination than it places on the cultivation of logical and dialectical skills.

Any attempt to use this form of narrative imagination in the development of capacities for civic freedom and civic rationality, however, must come to terms also with the difficulties and dangers attendant upon the narrative liberation of desire. We must understand that the complete narrative liberation of desire—that is, its complete disinvestment from any particular narrative reading of life events—is no less a danger than its exclusive investment in one such reading. A delicate balance must be struck between the detachment and the attachment of desire. Human desire flourishes most completely, as we have noted, not in being satisfied, but rather in the anticipation of its satisfaction. Human desire flourishes most completely when its objects are clearly identified and represented in narrative terms as attainable. The role of life narratives is to provide the linguistic means for this flourishing of desire. This means that, to some extent, human desire must indeed heavily invest in a narrative reading of life events that provides the conditions for its flourishing. On the other hand, exclusive and totalizing investments in such narrative readings make civic freedom and civic rationality impossible.

This leaves unanswered the difficult question we originally asked. In what sense can we understand civic freedom—as a component of the civic good, to be itself an object of desire, a substantive and final good? To the extent that the narrative over-investment of desire in its current object represents a danger, we can understand civic freedom, as the liberation of desire, as a good worthy of pursuit. But to the extent that civic freedom itself can produce a narrative detachment from all objects of desire, it represents a threat. Civic freedom is a component of the civic good. If we are to understand the civic good as a final and substantive good, it must provide some measure for determining the limits and boundaries of the liberation of desire. That measure can perhaps be provided by the second component of the civic good, the exercise of a capacity for civic justice.

Civic justice and the liberation of desire

Unfortunately, the development and exercise of a capacity for civic justice generates problems of its own for the narrative intelligibility of desire. Let us keep in mind the distinction made earlier between civic justice and communitarian justice. The life issue of justice in general arises from the specifically human desire for self-respect, or for a socially recognized and confirmed sense of relative worth. The rule of justice in general is "equals to equals"—that persons considered of equal rank, achievement, or desert in some respect and with regard to some standard should be treated equally. Civic justice is distinguished from communitarian justice by the unusual criterion of equality it applies.

The criteria of equality applied in judgments of communitarian justice are grounded in the way of life and the ranking systems of a particularistic cultural community. The criteria of equality applied in judgments of communitarian justice will therefore differ from community to community. Moreover, within any given particularistic cultural community, criteria of equality will differ, depending upon the life context and circumstances involved. Thus, in a community dependent upon agriculture for its livelihood, a communitarian standard of justice might dictate that the best farmers (other things being equal) be given priority in the overall, community-wide distribution of scarce goods and honors. It would dictate that farmers equal in merit (probably, in this case, as measured by productivity) be treated equally in the distribution of such goods and honors. However, in other life contexts within that same community—for example, in the contexts of family relations or religious practice—a communitarian standard of justice would typically dictate application of different ranking systems or criteria of equality. In the context of family relations, a communitarian standard of justice would typically dictate that qualities such as blood relationship or personal loyalty, rather than agricultural productivity, provide the basis for determining equal treatment. In the context of religious practice, a communitarian standard of justice would typically dictate that piety and faithful religious observance, rather than agricultural productivity, provide the basis for determining equal treatment. In meting out communitarian justice (i.e., in meting out equal treatment to equal persons within the various contexts of a particularistic cultural community), all such contextual nuances must be taken into account.

Thus, the development of an effective sense of communitarian justice requires the effective internalization of the system of overlapping and embedded ranking systems or equality criteria that are applied contextually within a given particularistic cultural community. This internalization of ranking systems typically occurs during the processes of socialization and education to which all community members are subject. In general, an ability to interpret and apply successfully the context-sensitive ranking systems and equality criteria proper to any community pretty much defines full cultural membership in that community. These standards of communitarian justice are grounded in and reflective of the total way of life of the community. They are embodied in its institutions, traditions, and mores. They articulate the community's totalizing view of the world, its comprehensive style of responding to the general human life issues of sex, friendship, work, suffering, sin, death, and salvation. As in the case of all other cultural factors that serve to give meaning and direction to human desire, these standards of communitarian justice also have a narrative dimension and function.

This narrative dimension is evident in the way that communitarian equality criteria and ranking systems are typically taught and communicated. Equality criteria are taught and expressed most effectively by storytelling. Stories in general, whatever else they do, provide model life narratives for their audiences, life narratives into which audience members can project themselves as the lead character and thereby apply them to their own lives. Stories of communitarian justice and injustice, in particular, give narrative embodiment to equality criteria and ranking systems. Standards of communitarian justice are internalized through the internalization of the model life narratives that represent them. These model life narratives show, by either positive or negative example, how a life story shaped in accordance with standards of communitarian justice is to be recognized and constructed. Such morality tales show the consequences of injustice, but also provide model narrative reconciliations of conflicting moral standards within the community (i.e., cases in which the ranking system to be applied in one life context conflicts with ranking systems applied in others). Further, stories of communitarian justice and injustice, in teaching a community's equality criteria or ranking systems, also articulate the overall concept of the good life proper to the community, providing narrative representations not only of community standards of justice, but also of the community's pursuit of a shared ideal of happiness. In this way, stories of communitarian justice and injustice are organically related to the larger set of narratives that tell the story of the community's pursuit of the good life from its founding to the present. In internalizing the model life narratives of communitarian justice and injustice, members of a particularistic cultural community thus internalize, also, elements of the life narrative of the community as a whole—the life narrative that provides the basis for the community's narrative solidarity, its collective sharing of a story of origins and of the pursuit of a common good.

Community or collective life narratives, like individual life narratives, are open-criterion narratives that have as their rhetorical function the representation of the current status of desire with respect to its object. They differ from individual life narratives in that community life narratives provide meaning and direction for a desire whose object is shared with others. Thus, ideally, community life narratives generate a sense of solidarity among those engaged in the pursuit of the same ideal of happiness. Because human desire flourishes most readily in anticipating satisfactions that are clearly defined and believed to be attainable, a community life narrative that in fact generates a sense of narrative solidarity in the group serves desire by providing a collective confirmation of the definition, desirability, and attainability of the shared goal. Members of a community develop and nurture bonds of narrative solidarity with its other members by incorporating their own individual life narratives into the larger collective life narrative of the group.

The narrative closure of such an ongoing collective life story typically consists in the community's attainment of the good life as its members currently define it. To support bonds of narrative solidarity, the collective good sought after typically must be broad enough in scope to define ranking systems in all or most of the general contexts of human life—the contexts of sex, friendship, work, suffering, sin, death, and salvation. Thus, lovers, families, villages, tribal or ethnic groups, trades, professions, religions, and nationalities construct stories of struggle and hope offering narrative readings of life events that create and support the sense of a common destiny. These stories are collective narratives of desire in which are inscribed individual narratives of desire. Because human desire gains its intelligibility, meaning, and direction from narrative representation, no bonds are stronger than those that can be created by the sharing of a common life narrative.

Thus, standards of communitarian justice are designed to nurture and support both the desire of individuals and the narrative solidarity of the group. The criterion of equality proper to civic justice, however, has a different function. Standards of civic justice, as components of a countervailing liberal democratic civic culture, are designed to weaken, or at least modify in a certain respect, the communitarian bonds of narrative solidarity. If not understood properly, standards of civic justice can even destroy those bonds. Just as the development of a capacity for civic freedom requires the achievement of an identity that is independent of any particularistic concept of the good, so also the development of an effective sense of civic justice requires the achievement of an identity freed of narrative definition by any shared life story governed by particularistic criteria of equality—that is, it requires the achievement of an identity capable of affirming the equality of all citizens. Insofar as capacities for both civic freedom and civic justice require the adoption of a standpoint independent of particularistic cultural concepts of the good, both of these capacities are produced and strengthened by the practice of life-narrational de-centering. However, in the case of civic justice, the focus is less on the imaginative practice of desiring differently, than on the imaginative practice of evaluating self and others differently through the application of a different sort of ranking system. Therefore, development of a capacity for civic justice entails the practice of a slightly different form of narrative imagination.

A community or collective life narrative (i.e., a life narrative whose rhetorical function it is to produce narrative solidarity) assigns meanings and values to persons in accordance with the particular ranking systems established by the community's current concept of the good. Accordingly, figures who are represented in collective life narratives as great or supremely significant are typically those who reflect the overall priorities and aspirations of the group. In a particular family narrative, for example, the character of a father may be assigned greatest importance or value, a grandparent or uncle a lesser importance, a neighbor virtually none. In the history of a particularly warlike tribe or nation, the stories of successful warriors or military leaders will typically be assigned greatest importance, the stories of tradespeople or producers less, the stories of domestic workers or slaves none at all. Thus, community life narratives, in their employment and selection of subject matter, reflect communitarian criteria of equality. A community life narrative can successfully create a bond of narrative solidarity only by reflecting, in this way, local standards of justice.

The criterion of equality proper to civic justice is different. The criterion of equality applied in judgments of civic justice is defined by the identical relationship that all citizens, as such, have to the basic institutional structure of a liberal democracy. Since all citizens, as citizens, stand in the same relationship to that basic institutional structure, all citizens are equal in that respect, whatever may be their relative value or status as assigned by one or another communitarian ranking system. To affirm this equality and act accordingly, a citizen is required to develop and maintain two opposing evaluational frameworks for dealing with questions of justice. As a member of a particularistic cultural community, a citizen must apply to self and others the relevant local standards of justice—those standards of justice that give meaning and structure to community life narratives, and that thereby forge the bonds of narrative solidarity. But, upon entering the public sphere, the citizen must put aside all such local standards of justice and call into play a very different evaluational framework, a framework that defines all citizens as equals. This means, however, that to apply this egalitarian evaluational framework, the citizen must externalize or step outside the narrative perspective proper to particularistic community life narratives. The citizen must develop the capacity to tell a different story about family, village, profession, or religion—a story that does not embody local communitarian criteria of equality in its employment and selection of subject matter. Thus, the father whose significance looms so large in the collective life narrative of a particular family must at the same time be imagined to be, as citizen, neither more nor less valuable or significant than a distant uncle or a far-off neighbor. The military leader whose story looms so large in the history of a nation must at the same time be imagined to be, as citizen, neither more nor less valuable or significant than a neighborhood merchant or a household domestic. Let us call the practice of this sort of narrative imagination "the practice of life-narrational equalization."

Let us note the differences between the practices of life-narrational de-centering and life-narrational equalization. Life narrational de-centering promotes development of a capacity for civic freedom by preventing the narrative over-investment of desire in its current object. In this form of narrative imagination, the goal is to recognize and affirm the narratively constructed character of all human identity. Practice in giving different narrative readings of the "same" life events, by referring them to different narrative closures, can produce the realization that human life narratives are open-criterion narratives. Only a person who has developed an external, authorial perspective on all life narrative can construct a particular life narrative freely and responsibly.

The practice of life-narrational equalization, on the other hand, promotes the development of a capacity for civic justice by preventing the over-investment of desire in one particular narrative-embodied ranking system, or in an exclusive bond of narrative solidarity. Community or collective life narratives embody, in their selection and representation of subject matter, social hierarchies based on particularistic communitarian standards of justice. A citizen must be able to adopt an external perspective on all such social hierarchies if a capacity for civic justice is to be developed. The criterion of equality proper to civic justice is a countervailing criterion. Unlike the criteria of equality proper to communitarian justice, it has no content in itself. The entire point of applying the egalitarian evaluational framework proper to civic justice is to neutralize particularistic local ranking systems so as to create a space, independent of all social hierarchies, wherein citizens can treat one another as equals.

Let us keep in mind that those who are to be treated as equal fellow citizens within the space of civic discourse are also those who, as members of one particular community or another, have been assigned either higher or lower rank in terms of local communitarian standards of justice. This rank or status does not simply disappear when citizens enter the public sphere. In fact, the egalitarian evaluational framework proper to the public sphere can be properly applied only in its difference from, or in its contrast to, the hierarchical evaluational frameworks defined by communitarian standards of justice. Civic equality is a property that persons gain only when they enter the liberal democratic public sphere, and that property is attributed to them by their fellow citizens always in spite of the rank or status those persons have within one particularistic cultural community or another. Civic equality does not abolish hierarchical rank or status, but achieves its force through the recognition of it—by affirming the equality of general and private, CEO and worker, billionaire and derelict, Pope and layperson, champion and also-ran—precisely in spite of, and with a view to, the large differences in their local status.

Furthermore, the treatment of fellow citizens as equals is not merely a formal procedural matter but, to be fully effective, requires its own special bond of affection. We call this bond "civic friendship." The bond of civic friendship differs greatly from the bond of communitarian solidarity. Because the liberal democratic public sphere, where the equality criteria of civic justice have their application, is itself limited in scope, so also is the bond of civic friendship limited in scope. The bond of civic friendship unites persons who share the same relationship to the basic institutional structure of a liberal democratic society. They may share nothing else, but they may often share membership in a particularistic cultural community—and thereby ties of communitarian solidarity. Here we see the complexity that is introduced into every relationship by liberal democratic citizenship. In a liberal democracy, every person has at least a two-fold relationship with every other person. First, every person is related to every other as either a member or a nonmember of a particularistic cultural community. That relationship is governed by the equality criteria and ranking systems proper to communitarian justice.

Second, every person is related to every other as citizen, a relationship governed by civic friendship and the standards proper to civic justice. To act justly within particularistic cultural communities, one must treat with appropriate respect persons assigned high status by local ranking systems. As citizen, on the other hand, to act justly one must treat as equals both high-ranking and low-ranking members of every particularistic cultural community, including one's own, regardless of their local rank. In short, a citizen must learn to cultivate with members of his or her own community not only the hierarchical bond of narrative solidarity, but also the egalitarian bond of civic friendship.

The practice of life-narrational equalization is designed to produce the capacity for developing and maintaining this twofold relationship to fellow citizens. This practice consists in giving alternative narrative readings to life events—to those events, above all, whose stories represent differentials in communitarian rank as properties inherent in the persons ranked. Any narrative reading of life events that represents differentials in communitarian rank as objective properties of persons is always the product of a particularistic narrative perspective or standpoint—the standpoint of narrative solidarity with the particularistic cultural community doing the ranking. The practice of life-narrational equalization is designed to lead to a recognition and affirmation of the narratively constructed nature of all communitarian rank differentials. This form of narrative imagination is designed to promote the realization that different narrative readings of the "same" life events can always be given—readings that overturn, or at least reinterpret, any differentials in communitarian rank assigned to persons as their inherent properties. These other readings adopt different narrative standpoints and apply different ranking systems—ranking systems either belonging to different life contexts, or identified with different cultural communities altogether.

Thus, in the case of a community life narrative of a particular battle or campaign that represents a military leader as an object of respect and foot soldiers as a persons of relative insignificance, the practice of life-narrational equalization would seek to recast this story in a way that produces at least a reinterpretation, if not a reversal, of the relative rankings of the individuals described. For example, the story of the battle or campaign could be recast from a narrative perspective expressing solidarity with the combat experiences of the common foot soldier. Told in this way, the story might represent the military leader as insulated from and untested by the rigors of combat, and the foot soldier as the true hero. The point of this exercise of narrative imagination would not be to discover the "truth" about some particular set of events, or merely to "bring down the mighty" by discrediting great military leadership. The purpose of such a narrative exercise would be, rather, to develop an external perspective on all communitarian life narratives, one that promotes the capacity to recognize and affirm the rank differentials assigned to persons as narrative constructions, as products of one or another particularistic narrative standpoint that can easily be reversed. To the extent that this sort of narrative exercise actually promotes development of this externalized perspective, it serves to develop a capacity to view all narrative-embodied, particularistic rank differentials as external to those who are ranked by them—thereby holding open the egalitarian space, outside of and against all particularistic ranking systems, within which citizens, as citizens, can address one another on equal terms and form bonds of civic friendship.

Thus, in different ways, both the practices of life-narrational de-centering and life-narrational equalization promote the liberation of desire—that is, the narrative transformation of the standpoint of desire that prevents an exclusive or total investment of desire in its current object. The practice of life-narrational de-centering focuses on narrative re-readings of life events in terms of different and conflicting happiness ideals. This form of narrative imagination promotes development of a capacity for civic freedom. It liberates desire by representing in narrative terms the desirability of many different life plans and goals. The practice of life-narration equalization focuses on narrative re-readings of life events that apply different and conflicting ranking systems or criteria of equality. As we have seen, this form of narrative imagination promotes the development of a capacity for civic justice by promoting the recognition that rankings applied to persons in community life narratives are not inherent properties of those persons, but rather are dependent upon the adoption of a standpoint of narrative solidarity with a particularistic cultural community. This form of narrative imagination liberates desire by overturning the narratively embodied social hierarchies and ranking systems in which desire can become over-invested.

This liberation of desire, however, is not an unproblematic good. We have seen how the liberation of desire required for development of a capacity for civic freedom moves in the direction of a general detachment from every particularistic object of desire, and therefore puts the intelligibility of desire itself at risk. This is because human desire is never desire-in-general. It is always particularistic desire. It is always desire for a particularistic concept of the good whose pursuit can be represented in a totalizing and coherent life narrative. In the same way, the liberation of desire required for development of a capacity for civic justice moves in the direction of a general detachment from every particularistic communitarian ranking system or standard of justice. Such detachment puts desire at risk in a similar way by promoting an attitude of alienation from all particularistic ranking systems—ranking systems that give direction to human aspiration and generate narrative solidarity with others.

When it produces this alienating effect, the practice of life-narrational equalization takes the form of a narrative debunking of every variety of particularistic human greatness and distinction, the sort of debunking typically carried on in scandal-mongering tabloid news stories and in unauthorized star biographies. In such news stories and biographies, persons who have been narratively exalted in terms of one ranking system are brought low by the narrative application of a different ranking system. The practice of life-narrational equalization in such cases becomes a practice of cultural leveling aimed at revealing every notable human achievement to be the result of chance, conspiracy, or moral failure. But this attempt to bring down the mighty, by showing all particularistic human distinction to be illusory, can also have the effect of stifling aspiration to distinctive human achievement in general. Ironically, this misguided practice of life-narrational equalization can even represent as fraudulent and ideologically deceived the aspiration to achieve a superlative sense of civic justice—so that the very practice of narrative imagination that should properly serve to develop a capacity for civic justice can have the effect of undermining the aspiration to achieve it. Thus, just as the practice of life-narrational de-centering can threaten the narrative coherence and intelligibility of desire, so also can life-narrational equalization both nullify the basis of narrative solidarity with others, and promote a general sense of the futility of particularistic desire itself.

So here, once again, the question of motivation must be raised. The practice of these forms of narrative imagination does not come naturally. Learning to adopt the externalized perspective on life narrative construction is difficult. It is hard to believe that anyone would undertake this project of the narrative liberation of desire without a belief in the goodness or desirability of its outcome. But what makes the civic good (i.e., the development and exercise of capacities for civic freedom and civic justice) desirable? How can this good become an object of desire when the transformation of desire that is required for its attainment can come to cast doubt upon the value of particularistic desire itself?

Let us be sure we understand the full scope of this question. We have taken what Rawls termed the two powers of moral personality as the capacities that define full cultural citizenship. These are the capacity for civic freedom and the capacity for an effective sense of civic justice. The development and exercise of these two capacities constitute the two primary components of the civic good. For those who have fully developed these two capacities, the exercise of these capacities is a highest-order interest. This means that, for such fully-developed citizens, where the civic good attained through the exercise of these two capacities comes in conflict with other goods, the civic good is to be preferred. The full realization of the normative standpoint of citizenship, then, consists of a modification of the effective ranking systems that persons typically bring to bear in daily decision making. In daily decision making, all human beings typically rank alternative courses of action in terms of one or another particularistic concept of the good. Their desire for that particularistic ideal of happiness, and the decisions it calls forth, are rendered intelligible through the ongoing construction of a coherent life narrative. This life narrative defines a specific identity in terms of the particularistic life ideal or object of desire currently being pursued.

Full cultural citizenship, then, in modifying the ranking systems applied in everyday decision making, modifies the narrative intelligibility of desire itself. To give highest priority to the civic good is to give highest priority to the adoption of an external perspective on all life narrative construction and, therefore, an external perspective upon every narrative interpretation of particularistic desire. To desire the civic good is to desire this narrative liberation of desire. As we have seen, this narrative liberation of desire can produce a certain detachment or alienation from particularistic ranking systems and forms of narrative solidarity that are necessary to give particularistic desire its meaning and direction. Clearly, the civic good cannot consist of this sort of detachment or alienation. To have a highest-order interest in the attainment of the civic good is not to desire the attainment of a perspective that undermines all particularistic desire. The question about the nature of the civic good is therefore the question of how the narrative modification of desire, required for the practice of civic freedom and civic justice, can itself be understood as an object of desire.

Furthermore, let us keep in mind that, in a viable liberal emocracy, citizens are united by their common pursuit of this civic good. Liberal democracy is a form of political association specifically established in order to provide the conditions under which, alone, this civic good can be attained by its members. It is a form of political association specifically established in order to make it possible for persons to accomplish this modification in the structure of desire, this narrative liberation of desire, that is the basis of the capacities proper to citizenship. Furthermore, liberal democracies (i.e., regimes of civic freedom and civic justice) can exist only to the extent that many or most of their members actually develop these capacities and actually desire the civic good. A proper understanding of this civic good, one capable of effectively motivating desire for its attainment, is therefore absolutely essential to the very existence of civic community. The question of motivation is the central cultural question facing any civic community. The contemporary demise of modernist civic culture raises this question in the most pressing possible way for us. The question of how to motivate pursuit of the civic good is thus not a matter of idle philosophical speculation, but rather of the most immediate and urgent political concern. How are we to answer it? What arguments can we offer to one another as citizens that will both make clear the demands of citizenship and effectively motivate the desire to attain it?

Let us keep in mind also that the required arguments cannot be generated from the cultural resources provided by civic community or the public sphere alone. As Rawls notes, liberal democratic political institutions must be supported by an overlapping cultural consensus. The diverse cultural communities included within a given liberal democracy must identify and cultivate within their own traditions resources supportive of citizenship. For many cultural traditions, this will be difficult or impossible. Cultural traditions wholly wedded to monocultural forms of desire will find that liberal democratic institutions constitute a relentlessly corrosive and hostile cultural environment. Where communities shaped by such monocultural values predominate, liberal political institutions themselves are not likely to succeed. Liberal political institutions can flourish only where the particularistic cultural communities subject to them can find a basis within their particular traditions for an affirmation of civic freedom and civic equality. A concept of the civic good, as understood only in terms of the limited cultural perspectives proper to the liberal democratic public sphere, can by itself never provide sufficient motivational resources rich enough to provide a cultural basis of social unity and stability. The civic good is a partial good. Civic culture is a "thin" culture. For citizens in the full cultural sense, attainment of the civic good is a highest-order interest. Yet pursuit of the civic good alone can never provide citizens with the resources for the creation of a comprehensive way of life.

A liberal democracy, then, requires the support of an overlapping consensus among the particularistic cultural communities that comprise it. However, this is not to say that the cultural perspectives proper to the liberal democratic public sphere can offer no supportive cultural resources at all. Arguments motivating desire for the attainment of the civic good can be drawn also from a concept of the liberal democratic public sphere itself. *Modus vivendi* arguments supportive of liberal political institutions are a case in point. But, as we noted earlier, *modus vivendi* liberalism is incapable of providing support for anything more than the most truncated and stunted forms of civic identity. *Modus vivendi* liberalism appeals only to the local self-interest of citizens as members of particularistic cultural communities. *Modus vivendi* liberalism argues for the support of liberal democracy only as part of a cultural and political compromise aimed at securing civil peace. What makes this compromise desirable is nothing beyond its promise to provide the conditions under which particular ethnic, class, and religious communities may continue to pursue their diverse concepts of the good life without the threat of interference from others. *Modus vivendi* arguments do not make clear in what sense citizenship itself is a good to be desired for its own sake. Such arguments cannot, therefore, generate motivation to undertake the transformation of desire required for full cultural citizenship. *Modus vivendi* arguments may be a permanent and even indispensable part of the rhetorical arsenal supportive of liberal democracy. But taken by themselves, in the absence of other means of cultural support, not only are they insufficient to generate the kind of motivation required for citizenship, they can actually weaken the cultural foundations of political community.

Beyond *modus vivendi* arguments, then, what other arguments can be drawn from the perspectives proper to the liberal democratic public sphere alone that can provide cultural support for the pursuit of the civic good? Perhaps such arguments might be discovered by examining another familiar concept of the goal of liberal democratic political association, one identified with modernist metaphysical concepts of liberal doctrine. According to this concept, the goal of liberal democratic political association is to secure the natural rights of individuals. If this concept of the civic good is to provide motivational resources for a postmodern civic culture, however, it must be reformulated in such a way as to strip the notion of individual rights of its metaphysical connotations—of any suggestion that civil and political rights are universal and essential properties of human beings as such. That could be accomplished in the following way.

Let us consider the fact that the criterion of equality proper to civic justice specifies that all citizens, as they enter the public sphere, must be treated as equals, regardless of their relative rank or status as measured by the ranking systems applied to them in accordance with communitarian standards of justice. As we have often noted, this civic criterion of justice is designed to have a countervailing impact on the hierarchical evaluational frameworks that typically order particularistic cultural communities. Particularistic cultural communities are governed by totalizing world views and united by narrative solidarity in the pursuit of a shared concept of the good life. As cultural communities that seek to nurture and provide direction to human desire, hierarchical standards of excellence and achievement are necessary. Without such standards, these communities cannot generate and guide the aspirations of their members. However, often within such communities hierarchical ranking systems and standards of communitarian justice are established that have the effect of stifling, rather than nurturing, particularistic human desire and aspiration. This occurs when members of particularistic cultural communities are excluded from positions of power, respect, and authority within those communities on the basis of quasi-natural traits such as birth, race, gender, age, and class. The establishment of liberal political institutions—the establishment of a regime of civic freedom and civic justice—is designed to free members of particularistic cultural communities from all such quasi-natural constraints on particularistic aspiration and desire. This is the countervailing force and intent of the criterion of equality proper to civic justice.

Let us explore this countervailing force and intent of civic justice a bit further. As we have seen, the development of the capacities for civic freedom and civic justice entails a modification of the structure of desire—what I have called a narrative liberation of desire—that can threaten the narrative intelligibility of desire itself, and weaken the sense of narrative solidarity with others. But this liberation of desire in the name of libertarian and egalitarian goals constitutes only one sort of threat to narrative solidarity and to the narrative intelligibility of desire. Another sort of threat to particularistic desire arises within the sphere of communitarian justice. We can understand the establishment of a regime of civic freedom and civic justice to be a response to this other threat.

Ideally, particularistic cultural communities nurture and direct the desire and aspirations of their members. Human desire flourishes most readily when its objects are clearly identified and narratively represented as attainable. The local culture generated by these communities—its narrative-embodied ranking systems, standards of excellence, virtue concepts, and so on—serves these goals, focusing desire and nourishing the hope of its satisfaction. The bond that unites members of particularistic cultural communities is rooted in the soil of biological life. Human life, like all life, requires hierarchy, ranking, command and obedience, authority and subordination. Only under these conditions can human desire, as a form of animal desire, flourish. But such communities, rooted as they are in the soil of biological life, can also set up obstacles that are destructive of human desire. This occurs when such communities assign rank, roles of command and obedience, or positions of authority and subordination, to members on the basis of quasi-natural traits such as birth, race, gender, age, and class. Members of a community who are systematically excluded from positions of power, respect, and authority on the basis of such quasi-natural qualities (i.e., qualities that they can neither gain by effort nor lose by human fault) cannot aspire to those positions. On the other hand, neither can those who hold such positions as a result of birth, race, gender, age, or class aspire to them—or at least their aspiration is limited by the fact that the positions are delivered over to them solely by virtue of their possession of such quasi-natural traits. In this way, the establishment of such obstacles to desire has the effect of blocking the aspirations not only of those whose life possibilities are limited by those obstacles, but also of those who benefit from them.

When any particularistic cultural community establishes such quasi-natural obstacles to the aspirations of its members, justification for such limitation is ordinarily incorporated into the official culture of the community—that is, into the official world view and community narratives. In some Christian communities, for example, women are excluded from positions of ecclesiastical power and authority by appeal to Biblical precepts and narratives. Again, in modern liberal democracies, racial groups have been excluded from positions of power and respect by appeal to "scientific" genetic theories. Because the justification for quasi-natural obstacles to desire are incorporated in this way into the official world views and narratives of these communities, community members whose aspirations are blocked by these obstacles and who remain in the community have only two choices: (1) they must incorporate those quasi-natural obstacles into their own identities and narrative self-understanding, or (2) they must generate counter-narratives and counter-world views opposed to the official culture of the community. In either case, the capacity of the local community culture to carry out its essential function of nurturing and directing human desire is undermined and diminished.

Thus, in the first case, when community members who are victims of this discrimination incorporate into their own life narratives community beliefs about the disqualifying character of traits such as birth, race, gender, age, and class, then the life narratives of those community members become the internalized mechanism by which desire is stunted and impeded. Under such circumstances, life narratives fail to carry out the function of rendering human desire intelligible to itself. The life stories of those whose birth, race, gender, age, or class constitute obstacles to aspiration are inevitably stories of unjustified desire, forbidden aspiration, and repressed hopes.

In the second case, when persons who are victims of discrimination reject their exclusion from positions of power and respect and, in this rejection of the official culture of the community, generate counter-narratives and counter-world views as a response, the basis for the narrative solidarity of the community is destroyed. When this occurs, the local culture of such a community becomes a theater of conflict, a distorting mirror of intergroup rivalry, rather than the medium through which a collective desire for attainment of a shared concept of the good life is made transparent to itself.

Rather than describing the goal of liberal democratic regimes as the securing of the universal human rights of individuals, we can now describe this countervailing intent of regimes of civic justice in a non-metaphysical way. We can say that liberal democracy is a form of political association established for the purpose of eliminating all quasi-natural obstacles to human desire and aspiration. Liberal democratic regimes accomplishes this through the creation of a civic culture whose countervailing premise is the freedom and equality of all citizens. The criterion of civic equality is not intended to subvert or nullify the ranking systems, virtue concepts, or standards of excellence proper to particularistic cultural communities. As we have noted, these ranking systems, functioning properly (i.e., as conceived of by liberal doctrine), are absolutely necessary for the nurturing and direction of human desire. Civic equality is a political and not a metaphysical concept. It applies to the part and not to the whole of life. Human beings are defined as equals only in their relationship to the basic structure of liberal democratic society as a whole, only with respect to their participation in the liberal democratic public sphere. The criterion of civic equality is properly applied, within particularistic cultural communities, only to those local ranking systems that assign roles of power and authority on the basis of quasi-natural qualities such as birth, race, gender, age, and class. Such ranking systems apply criteria for evaluation based upon human differences that can be neither gained nor lost. Such ranking systems therefore establish obstacles to particularistic human desire and aspiration that threaten the narrative intelligibility of human desire and the narrative solidarity of communities.

Civic justice requires that all such obstacles be removed.

Liberal democracy makes this demand in the name of the narrative intelligibility of desire itself, and for the sake of strengthening the narrative solidarity of particularistic cultural communities. Of course, beyond absolutely clear-cut violations of civic equality found in such communities, such as racial segregation and gender discrimination, the principles of civic justice that determine how the criterion of civic equality is to be applied in particular cases can never be specified in advance. In other words, there can be no general "theory" stating the principles of civic justice once and for all. Application of the criterion of civic equality is always a matter of political judgment and civic consensus. In its affirmation of human desire and aspiration, liberal democracy not only establishes an order of civic equality, but also affirms and underwrites orders of inequality determined by talent and merit. In liberal democratic societies, ongoing political discussion and conflict has much to do with striking the proper balance between civic equality and social hierarchy. Determining where that line is to be drawn in any particular case or for any particular era is a task for public political debate and not for political philosophy.

This way of reformulating the goal of liberal democratic political association can perhaps suggest a way of addressing the issue of motivation in the project of inventing a viable postmodern civic culture. As we have seen, if citizens are going to be motivated to develop and exercise capacities for civic freedom and civic justice, the desirability of these capacities must be made clear to them. Development of these capacities requires a modification of the structure of particularistic desire—a certain detachment of particularistic desire from its current object that, if taken too far, can become a general alienation from every object of desire, an alienation threatening the narrative intelligibility of desire itself. The civic good (i.e., the exercise of capacities for civic freedom and civic justice) can be understood, as an object of desire, only if this detachment of particularistic desire from its current object can be understood as an object of desire. But how is that possible?

It is possible only if this detachment is subject to the limits defined by the goal of liberal democratic political association. The point of learning to adopt a standpoint of detachment from every object of particularistic desire—an external perspective on all life narrative construction—is, for purposes of attaining the civic good, not to nullify particularistic desire, but rather to affirm it by removing all quasi-natural, socially imposed obstacles to its fulfillment. The paradoxical aspect of the pursuit of the civic good is that in order to create and maintain the political institutions capable of removing socially imposed obstacles to the fulfillment of particularistic desire, a culture is necessary that motivates persons to abandon the standpoint proper to the pursuits of their own particularistic objects of desire. The reason why the civic good can become the highest-order interest of citizens is not because the civic good itself has a specific content over and above the pursuit of one particularistic concept of the good or another, but because it consists in the realization of a standpoint capable of affirming all particularistic desire *as* particularistic desire. To put it in a slightly misleading, but nevertheless perhaps useful way, the civic good consists in the attainment of a standpoint from which the desires proper to "this world" (i.e., proper to earthly, natural human life) can be affirmed precisely *as* desires of "this world," precisely *as* desires for objects that are contingent, of only relative value and of local significance.

As long as the practices of life-narrational de-centering and life-narrational equalization are undertaken with this purpose clearly in view, they will not produce the general detachment or alienation from all objects of particularistic desire that can produce a sense of the futility of all particularistic desire. Attainment of the civic good is made possible by an abandonment of the standpoint of particularistic desire that nevertheless affirms all particularistic desire as such. Thus, liberal democracy, as a form of political association, is grounded upon the most complete possible affirmation of particularistic desire, the most complete possible affirmation of earthly, natural human life. Nevertheless, in the service of particularistic desire, in the name of its narrative intelligibility, and for the sake of human narrative solidarity, liberal democracy requires particularistic desire to examine itself critically. According to this concept of the civic good, it is the claim of liberalism that the greatest threat to particularistic human desire lies in its being captured by monocultural forms of narrative solidarity. To attain full cultural citizenship, persons must learn to break open closed cultural worlds and to overturn rigid hierarchies and ranking systems. Persons must learn to do this not in order to destroy those worlds and hierarchies, but rather to let them function in the open space of a more encompassing sphere that is free of intrinsic hierarchy and unbounded by any closed narrative horizon.

Is such a concept of the civic good capable of motivating citizens to undertake the uncomfortable work of becoming full cultural citizens? Certainly not. Yet it possibly does provide a basis for such motivation and a framework within which citizens can work, as members of particularistic cultural communities, to discover within their own local traditions richer and more effective sources for motivating the pursuit of the civic good.

5 God and the Space of Civic Discourse

Inventing postmodern civic culture

What will a postmodern civic culture look like? Whatever form of civic culture, if any, finally succeeds modernist liberal civic culture, it is bound to be different in certain important respects. Some of these differences are suggested by the directions taken by postmodern liberal political philosophy—what I have called the rhetorical and teleological turns.

Consider, for example, the implications of the rhetorical turn. A political or rhetorical concept of liberal doctrine permits liberal democratic civic culture to have a name and an identity. For a rhetorical concept of liberalism, a civic culture is a countervailing culture addressed to the citizens of a liberal democracy. It is a culture that is limited with respect to its content and scope. Its purpose is to provide the citizens with the insight and motivation required for the attainment of full cultural citizenship. As such, it is a culture that should have an official public status and role of some sort. Public education, for example, should include elements of this culture as a clearly identified component of the curriculum.

Modernist metaphysical concepts of liberalism prevented this sort of clear identification of the role and content of civic culture. Modernist liberal political theory conceived of liberal doctrine as a totalizing world view. It presented liberal moral ideals not as components of a certain historical form of civic culture, but rather as articulations of universally valid moral standards. Because modernist liberalism depended on Enlightenment concepts of reason and knowledge to support its universalist and essentialist claims for liberal moral ideals, the vital role of the non-cognitive or narrative dimensions of civic culture in the production of full cultural citizenship were systematically ignored. Scientific education became a surrogate for civic education. Civic education was carried on surreptitiously under different names, and was often identified with the modernist ideals of culture-neutral, value-free knowledge. The liberal democratic state itself was represented as having no particularistic cultural point of view at all, its culture-neutral and value-free standpoint advertised as the political analogue of the value-free objectivity of scientific knowledge.

Once the nature and political function of a liberal democratic civic culture has been clearly recognized, we should expect the content of civic culture increasingly to become an issue for public debate. Indeed, the political struggle over the definition and content of a postmodern civic culture has already begun. This struggle is evident in the "culture wars" being fought in America today in virtually every area of public life. In these culture wars, the forces of progress and liberal "enlightenment" find themselves opposed by the forces representing cultural orthodoxies of all types. The progressive forces are armed with the rhetorical weapons provided by modernist liberal civic culture. On this side are those who still appeal to the modernist liberal moral ideals of authenticity and autonomy, who identify with the rationalism of the Enlightenment and who continue to advocate universalist and essentialist concepts of civic justice. But the rhetorical weapons wielded by the forces of cultural orthodoxy have also been shaped by modernist liberal ideas. These forces appeal to traditional communitarian values of various sorts. On this side are those who oppose public use of the culture-neutral, value-free vocabulary of modernist liberalism on the grounds that it embodies a world view hostile to the moral ideals and beliefs of particularistic cultural communities. However, because they identify liberalism exclusively with comprehensive or metaphysical concepts of liberal doctrine, the orthodox tend to speak exclusively the language of communitarian as opposed to civic justice. Their political and cultural agenda is anti-modernist, but all too often also anti-liberal.

The rhetorical turn in contemporary liberal political philosophy addresses the issues raised by this political struggle by remapping the terrain on which the culture wars are being fought—by providing a new moral vocabulary capable of defining a common ground on which the opposing sides can meet. A political or rhetorical concept of liberalism is capable of affirming fully, at the same time, both civic and communitarian standards of justice. It accomplishes a de-totalization of civic culture and of the liberal democratic public sphere itself. It denies the universalist and essentialist interpretations of liberal moral ideals typical of modernist metaphysical concepts of liberal doctrine. Liberalism thus ceases to be identified with the scientific world view of the Enlightenment, or with any other totalizing world view hostile to religious belief and moral ideals. A political or rhetorical concept of liberal doctrine, in effect, makes adherents of the modernist "individualist" moral ideals of authenticity and autonomy into just one more particularistic cultural community, with no special rights over the vocabulary used in public life or for purposes of civic education. On the other hand, a political or rhetorical concept of liberalism makes clear the obligation of every citizen to develop fully and exercise the capacities proper to citizenship. As we have seen, the development and exercise of these capacities, even though they pertain only to a part and not to the whole of life, nevertheless introduce certain complexities and tensions into the orthodox moral beliefs and practices proper to particularistic cultural communities. Thus, while a political or rhetorical concept of liberal doctrine breaks the connection between the liberal democratic public sphere and the rationalist world view of the Enlightenment, it also affirms the obligatory nature and the full countervailing force of the civic ideals of individual freedom and equality.

Perhaps the most significant and notable difference between modernist liberal civic culture and the postmodern form of civic culture now emerging is suggested by the teleological turn in contemporary liberalism. A postmodern liberal democratic civic culture must provide cultural resources for motivating citizens to develop and exercise the capacities proper to full cultural citizenship. It must represent the attainment of capacities for civic freedom and civic justice not merely as a matter of obligation, but also as a matter of desire. Liberal democracy is a form of political association that presupposes the shared pursuit of a particularistic concept of the good. The peculiarity of this way of life is that the concept of the good shared by citizens of a liberal democracy is a limited good, a good applying to only a part of life, a good incapable of generating a comprehensive strategy for addressing the full range of general human life issues. As we have seen, that civic good consists in a certain liberation and affirmation of particularistic desire as particularistic desire. A postmodern liberal democratic civic culture must provide the cultural resources (e.g., discourses, narratives, representations of various sorts, etc.) capable of presenting the civic good persuasively as a good to be desired and attained for its own sake.

This particularistic concept of the good distinguishes the general culture or civilization proper to North Atlantic liberal democracies from other regional cultures and civilizations that remain powerful and vital forces today—including the Islamic, the Japanese, the Confucian, the Hindu, the African, and so on. The liberal democratic state must understand itself as the caretaker and cultivator of this particularistic Western way of life. This requires a break with all modernist liberal concepts of the liberal democratic state as embodying a standpoint of cultural and moral neutrality. A postmodern liberal democratic state must view itself as a perfectionist regime like any other, insofar as its role is to foster the desire of its citizens to pursue a certain ideal of happiness and to the extent that any particular liberal democratic form of government or administration will be judged by its capacity to provide the conditions required for the realization of that ideal.

While it is the role of the postmodern liberal state to support a civic culture capable of motivating its citizens to pursue the civic good, the state must also acknowledge, as we have seen, that its resources are inadequate to that task. The cultural perspectives proper to the liberal democratic public sphere can provide some motivational resources supportive of the pursuit of the civic good—but the greatest part of those resources must come from an overlapping consensus among particularistic cultural communities in support of the liberal democratic moral ideals of civic freedom and civic justice. This support cannot be mandated by the liberal state. It must be generated by members of particularistic cultural communities who, acting as citizens, succeed in discovering or inventing within their own local cultural traditions motivational resources supportive of the pursuit of the civic good. This discovery or invention of motivational resources supportive of civic moral ideals will generally take the form of identifying independent grounds within particularistic cultural traditions that are supportive of the recognition and institutionalization of standards of civic justice.

For example, consider professional associations. Professional associations belong to the general category of communities based upon shared social class and occupational roles. They are associations formed to pursue collective economic goals and carry out a specific social function. Members of such associations, acting as citizens, might discover in their local traditions or organizational assumptions independent (i.e., not specifically mandated by the state) cultural justifications for the establishment of codes of ethical conduct informed by standards of civic justice—codes of ethics embodying libertarian and egalitarian ideals, and requiring the development of libertarian and egalitarian attitudes. The basic goal governing all such efforts aimed at achieving an overlapping consensus is the achievement of a congruence between the communitarian standards of justice and civic standards of justice, so that praise given to a person as a member of community X (on the basis of purely local standards of justice) is, to some degree, consistent with praise of that same person as a good citizen.

Different cultural communities will contribute differently
to this overlapping cultural consensus in support of civic
moral ideals. In the remainder of this chapter, I want to consider in some detail how citizens who are members of one particular group of cultural communities might go about the
process of discovery or invention that could make a uniquely
powerful contribution to the motivational resources of a postmodern civic culture. I have in mind those cultural communities founded in the broadest sense on the biblical religious
tradition, and specifically those communities that identify
themselves as Christian.

God and the civic good

As we have seen, modernist liberal political theory arose in
part as a mediating cultural response to wars of religion. As a
result, it generally regarded most forms of religious belief with
some suspicion. The Enlightenment intellectuals and scholars, who identified their own standpoint of cognitive objectivity with the normative standpoint of citizenship, typically considered religious belief to be an impediment to the
development of civic attitudes and dispositions. The particularism of religious belief and moral ideals seemed opposed to
the universalistic and humanistic cultural standpoint that
seemed necessary to support liberal political institutions. A
postmodern civic culture must reverse this pattern of suspicion and hostility to religion, and learn to exploit whatever
motivational resources supportive of civic moral ideals that
religious belief can offer. Reversal of this pattern might even
be essential to the success of a postmodern civic culture, for
religious belief alone can provide cultural support for civic
moral ideals precisely at the point where they are most in
need of support, the point at which they expose citizens to the
dangers and discomforts of liberty—above all, to the dangers
of nihilism and alienation. But, in reversing this pattern of
suspicion, it is important to keep two points clearly in mind.

First, acknowledging that religious belief can make an
important contribution to a postmodern civic culture does

not entail the public endorsement of any particular form of religious belief, Christian or otherwise. It does not entail any sort of violation of the principle of the separation of church and state. The cultural perspectives proper to the liberal state, and to the liberal democratic public sphere in general, encompass only a part and not the whole of life. Christian religious community, on the other hand, is governed by a totalizing and comprehensive concept of the good. Christianity offers a world view that addresses all the general issues of human life—sex, friendship, work, suffering, sin, death, and salvation. Christian belief and moral ideals thus belong to a cultural sphere radically distinct from the liberal democratic public sphere, the sphere of civic culture. These two cultural spheres must not be confused. Furthermore, Christian religious communities constitute only one group of religious communities among the many that comprise any particular liberal democracy. Christian religious belief can offer cultural resources supportive of civic moral ideals—but, in varying degrees, other forms of religious belief can do that also. In this respect, Christianity is to be distinguished from other totalizing concepts of the good only in view of the fact that, in North Atlantic liberal democracies, large numbers of citizens are members of Christian religious communities or are influenced by a Christian world view. In nations little influenced by Christianity, native forms of religious belief may offer lesser or greater resources for the support of civic moral ideals than Christianity, should the establishment of liberal democratic institutions ever become a real possibility in those countries.

Second, my focus on Christianity as a resource for postmodern civic culture should definitely not suggest that I am operating with any sort of essentialist concept of Christian religious faith. For present purposes, I assume a great diversity among the forms of Christian belief and practice, and I identify none of them as the unique embodiment of the essence of Christianity. I take the similarities among these diverse forms of Christian belief to be family resemblances. Moreover, I assume that, as in the case of every other sort of cultural tradition, each generation of Christians in each Christian community invents Christianity anew through a dialogue with the past. As each generation reinvents Christianity, the forms taken by Christian belief can be either friendly or hostile to civic moral ideals. I assume that, if Christian religious belief is actually to contribute motivational resources supportive of a postmodern civic culture, this will happen only because Christians, who are also citizens, have perceived an analogy between civic moral ideals and Christian moral ideals—and, as a result, invent a Christianity that will flourish in liberal democracies because it is both (and equally) Christian and civic. This perception is a creative act. This perception is a call to the theological and narrative imagination. It emphatically is not a direct insight into the essential nature of Christianity because, for present purposes (i.e., for purposes of exploring the possible contribution of Christian belief to an overlapping cultural consensus) we must take Christianity as having no such essential nature.

These points understood, then, we can now ask precisely what sort of analogy might be perceived between civic and Christian moral ideals that could be exploited in the invention of a postmodern civic culture. Early modernist liberal political philosophers seized upon an analogy between the normative standpoint of citizenship and the standpoint proper to an autonomous faculty of reason, as articulated in the work of Descartes and others. This was the creative and defining moment out of which arose the Enlightenment project and modernist liberal civic culture in general. Modernist liberals, in perceiving and developing this analogy, brought together two standpoints that had been radically distinguished by classical political philosophers—the practical, engaged standpoint of the citizen-ruler, and the detached, purely contemplative or theoretical standpoint of the metaphysician. Following a similar pattern, can an analogy be perceived today between the normative standpoint of citizenship and the normative standpoint of Christian religious belief? If members of different Christian communities—acting *both* as citizens concerned about the fate of liberal democracy, *and* as Christians concerned with enhancing Christian practice in the context of an emerging postmodern culture—were to set out today to identify and develop such an analogy, where would they look?

Perhaps such an analogy can be discovered through an examination of what we might perceive as a certain paradoxical aspect common to the pursuit of both the civic good and the good proper to Christian life. I might formulate this paradoxical aspect as follows: both the pursuit of the civic good and the pursuit of the Christian good follow a pattern that can be expressed in the most general terms as one of attainment through abandonment. What I have in mind is that, in both cases, the object of desire consists (although in very different ways) in the adoption of a standpoint affirming particularistic human desire in general (i.e., affirming life "in this world") but, in both cases, this object is attained through a certain abandonment of the standpoint proper to particularistic desire (i.e., the standpoint proper to "this world"). Furthermore, we might note that this paradoxical aspect of the pursuit of both the civic good and the Christian good is linked to a special, shared characteristic: in both cases, attainment of the object of desire itself, attainment of the standpoint affirming particularistic human desire in general (i.e., affirming life "in this world"), excludes representation in narrative terms (i.e., cannot be understood as a standpoint "within time"). These two points constitute only the barest and most abstract statement of one analogy that might be perceived between Christian religious belief and a civic concept of the good. In the rest of this chapter, I will attempt to flesh out this analogy a bit, with the aim merely of providing a rough model of the sort of thinking that will be required of all citizens who wish, as members of one particularistic cultural community or another, to contribute toward the development of an overlapping consensus supportive of a postmodern civic culture.

Let us consider first in what sense the pursuit of the civic good can be understood to display this paradoxical pattern of attainment through abandonment. As we noted in chapter 4, the establishment of liberal democracy as a form of political association is intended to remove constraints on human aspiration attributable to relations of cultural, social, and economic domination. However, in order to establish this form of political association, citizens must develop the capacities prop-

er to liberal democratic citizenship, the capacities for civic
freedom and civic justice. Development of these capacities
requires what I characterized as a certain liberation of particularistic desire. This liberation of particularistic desire is
attained through the formation of an identity that is independent of the ranking systems and the world views associated
with any particularistic cultural community or concept of the
good. It is the attainment of this identity or standpoint—the
standpoint that provides the basis for the capacities of civic
justice and civic freedom—that is desired in the desire for the
civic good. Here we see the paradox. In order to establish and
maintain a form of political association aimed at removing
constraints on particularistic desire produced by cultural,
social, and economic domination, persons must adopt and
desire to adopt a standpoint detached from every particularistic object of desire. A form of political association aimed at
removing constraints on particularistic desire produced by
domination is a form of political association governed by a
standpoint affirming particularistic desire in general, affirming life "in this world." Attainment of this standpoint proper
to an affirmation of particularistic desire in general, however,
requires an abandonment of the standpoint proper to the
exclusive pursuit of any given object of particularistic desire.

   This pattern of attainment through abandonment is
linked to another feature of the pursuit of the civic good—the
fact that the standpoint proper to civic justice and civic freedom excludes representation in narrative terms. The external
and authorial standpoint proper to a capacity for civic freedom is not a standpoint that can itself be represented narratively. The pursuit of the civic good defines the liberal democratic public sphere, the space of civic discourse. But the space
of civic discourse encompasses only a part of life. It does not
constitute a totalizing order of meaning that comprehends all
the general issues of human life. It does not constitute a
"world" in the sense that particularistic concepts of the good
define totalizing views of the world. While the space of civic
discourse encompasses all citizens, it encompasses all citizens
only as free and equal individuals, leaving out of consideration differences and properties relevant to other life

concerns—gender, wealth, talent, beauty, ethnicity, age, birth, class, and so on. Citizens create and enter the space of civic discourse motivated to attain the good proper to it (i.e., the liberation of particularistic desire). Bound together by the pursuit of this good, citizens form a limited community of a certain kind—what we can call a "civic community." But this civic community is unlike the particularistic cultural communities founded upon the pursuit of a comprehensive ideal of happiness. Particularistic cultural communities are bound together by the sharing of a common history, a shared communitarian life narrative that gives meaning and direction to human desire in its totality. Particularistic cultural communities enjoy a narrative solidarity that is global, a narrative solidarity grounded upon shared stories that serve to foster and direct desire in all significant life activities and relationships. But the narrative solidarity proper to a civic community is very different.

The story of any civic community is a story of the pursuit of liberty, the civic good. It is a story about human beings as public persons, human beings who, as citizens, assign priority for the moment to their identities as free and equal individuals. To assign priority in this way to civic identity is to leave behind the distinctions, the honors, the rank, the privileges (or lack of them) attaching to communitarian identity. Communitarian identity is shaped by the ranking system, the virtue concepts, and the standards of excellence proper to a particularistic cultural community. The attributes of a person assigned on the basis of local community ranking systems reflect the totalizing world view or happiness ideal of that particular community. These attributes are incorporated into personal life narratives and, in this way, personal life narratives are incorporated within collective life narratives. The narrative solidarity that a member of a particularistic cultural community enjoys is, thus, a solidarity based upon the member's internalization of these personal attributes—the member's internalization of the relative position of rank and honor he or she holds within the community. To assign priority to civic identity, however, is to externalize all such personal attributes. As members of a civic community, all citizens are

free and equal individuals. The honors they receive or the
rank they hold within particularistic cultural communities is
irrelevant. To the extent that the political community itself
assigns rank and awards honor, these attributes also must
remain externalized by their recipients. Any citizen who, as a
citizen, views the distinctions and honors awarded by a civic
community as tokens of a status higher than that of other citizens has interpreted those distinctions and honors in the
wrong way.

Thus, civic identity exists only as an externalization of all
attributes of rank and relative esteem. The narrative solidarity
of any civic community is a solidarity based upon this externalization. The story of liberty is a story that assumes the equality
of all particularistic desire. It is a story that affirms all particularistic desire equally, without regard to the rank or relative
esteem of those who pursue it. In short, the narrative solidarity of a civic community is not the sort of narrative solidarity
that can ever give specific direction and meaning to particularistic desire. The civic identity created by the externalization
of all attributes of rank and relative esteem, as I noted in
chapter 4, has, at the limit, a peculiar non-narrative property.
Human life-narratives are stories relating the pursuit of a particular comprehensive concept of the good life. The function
of these stories is to provide intelligibility to human desire in
terms of a representation of time. Human desire flourishes
most abundantly in the anticipation of its satisfaction. Human
life narratives define the status of desire with respect to that
anticipated satisfaction. Rank, esteem, honors granted to the
main character of any particular life narrative are measures of
that status. Life narratives are stories of ongoing success or
failure. But civic identity, based upon the externalization of
all attributes of rank and relative esteem, can never serve as
the primary identity of the main character of any life narrative. By virtue of civic identity alone, the narrative status of
one person's desire cannot be distinguished from that of any
other person. Thus, at the limit, in its full development, civic
identity resists life-narrative representation altogether. The
civic good, in the pursuit of which civic identity is formed,
consists in the liberation of particularistic desire in the name

of an affirmation of particularistic desire in general. As an affirmation of particularistic desire in general, it implicitly carries an affirmation of the pursuit of life-narrative significance. Yet, the civic identity that must be given priority in the pursuit of the civic good is itself constituted by the externalization of all life-narrative significance. Thus, in attaining the standpoint from which narrative significance in general can be affirmed, one attains a standpoint whereby all specific narrative significance must be abandoned. Here once again (but now in terms of life-narrative representation), we see the pattern of attainment through abandonment as it is exemplified in the pursuit of the civic good.

Let us now see whether we can use this pattern in order to draw a useful analogy between the civic good and the object of Christian desire. Needless to say, the analogy will not be perfect, since we are speaking here about two very different spheres of life. The only question is whether the analogy between the normative standpoint of religious faith and the normative standpoint of citizenship can be exploited in the process of forming an overlapping cultural consensus supportive of a postmodern civic culture. The question is, then, in what sense can we understand the Christian good to involve this paradoxical pattern of attainment through abandonment—that is, of offering a certain kind of affirmation of particularistic desire, in general, through a relinquishing of the standpoint proper to particularistic desire?

We can perhaps best perceive this pattern by describing in a symmetrical way the elements of both the civic good and the Christian good. The civic good consists of the *liberation* of particularistic desire by means of the formation of a desire for civic freedom and civic justice, a desire whose realization requires the formation of a civic identity characterized by a certain externalization of all personal life-narrative attributes derived from the pursuit of any specific particularistic good. For purposes of symmetrical comparison, we might characterize the Christian good in this way: the Christian good consists in the *salvation* of particularistic desire by means of the formation of a different kind of desire, a desire whose realization requires the formation of an identity characterized by the

externalization of all personal life-narrative attributes derived
from the pursuit of any specific particularistic good. To flesh
out this comparison and to render plausible the analogy that
it seeks to articulate, it will be necessary to fill in some blanks
remaining in the characterization of the Christian good. We
must briefly explain: (1) what it means to speak of the salvation of particularistic desire, and (2) what sort of desire is
formed that might achieve this end.

The salvation of particularistic desire

As I observed earlier, human desire is a form of animal desire.
It is distinguished from other forms of animal desire in that,
through speech, it can be given narrative representation. This
fact that human desire can be experienced in terms of a representation of time affects desire, both qualitatively and quantitatively. The narrative representation of desire constitutes an
intensification of animal desire because to the experience of
present satisfaction can be added a representation of continued and increased future satisfaction. Narrative representation also constitutes a modification of animal desire to the
degree that the very anticipation of continued and increased
future satisfaction can become itself satisfying, and can therefore become itself an object of desire. As a result, perhaps the
most characteristic form of specifically human desire is the
desire for desire itself. The state of desire is a state of both dis-
satisfaction and anticipation of satisfaction. This "desire for
desire" is a desire for that state of anticipation. In other
words, as I have said many times, human desire flourishes
most completely not by being satisfied, but in the anticipation
of satisfaction. But this characteristic form of human desire is
potentially a source of danger and a point of vulnerability.
    The characteristically human desire for desire invests
human life in the logic of narrative representation (i.e., in the
logic of "temporality"). Narrative representation serves the
desire for the anticipation of desire's satisfaction by linking
events to one another in terms of a narrative closure constituted by the attainment of desire's object. Events that are linked
narratively in this way to an anticipated satisfaction gain a cer-

tain kind of narrative significance. By virtue of the very logic of narration, all narrated events are assigned narrative significance in terms of the narrative closure, the end of the story, to which they are referred. But in the case of human life narratives, events are assigned a special surplus of meaning in this way. The rhetorical function of human life narratives is to articulate the current status of desire in terms of a representation of time. The narrative significance assigned to events in a life narrative is defined by the link between those events and some desired and anticipated narrative closure. The narrative significance of events in an ongoing human life narrative articulates, in this way, the current status of desire. Events have narrative significance to the extent that they can be defined in their relevance to an anticipated satisfaction. The characteristically human desire for desire itself thus typically takes the form of a desire for narrative significance. To the extent that human desire takes this form, it invests itself in the logic of narrative representation. When human desire takes this form *exclusively*, it is captured by this logic and becomes its servant.

This condition of servitude to the logic of narrative representation is likely to affect the current status of human desire only when the narrative significance of events is threatened. Such a threat emerges when events occur or promise to occur that are incompatible with the currently anticipated closure of an ongoing life narrative. War, illness, unemployment, natural disasters—all such events can disrupt ongoing life narratives, and thus strip life events of their current narrative significance. The paradigmatic event of this kind, of course, is death. Death is an event that marks the end of a life narrative, but an event that, in most cases, cannot be taken as a narrative closure. Events generally cannot receive human life-narrative significance by reference to an end of the story that is not an anticipated satisfaction. Death rarely is such an anticipated satisfaction. Death, as an event, for the most part constitutes a narrative disruption for the person suffering it, a narrative disruption that can not only strip life events of their current narrative significance, but—at the limit, given the finality of death—can destroy all narrative significance as such.

It is the narrative encounter with the event of death, then, that above all makes evident the condition of the servitude of desire to the logic of narrative representation. When human desire has been captured by narrative representation, it takes exclusively the form of a desire for narrative significance. In the narrative encounter with death, in the encounter with death as a narrative disruption, the narrative significance of life events is threatened. To the extent that the threat is realized or seems inevitable, human desire for desire itself is threatened. If human desire flourishes most abundantly in the anticipation of satisfaction, it flourishes least abundantly not in the anticipation of the failure to attain satisfaction, but rather in the condition where no narratively representable anticipation makes sense at all. In this condition, all events, and even human desire itself, seem completely pointless and in vain. This is the condition invited by desire's servitude to the logic of narrative representation.

Let us characterize this condition, to speak in a semi-religious vocabulary, as the condition of desire's capture by the things of this world (i.e., desire's attachment to the temporal order). The temporal order is the narrative order. "This world" is the sphere of personal and collective life narratives shaped by the pursuit of particularistic desire. Particularistic desire aims at a satisfaction that can be anticipated and represented, in narrative terms, as a narrative closure. The goods sought by particularistic desire are the goods of this world, the goods whose pursuit gives narrative significance to the life events instrumental to their attainment. However, the servitude of desire to the logic of narrative representation constitutes a threat to particularistic desire. To the extent that desire has exclusively bound itself to narrative representation, the narrative encounter with death can cast doubt upon its validity. To the extent that particularistic desire has been captured by narrative representation, the characteristically human desire for desire can be weakened and even (at the limit) extinguished by the threat of narrative disruption. Such desire stands in need of a liberation from its condition of servitude to the temporal order. Such desire stands in need of salvation.

The Christian transformation of desire

In this notion of the salvation of particularistic desire, the rough outlines of an analogy between the civic good and the Christian good can perhaps begin to become visible. The civic good consists of the liberation of particularistic desire for the sake of the free pursuit of particularistic desire. Affirmation of the civic good achieves its goal of liberating particularistic desire by forming a new desire, a desire that takes precedence over the pursuit of any particularistic good—namely, a desire for civic freedom and civic justice. Christian belief and practice proceed in the same way. The Christian good consists of the salvation of particularistic desire—that is, the liberation of desire from its attachment to the temporal order, for the sake of the preservation of particularistic desire itself. Christianity achieves its goal of liberating particularistic desire from its servitude to the logic of narrative representation by forming a new desire that takes precedence over the pursuit of any particularistic good—in this case, a desire for a good that cannot be represented in narrative terms at all. We must now ask: In what way does Christianity accomplish this liberation? What is the nature of the transformation of desire fostered by Christianity? Further, how does this way of accomplishing the liberation of particularistic desire evince the pattern of attainment through abandonment?

As I noted earlier, human desire is a form of animal desire that is distinguished from other forms of animal desire by the fact that it can be experienced and rendered intelligible in terms of a representation of time. It is the very fact that human desire can be experienced in this way that gives rise to the characteristic form of human desire—namely, the desire for desire itself. The desire for desire itself is a desire for the anticipation of desire's satisfaction. This satisfaction is represented in narrative terms as a relationship between a present event, the present moment or condition of desiring, and the event of satisfaction, represented as a narrative closure, an end of the story. This relationship defines the narrative significance of the present event or condition of desiring. In this way, the characteristic form of human animal desire consists in a sort of second-order desire—that is, a desire not merely for a particular satisfaction, but rather for a relationship between the present state or condition of desiring and an anticipated satisfaction. This characteristic form of human desire thus refines and intensifies animal desire by taking a step back from the immediacy of animal desire. In this form, human desire for desire is experienced as a desire for the narrative significance of the present. Desire becomes not merely the desire of a particular satisfaction (as in the immediacy of animal desire), but rather a desire for the successful construction of a coherent and complete life narrative.

Human desire for desire, then, as the desire for narrative significance, includes within itself a representation of the present incompleteness of desire. The object of desire is the present state or condition of desiring, but understood through its relationship to its object. As we have seen, this characteristic form of human desire constitutes both a qualitative and a quantitative change in animal desire. It constitutes a qualitative change in animal desire because the object of desire becomes the very state of anticipation of future satisfaction. It constitutes a quantitative change in animal desire because what is desired is not only the object of satisfaction, but the anticipation of that satisfaction as well. But this characteristic form of human desire can take one further step away from the immediacy of animal desire, and experience in a another way both a quantitative and qualitative transformation. The desire for desire, as a desire for the anticipation of future satisfaction, has for its object the present event, state, or condition of desiring itself. But that condition is still tied to the immediacy of animal desire by virtue of its connection to some anticipated satisfaction. Such desire for desire takes for its object the present state of desiring, with respect to its incompleteness and to its promise. By virtue of this incompleteness and promise, the present state of desiring possesses narrative significance. Human desire for desire, however, can become fully itself only as a desire for the present event, state, or condition of desiring, without regard to its relationship to an anticipated satisfaction. In this case, desire becomes truly and fully its own object. In this case, there is no longer a question of the incompleteness of desire or a promise of satisfaction. The satisfaction of desire is attained through the act of desiring itself. This constitutes the most radical transformation of human animal desire possible, both quantitatively and qualitatively.

When the present event, state, or condition of human desire becomes its own object in this way, human desire possesses explicitly the object possessed, but only implicitly, as the desire for narrative significance. Human desire characteristically flourishes most abundantly not in the satisfaction of desire, but in the anticipation of its satisfaction. This is because human desire is characteristically the desire for desire, the desire for the present event or condition of desiring. When this present of desire becomes the explicit object of desire, the previously open circle of human desire is closed—and human desire finds its greatest and most intense completion in its present moment. Since desire in this state finds completion in its present moment, this moment itself can have no narrative significance whatever. An event gains narrative significance only through reference to some other event and, finally, through reference to a narrative closure. But the present moment of desire, taken as desire's own absolute object, is referred to no other event. The completion experienced by desire in this condition cannot be represented in narrative terms at all. The present of desire's self-completion constitutes neither beginning, middle, nor end of a story. This present is an unnarrated, dateless present, a *nunc stans*. Such an unnarrated, dateless present, using a more or less traditional religious or theological vocabulary, may be termed the "eternal present." The order of desire to which this present belongs is the eternal order. This eternal order of desire is opposed to the temporal order (i.e., the order of narrated desire, the order of narrative significance).

Christianity fosters and mandates this transformation of desire, whereby the object of desire becomes the eternal present. Let us call the desire that has been thus transformed the "love of God." But such terms can be misleading. In speaking of this transformation of desire, language itself becomes increasingly strained and problematic. This is, above all, because there can be no human speech addressed to others from the standpoint of the eternal present. All human speech must take into account the elements of the rhetorical situation it addresses. Among those elements are the specific place and time of the communicative act itself. Furthermore, all human speech offers, at least implicitly, a narrative interpretation of the rhetorical situation itself, a story of its very occasion, to its hearers for their acceptance or rejection. In these ways, human speech belongs completely to the narrative order of desire, to the temporal as opposed to the eternal order. The standpoint of the eternal present consists in an absence from this narrative order. The form of human speech native to the eternal present is in fact no speech at all, but rather a silence that bespeaks a completion of desire that is always already fully achieved.

Nevertheless, if Christianity is to foster the desire for this completion, it must be spoken about in some way. In Christianity, human speech about the eternal present typically adopts the vocabulary and perspectives proper to the rhetorical situation of human speech and to the narrative order of desire—the vocabulary and perspectives of "this world." The standpoint of the eternal present, the perspective proper to the eternal order of desire, thereby comes to be framed in speech as a realm absent to or beyond the temporal realm within which dwell the speakers who refer to it—it comes to be framed in speech as the world beyond this world, the "after-life." The discourse through which Christianity seeks to foster and mandate the transformation of desire thus becomes a discourse about this life and the next, the temporal order and the eternal order, the love of this world and the love of God. This discourse is then addressed to those who have encountered the threat to particularistic desire posed by an exclusive dependence upon a representation of that desire in narrative terms. In other words, Christian discourse becomes a discourse addressed to those in this world who have understood the need for the salvation of particularistic desire. This discourse seeks to affirm and preserve particularistic desire that has fallen into this condition of servitude to the temporal order by breaking the bonds of narrative representation and nurturing a desire for the unnarrated, dateless present—that is, by nurturing the love of God and the desire for eternal life.

Keeping the import of this language clearly in view, perhaps we may now perceive more clearly and work out more fully the analogy between the pursuit of the civic good and the Christian love of God. Both liberalism and Christianity aim at a transformation of desire that serves to affirm and support the pursuit of particularistic desire or life in "this world." Liberalism does so through the establishment of a distinction between the realm of public life and the realm of private life. Persons who become citizens in the full cultural sense in fact develop the capacities that permit them to participate in the public realm, the space of civic discourse. These capacities for civic freedom and civic justice require citizens to form an identity that is not exclusively defined by any single personal or collective life narrative. Citizens must learn to identify themselves and others effectively in action and speech as free and equal individuals, individuals whose self-understanding is not exclusively determined by the ranking systems and virtue concepts of any particular cultural community. Citizens who have actually developed civic identities have the capacity to give priority to the civic good over the communitarian good whenever the civic good comes into conflict with particularistic desire. They develop a love of civic freedom and civic justice. Through this transformation of desire, citizens permit the establishment of a civic community that guarantees the free pursuit of particularistic desire, that guarantees a pursuit of happiness freed from obstacles produced by interests in social and economic domination. Thus, for liberalism, the liberation of particularistic desire is achieved only to the extent citizens subordinate its pursuit to the pursuit of the civic good.

Now Christianity, as opposed to liberalism, is a comprehensive doctrine. It constitutes a particularistic cultural concept of the good life. It offers a totalizing world view that addresses all the general issues of human life. On the other hand, Christianity, like liberalism, aims at a transformation of human desire that seeks to affirm and support the pursuit of particularistic desire. Christianity, like liberalism, does this through the establishment of a distinction between two realms of desire—in the case of Christianity, a distinction between the temporal order and the eternal order, "this world" and "the next." Christian faith thereby preserves and perfects human desire as the desire for desire itself. Particularistic desire can undermine itself by becoming exclusively dependent upon a narrative representation of its status. Human desire for desire then becomes exclusively a desire for narrative significance, a desire for the ongoing construction of a coherent and complete life narrative. Events incompatible with the narrative coherence of life—above all, death—can, when encountered or anticipated, strip life events of their narrative significance and therefore seem to deprive desire of its object.

Christianity is addressed to those whose desire has been captured by the logic of life narrative representation, and who have recognized the threat to narrative coherence and, therefore, to desire itself. To save particularistic desire, Christianity fosters a different form of desire, a form of desire that supplements and transforms the desire for narrative significance and coherence. For those Christians who have attained the standpoint normative for the Christian community, this desire—a desire for the eternal present—takes precedence over the pursuit of all particularistic goods. This priority given to the eternal order of desire over the temporal or narrative order, however, is not intended as a depreciation or disparagement of the narrative order or of "this world." Its purpose is to break the exclusive power over desire of the logic of narrative representation. The desire for the eternal present cannot replace the pursuit of particularistic goods. Human beings, as human beings, cannot live in the unnarrated, dateless present, beyond speech and beyond world. Human animal desire requires the order, meaning, and direction that only a narratively coherent pursuit of particularistic goods can provide. The salvation of desire sought by Christians is a salvation of human animal desire, a salvation of the temporal order. But it is a salvation of the temporal order that can be realized only through the formation of a desire for the eternal order. Particularistic desire can be saved only through the development of a desire to be free of all particularistic desire. The desire for "this world" and its goods can be saved only by placing the love of God first.

Thus, though in different ways and with a different content, both liberalism and Christianity evince the pattern of attainment through abandonment—the affirmation and support of particularistic desire through a relinquishing of particularistic desire. Recognition of this pattern in both liberalism and Christianity, by Christians who are also citizens, conceivably could promote the shaping of postmodern forms of Christian belief and practice along lines that would support a new culture of citizenship. If Christian communities explicitly undertook the project of developing the analogy sketched here, Christianity could make an absolutely crucial contribution to the development of an overlapping cultural consensus that would provide the foundations of a postmodern liberal civic culture. A congruence could be established between the pursuit of the civic good and the pursuit of the Christian good, such that civic life and Christian life would mutually enlighten and reinforce one another. This certainly would not mean that the civic community would become identical to the community of Christian faith. Such an identification would, without doubt, destroy the civic community and almost certainly corrupt the Christian community by entangling it unduly in the affairs of this world. Yet a Christian community, formed in belief and practice with a view to the pursuit of the civic good, would be a Christian community whose members would find themselves to be, as citizens, more fully Christians ˙ ı their pursuit of the civic good and, as Christians, more deeply committed to the civic good in their love of God and pursuit of eternal life.

Civic friendship, Christian love, and
the providential order of history

A perception of the basic analogy between the civic good and the Christian good depends on perception of the following similarities:

(1) Both liberalism and Christianity seek to produce a global affirmation of particularistic human desire.

(2) Both seek to accomplish this by producing a transformation of desire, so that attainment of the new object of desire involves an abandonment of the standpoint proper to particularistic desire, and thus a modification of particularistic desire itself.

(3) The standpoints proper to the new objects of desire—in the case of liberalism, the standpoint of the love of civic justice and, in the case of Christianity, the standpoint of the love of God—are standpoints that, in different ways, cannot be represented in narrative terms and require the development of identities characterized by the externalization of all narratively defined traits.

Once again, the perception of this analogy is not the assertion of an identification of the civic good with the Christian good, nor is it an identification of the space of civic discourse with the eternal order. As in the case of all analogies or metaphors, the perception of this analogy is a creative act. It is not some sort of direct intuition of a preexisting essential relationship between liberal democratic cultural values and the values of Christianity. On the other hand, analogies also can transform in a profound way our understanding of the analogues. This is the sort of creative process that must occur among the members of a number of different cultural communities if a new overlapping cultural consensus in support of liberal democratic institutions is to be achieved. Christians (like Jews, Muslims, Buddhists, etc.) in North Atlantic liberal democracies are also citizens. As citizens, it is their civic duty to identify and strengthen the resources within their own cultural tradition that support the practice of citizenship. As Christians, love of God and neighbor dictates the identification and strengthening of Christian theological, confessional, and pastoral resources that can enhance the practice of Christianity by persons who are citizens of liberal democracies. In this way, the perception and further development of this analogy between the civic good and the Christian good would support Christians in the performance of both their civic and their Christian duties. But the development of an explicitly civic form of Christianity is not only a matter of duty. The very survival of liberal democratic political institutions in the postmodern era may depend on it. Given the fact that a large majority of citizens in North Atlantic liberal democracies are Christians, or at least strongly influenced by Christianity, it may be the case that only the emergence of an explicitly civic form of Christian belief and practice can provide the motivational support necessary for an effective postmodern civic culture.

There is good reason to believe, however, that a civic Christianity can emerge that can play this role. The analogy between the civic good and the Christian good can be extended further in many different directions. For example, let us consider briefly a possible analogy that could be developed between civic friendship and the Christian love of neighbor.

Civic friendship first must be clearly distinguished from a different sort of friendship: the sort of friendship that unites persons who are members of the same particularistic cultural community—persons who share a common world view and use the same primary moral vocabulary. Let us call this sort of friendship "communitarian solidarity." Communities whose members are united by this kind of solidarity are exclusive in a special, but familiar, sense. Such communities include and exclude persons on the basis of a set of criteria drawn from a particularistic concept of the good life. Qualifications for membership in particularistic cultural communities include not only specific beliefs, commitments, and behaviors, but often also personal traits such as birth, class, gender, talent, educational credentials, ethnicity, nationality, and so on. Consequently, built into this bond of affection is an awareness and affirmation of distinction and difference. This awareness of distinction contains an at least implicit reference to others who have been excluded. Where persons are united in communitarian solidarity, an "us" is distinguished from a "them."

This opposition between the "us" and the "them" is not just incidental to communitarian solidarity. Communitarian solidarity increases in intensity as awareness of this opposition grows. For this reason, communitarian solidarity actually seeks out ways to enhance this awareness, using means such as distinctive clothing, distinctive speech, distinctive patterns of consumption, distinctive rites of initiation and passage, and so on. This awareness of distinction necessarily involves the imposition of a certain minimal level of conformity in belief and behavior on those united in communitarian solidarity. The condition for the maintenance of the communitarian bond of affection is continued adherence to the ranking systems, the standards of excellence, and the virtue concepts of the particularistic cultural community. Any weakening of this adherence on the part of any member of the community weakens the solidarity that binds him or her to the other members.

The primary means of establishing and shaping communitarian solidarity is through the construction of collective life narratives. Such collective life narratives tell the story of how a particular community (whether consisting of lovers, family members, villagers, or persons sharing a common ethnic, class, or religious identity) came to be, and where its future lies. Human bonding of all kinds, as a bonding of desire, is achieved most effectively and fundamentally through the sharing of a common story. As in the case of all life narratives, the rhetorical function of collective life narratives is to represent and render intelligible the current status of desire with respect to its satisfaction. The form of desire proper to the communitarian bond of affection is a desire for narrative significance. By constructing a common narrative representation of events, persons united in communitarian friendship reinforce one another's readings of the narrative significance of those events. Thus, communities in the process of formation create for their members a common past and a common future. On the other hand, members of communities in the process of disintegration express that disintegration by warring over the interpretation of past events as they bear upon future prospects. Furthermore, communities characterized by oppression of one group by another generate among the oppressed collective counter-narratives that tell a very different story of what the community has been and will be.

Because collective life narratives provide the basis for communitarian solidarity among persons sharing a common life ideal, they are always stories told from the "inside"—that is, they are always moral histories, histories whose reading of events is governed by the ranking system and virtue concepts proper to the group. A collective life narrative is written in the primary moral language of a particularistic cultural community. It assigns to actions and persons attributes of rank and relative esteem reflective of the community's standards of excellence. Members of the community who incorporate their own personal life narratives into the larger collective life narrative of the group get their heroes and villains from these stories. Community solidarity is thus a bond of affection between persons who in some measure share the same heroes and villains.

Civic friendship differs radically from communitarian solidarity. The members of a liberal democracy are not united on the basis of a shared concept of the good life or a shared collective life narrative. Liberal political community is indeed an exclusive community, but the criteria of exclusion and inclusion applied by a civic community are not defined by the possession of shared personal traits, as evaluated by some particularistic cultural ranking system. Criteria for membership in a civic community are defined constitutionally without regard to the differentiating biological, economic, and cultural properties of its members. The citizens of a liberal democracy are defined constitutionally as free and equal individuals. The friendship proper to citizens must be a friendship proper to free and equal individuals, a friendship that disregards, for the purposes of civic friendship, personal traits that are evaluated differently by different local ranking systems.

This fact gives to civic friendship a certain appearance of paradox. Communitarian solidarity is built out of an awareness of distinction. Where communitarian solidarity exists, an "us" is opposed to a "them." But in the case of civic friendship, the bond of affection is built out of an awareness of a very different sort of distinction. This distinction cannot in principle be understood properly as an opposition of an "us" to a "them." The "us" defined by the bond of civility embraces, at least potentially, all human beings. Citizens united in friendship as citizens are united as free and equal individuals, precisely in their difference from all those differences in personal traits, values, and beliefs that define the criteria for membership in particularistic cultural communities. Civic friendship is a bond of affection that is effective between persons precisely to the extent that those persons do not distinguish themselves from one another on the basis of the biological, economic, and cultural properties that are fundamental to communitarian solidarity. Thus, civility also bases itself on a distinction between sameness and difference, but the affirmation of sameness in civic friendship is really an affirmation of difference in two respects: (1) an affirmation of difference in world view, values, and personal traits; and (2) an affirmation of the difference of both self and other from all such differences—that is, an affirmation of the freedom of self and other as citizens.

Civic friendship, then, is a very complex and peculiar phenomenon. Communitarian solidarity creates and nurtures the awareness of biological, economic, and cultural differences distinguishing those who belong to a given community from those who do not. As an affirmation of difference, communitarian solidarity consists of a relatively straightforward affirmation the difference of self from other. On the one side stands the "us," on the other side the "them." Communitarian solidarity flourishes where members of a given particularistic cultural community perceive in one another an exclusive identification with the "us," as opposed to a "them." But the impulse behind civic friendship is very different. Civic friendship follows a logic very different from that of communitarian solidarity because civic friendship is a bond uniting those who pursue the civic good. Civic friendship flourishes where members of a civic community perceive in one another an identification with and commitment to the civic good. The civic good is to be distinguished from the communitarian good in that the civic good is a partial good. Its pursuit does not comprehend the whole of life. The civic good consists of the liberation of particularistic desire. Those who pursue the civic good do not abandon their commitment or allegiance to a particular cultural community. Rather, pursuit of the civic good seeks only a modification of that commitment—a modification whereby it becomes a commitment undertaken in full freedom and responsibility. Those who are united in civic friendship wish for one another the attainment and exercise of this capacity for freedom and responsibility.

Civic friendship is thus a bond of affection between free and responsible individuals who are, and wish to be, *freely* committed to a particularistic way of life or ideal of happiness. Civic friendship nurtures the capacity for free and responsible choice. It does this by establishing a bond of affection between persons that is not based upon similarities of biological, economic, or cultural traits. Civility establishes a sameness, an equivalence between persons that lies beyond all such differences. One citizen, in behaving civilly toward another (i.e., in affirming this equivalence), affirms his or her own civic identity as one that is not exclusively determined by any particularistic ranking system or world view. Citizens united by civic friendship are the same—precisely insofar as they grant to themselves and to one another the possibility of being different. Their unity is constituted by an affirmation of their difference from all particular differences that determine particularistic community identifications. Accordingly, the mark of civility is not a wish to change others, to make them conform more completely to the requirements of some particularistic ranking system. Nor is the mark of civility a mere willingness to live and let live, a tolerance bordering on indifference to the other. Rather, the mark of civic friendship is an affection that actively grants to the other an open space for the free play of desire, an active affirmation of both mutual difference and an identity beyond all differences.

Thus, while communitarian solidarity thrives where there exists an identity of interests and tastes, civic friendship is libertarian, empowering otherness and difference. While communitarian solidarity thrives where there exists shared measures of excellence and personal worth, civic friendship is egalitarian, establishing a bond that disregards all measures of relative rank and merit. Given their very different logics, civic friendship and communitarian solidarity coexist uneasily with one another. In a civic community, persons are expected to develop and exercise equally a capacity for both—another example of the extraordinary cultural demands made upon those who live under liberal democratic regimes. Just as liberal democracy in general requires citizens to be both committed to a particular way of life and detached from it sufficiently to exercise the capacities of civic freedom and civic justice, so also liberal democracy requires citizens to cultivate solidarity with the members of their family and their ethnic, class, and religious communities—while at the same time cultivating a bond of civility with those who pursue very different and even conflicting life ideals. The difficulties involved in the realization of this ideal of the equal cultivation of both communitarian solidarity and civic friendship are enormous.

The cultivation of civic friendship can very often seem actively hostile to the cultivation of communitarian solidarity. Communitarian solidarity supports the pursuit of a particularistic concept of the good life. It seeks to nurture and perfect in fellow community members those attitudes, dispositions, and skills necessary for the attainment of a particularistic ideal of happiness. The mark of communitarian solidarity is thus a desire and even a commitment to change others, to help them to conform more completely to the highest standards of the community. In order to flourish, human desire needs such direction. The nurture and direction of particularistic desire very often requires a strong assertion of authority and a demand for exclusive compliance with a specific ranking system. Communitarian solidarity has, for this reason, a certain priority in relation to civic friendship. In contexts where clear and firm direction is most needed—say, in family relationships, in education, in economic, partisan political, or religious affairs—the libertarian nature of civic friendship, in its affirmation and nurturing of difference, can express personal disengagement and even a positive indifference to others.

The civic good, we must recall, is a partial and not a comprehensive good. The free space granted to others by civic friendship in pursuit of the civic good cannot encompass the whole of life. Just as civic identity exists only as a modification of communitarian identity, so also civic friendship exists only as a modification of communitarian solidarity. The very possibility of civic friendship therefore depends upon strong communitarian identity. Citizens who are not firmly anchored in communitarian solidarity will neither understand nor appreciate the practice of civility. Accordingly, the affirmation of otherness and difference proper to civility is inappropriate when it has the effect of undermining the ordered and disciplined pursuit of a particularistic ideal of happiness. The practice of civility as a civic virtue, then, requires moral insight. It requires a prudence guided by a clear understanding of the good civility serves.

Cultivation of civic friendship also can have the effect of weakening the narrative foundations of communitarian solidarity. Communitarian solidarity is forged and maintained by the sharing of a collective life narrative. The rhetorical function of collective life narratives is to create a bond between the members of a given cultural community, a bond that supports the pursuit of a particularistic concept of the good life. Civic friendship is also forged and maintained by the sharing of a common narrative, but the rhetorical function of this civic narrative is quite different. The story of a civic community is the story of the pursuit of the civic good, the pursuit of civic freedom and civic justice. But the desire for the civic good is not a desire for a comprehensive good that can give direction and meaning to life as a whole. The story of liberty is a story that affirms the pursuit of particularistic desire in general, and affirms all particularistic desire equally without regard to any specific ranking system or world view. A citizen identifies with the story of liberty to the extent that he or she externalizes all attributes of rank or relative esteem gained by identification with the collective life narrative of any particularistic cultural community. This identification with the story of liberty is perfected by what I have called the practice of life-narrational equalization.

Civic friendship is a bond of affection based upon this equalization of all particularistic desire, and this externalization of all attributes of local rank and status. But a developed capacity for this equalization and externalization of rank can have a corrosive effect upon belief in the collective life narratives of particularistic cultural communities. Affirmation of the community life narrative of a civic community, in effect, requires a certain relativization of local collective life narratives. It requires that these local collective life narratives be placed in the context of an encompassing narrative that equalizes all particularistic desire and represents the histories of all particularistic cultural communities, as it were, from the outside. Yet the narrative of the civic community is a moral history. It tells the story of the struggle for and defense of civic freedom and civic justice. It has its heroes and villains.

It is important to see, however, that genuinely civic heroes, unlike the partisan heroes proper to communitarian moral histories, are heroes precisely to the extent that their actions have affirmed the equalization of all particularistic desire and the externalization of all local measures of rank and relative esteem. Such heroes do not serve well as models for the shaping of particularistic desire and aspiration over the course of an entire life. They offer no specific direction beyond that of an affirmation of individual liberty to choose and follow a particular ideal of happiness. Thus, the narrative requirements of civic friendship come into conflict with the narrative requirements of communitarian solidarity. This conflict is not inevitable, but its proper mediation requires, once again, a moral insight informed by a clear understanding of the end served by civic friendship. When civility is cultivated without the guidance of such insight, the affirmation of otherness and difference proper to civic friendship—its libertarian and egalitarian nature—can actually make citizens even more vulnerable to the cultural dangers endemic to liberal democracy, the dangers of nihilism and alienation.

Christians, like all citizens of liberal democracies, are called upon to cultivate both civic friendship and communitarian solidarity. They are therefore called upon to develop the moral insight or prudence required for the full and proper development of both. As citizens, it is the civic duty of Christians to locate within their own cultural tradition resources supportive of a liberal democratic civic culture. As I have shown earlier in this chapter, the potential resources of that tradition for such a purpose are vast. Another case of this might be noted in the congruence between civic friendship and the Christian love of neighbor. Let me point out a few general parallels.

Christian love of neighbor, however greatly it may differ from civic friendship, is paradoxical in many of the same ways. To see the similarity, we must remember that liberal democracy requires persons to move within two very different moral contexts, contexts that stand in a relationship of tension with one another: the sphere of local community life, and the liberal democratic public sphere. Participation in the public sphere, in the space of civic discourse, requires a kind of abandonment or surrender of the standpoint proper to membership in a particularistic cultural community. Liberal democracy requires citizens to develop and cultivate a standpoint and an identity proper to civic life, one that involves a significant modification of communitarian identity. The development and cultivation of civic identity includes, among other things, the cultivation of a capacity for civic friendship, a friendship uniting all citizens without regard to their diverse and conflicting communitarian commitments and interests. But a cultivation of this civic bond of affection can be disruptive to relationships of communitarian solidarity, because the libertarian and egalitarian nature of civic friendship can seem incompatible with the exclusivist and rank-sensitive nature of communitarian friendship.

Now, Christianity draws distinctions and imposes responsibilities similar to these. Like citizens of liberal democracies, Christians also belong to two worlds—the world of temporal affairs, or the City of Man, and the world of eternal things, or the City of God. Full membership in the City of God, like full liberal democratic cultural citizenship, requires a relinquishing of the standpoint proper to particularistic desire. Like citizens of liberal democracies, citizens of the City of God must develop and cultivate a new standpoint and an identity—in the case of Christianity, a standpoint distinct from and even alien to identities and roles adopted within the sphere of temporal affairs. Like liberal democratic citizens, Christians must also cultivate a new kind of friendship as citizens of the "heavenly" City—in the case of Christianity, a kind of friendship that is alien to the communitarian solidarity that unites members of the City of Man. This friendship that unites the citizens of the City of God is Christian love of neighbor, or "charity." Further, just as civic friendship and communitarian solidarity coexist uneasily, so also the Christian love of neighbor introduces tension and ambiguity into the communitarian relationships proper to the City of Man. Let us now fill in a few details of this comparison in an attempt to show precisely how the Christian love of neighbor might become a vital element of a postmodern civic culture that supports the cultivation of civic friendship.

We must keep clearly in view the fact that, within the civil order, the Christian community constitutes one cultural community among others. As a particular cultural community united by a shared concept of the good life, the Christian community has all the general features of every other such community. Christianity is a comprehensive doctrine that addresses (at the limit) all the general issues of human life. It offers to its adherents a totalizing world view that encompasses human life in its entirety. Moreover, the Christian community is embodied in institutions with different types and various degrees of organization. These institutions—Christian churches—have a variety of functions beyond their strictly religious function. They are political organizations, advancing the political interests of Christians as Christians within the encompassing civil order. They are welfare organizations, satisfying the material, psychological, and social needs of Christians. They are economic organizations, often owning property, buying and selling goods, raising and spending money in pursuit of various other goals. They are educational institutions, teaching their members not only about Christian faith, but also offering them information, narratives, and arguments relating to current issues of concern to all citizens. As political, welfare, economic, and educational organizations, Christian churches generate institutional structures not unlike those of non-religious organizations. Organizational activities must be initiated and managed. Some minimally hierarchical system of responsibility must be established to direct and oversee such activities.

As political, welfare, economic, and educational organizations, Christian churches create their own distinctive and separate cultural identity within the larger society. They constitute more or less exclusive particularistic cultural communities, and their members are necessarily united by an awareness of their differences from members of other such communities. Governed by this awareness of difference, Christian churches generate their own forms of communitarian solidarity. They generate their own local cultures—their own ranking systems, styles of speech and dress, rites of initiation and passage, preferences in entertainment and leisure activities, and so on. But the Christian community, understood in this way as a community united by communitarian solidarity, an institutionally organized association serving many different purposes, is not yet understood with respect to what makes it a specifically Christian community. In the vocabulary of theology, the Christian community, understood as a community united in communitarian solidarity, belongs to this world, the world of temporal affairs, the City of Man. Christian churches, as political, welfare, economic, and educational institutions, constitute the visible church, the church that stands organizationally distinct from all other forms of association found within the encompassing civil order. However, what unites Christians specifically as Christians is not a form of communitarian solidarity. To the extent that persons who are members of Christian churches have developed and cultivated a specifically Christian understanding of who they are and what their lives are about, they are united in a different way. The bond of affection that unites Christians as Christians is the bond of charity, the Christian love of neighbor. How does charity differ from all forms of communitarian solidarity?

Whatever other pursuits may unite Christians in communitarian solidarity, the pursuit that unites them specifically as Christians is the pursuit of the Christian good, the love of God. As we have seen, the love of God consists in that transformation of human desire that Christianity seeks to accomplish in its adherents. Christian faith seeks the salvation of particularistic desire. Human desire characteristically takes the form of the desire for desire, or the desire for narrative significance. But the desire for narrative significance in human life is vulnerable to a variety of obstacles and frustrations. As we have seen, to the extent that human desire is exclusively bound to the logic of narrative representation, those obstacles and frustrations pose a threat to the affirmation of particularistic desire itself. One obstacle in particular—death—appears to constitute an insuperable narrative disruption that seems to be alone sufficient to destroy the narrative coherence and significance of a human life. In order to overcome this appearance and to save particularistic human desire from this apparent threat of defeat, human desire must be freed of its bondage to the logic of narrative representation. The problem is not death, but this bondage. As we have seen, what is desired in the desire for narrative significance is the desire for desire itself, the closing of the circle of desire that escapes all narrative representation utterly. Christianity seeks to foster a kind of desire for desire that escapes its bondage to narrative representation, and that closes the circle of desire. This desire is the desire for the unnarrated and dateless present, the desire for the eternal present, for the love of God. Members of Christian churches whose desire for desire has been successfully transformed in this way are united by their shared love of God. The bond of affection by which such Christians are united is charity.

This specifically Christian form of fellowship differs from communitarian solidarity in many of the same ways that civic friendship differs from communitarian solidarity. Christians who are actually united in the love of God, in the desire for the eternal present, are united in a different way than when they are joined in communitarian solidarity. United in charity, they are citizens of the City of God. United in communitarian solidarity, they are citizens of the City of Man. United in communitarian solidarity, Christians are members of the visible church, an institutionally organized association that is distinct, and which seeks to be distinct from other kinds of association. Members of the visible church know who numbers among them and who does not. The visible church has public criteria for inclusion and exclusion. Members of the visible church actively differentiate themselves from members of other religious communities as a means of strengthening their communitarian bond.

This awareness of difference and distinction introduces pressures for conformity and submission to authority into Christian forms of communitarian solidarity, as it does into all forms of communitarian solidarity. But charity follows a different logic. Charity follows a libertarian and egalitarian logic similar to that of civic friendship. Charity is libertarian (i.e., affirms and empowers otherness and difference) and egalitarian (i.e., establishes a bond that disregards all measures of relative rank and merit) by virtue of the good that it serves and attains. Christians are united in charity through their shared love of God. But the love of God is a love for the eternal present that releases human desire from its bondage to the logic of narrative representation. This transformation of desire also produces a transformation of identity. These transformations are the sources of the libertarian and egalitarian nature of specifically Christian friendship.

Christians who have fully attained the standpoint of faith, the standpoint proper to the love of God, gain an identity that is no longer defined by any particular personal life narrative. The standpoint of completed desire, the standpoint of the eternal present, is dateless and not subject to narration. The personal identity that is shaped by a particular life narrative is formed by the narrative internalization of personal traits and attributes of rank assigned through a process of comparison with others. This narrated personal identity is defined by a reading of life events that distinguishes a person in terms of biological and economic properties, goals, interests, and achievements. A person, thus defined, becomes the central character in the ongoing construction of his or her personal life narrative. In attaining the standpoint of faith, however, the Christian gains an identity that is different from any narrated identity, an identity that cannot be defined or expressed in narrative terms. In the standpoint of completed desire, the object of desire is always already fully possessed. The identity proper to this standpoint thus cannot in principle be understood as one belonging to a character undergoing a process of life narrative construction, a character on the way to some specific narrative closure. As a result, the differentiations and distinctions that define any narratively constructed identity fall into irrelevance. In the Christian love of neighbor, persons are united on the basis of the sharing of an identity that stands beyond all differences and distinctions subject to narrative representation. This includes, at the extreme, even those differences produced by injurious and hostile actions. The Christian love of neighbor thus encompasses (at the limit) even the love of enemies. Of course, who is loved in the love of enemies is not the other as enemy, for the characterization of actions as injurious and hostile belongs to the sphere of narrative representation. In the Christian love of neighbor, even the enemy becomes neighbor as the entire sphere of narrative representation itself falls into the oblivion of the eternal present.

Furthermore, the Christian love of God and neighbor transforms not only personal identity, but particularistic desire as well. The Christian good is the salvation of particularistic desire. Christian faith achieves this not by the denial or disparagement of particularistic desire, but rather by freeing it from its bondage to the logic of narrative representation. The Christian love of God fulfills human desire for desire by transforming it completely into itself, as the desire for the unnarrated and dateless present. But no human life could ever live wholly within an unnarrated and dateless present. In human life, contemplation of the eternal present, the silencing of the narrative imagination, is inevitably an affair of the moment. Human beings are living things whose desire is distinctively qualified by the human power of narrative representation. The love of God closes the circle of desire momentarily—not in order to close it permanently, but rather to permit this momentary completion of desire to liberate particularistic desire from the constraints of an exclusively narrative self-understanding.

This liberation of particularistic desire abolishes permanently any appearance that desire can remain incomplete as a result of events that disrupt the construction of coherent personal life narratives. The power of death, as one such event, is thereby overcome. The result of this liberation of particularistic desire, from bondage to the logic of narrative representation, is a global affirmation of the narrative significance of human life in the face of all narrative disruptions. In the vocabulary of Christian faith, this global affirmation of narrative significance is the theological virtue of hope. In any case, this global affirmation of narrative significance is an affirmation not of any particular life narrative pattern, but rather of any and all life narrative patterns. In short, this affirmation entails an equalization of particularistic desire, an equal affirmation of every human project of constructing a coherent personal life narrative. Therefore, the Christian love of neighbor, as a bond of affection between persons based upon an identity beyond all differences, is also a bond of affection that embraces equally every life in its particularity.

Thus comes into view clearly the intrinsically libertarian and egalitarian nature of Christian charity. Christian love of neighbor is libertarian, because it imposes no conformity and requires no submission to authority. Charity flourishes where differences are greatest—even at the point of the most extreme difference, as in the Christian love of those who hate Christianity. Furthermore, Christian love of neighbor is egalitarian, because the Christian salvation of particularistic desire is a salvation of narrative significance in general, without regard to the particular life project or to the person who undertakes it. Thus, once again we see a possible congruence between the pursuit of the civic good and the pursuit of the Christian good, between Christian charity and civic friendship. If guided by this perception of congruence, those who attain fully the standpoint of faith and who practice the Christian love of neighbor will find the practice of civic freedom and civic justice to be an inevitable and natural extension of their Christian way of life. In fact, if this analogy between Christian charity and civic friendship is plausible at all, Christian charity is bound to appear as an even more radical, extreme, and demanding form of civic friendship than that required by liberal democracy itself. The friendship of citizens of the City of God might then be viewed as the fulfillment of that bond of affection, which is realized in civic friendship only as promise.

We may press this analogy between civic friendship and Christian charity one step further, a step that reveals what may be the most important contribution Christianity can make to the invention of a postmodern civic culture. We have noted the way in which libertarian and egalitarian civic friendship stands in a relationship of tension with communitarian solidarity. Communitarian solidarity is a vital force in the shaping and direction of human desire. Communitarian friendship nurtures and supports human aspiration by grounding it in collective life narratives that provide models of human achievement and success. But the equalization of all particularistic desire that is affirmed in civic friendship seems to involve a certain relativization of all models of achievement and lead to a general debunking of heroes. In other words, the egalitarian character of civic friendship can seem to promote a general disaffection from all particular ranking systems—a disaffection that, at the extreme, becomes full-blown nihilism.

Furthermore, the sort of collective narrative that supports civic friendship (i.e., the narrative of the liberal political community's quest for civic freedom and civic justice) is not the sort of narrative that can give human desire specific direction. In the narrative identification with the story of liberty, a citizen must adopt a narrative standpoint external to the particular collective life narrative that frames his or her own personal life narrative. The cultivation of this narrative standpoint that looks at all local collective life narratives from the outside, so to speak, is necessary for the development of a capacity for civic friendship. But it can also promote a skepticism toward every community narrative that is presented with moral or inspirational intent. Such skepticism can in turn promote a generalized disengagement from the particular cultural communities whose members are motivated by these local moral histories. In other words, the libertarian character of civic friendship can foster a detachment from community life that, at the limit, can become full-blown alienation. In this way, the cultural resources required to support civic friendship seem to conflict with the cultural resources required to support communitarian solidarity. The citizen's civic duty to cultivate equally both civility and communitarian solidarity can thus seem to be self-defeating, to require the development and rec-

onciliation of hopelessly contradictory and mutually undermining normative standpoints.

The Christian love of neighbor coexists with communitarian solidarity no more comfortably than does civic friendship.
The libertarian and egalitarian nature of Christian charity,
however, gives rise to different tensions for different reasons.
As we have seen, Christian love of neighbor also affirms the
equality of all particularistic desire. The proper Christian
response to the question, "Who is my neighbor?" is "Anyone
at all." But the Christian community is also a particularistic
cultural community, among others, with its own identity and
organizational structure. The members of the Christian community are united in communitarian solidarity as they carry
out the political, welfare, economic, and educational tasks
that constitute part of the mission of Christian churches.
Christianity, in order to survive as a doctrine and way of life,
must create organized and institutionalized forms of association, forms of association that cannot flourish in the absence
of communitarian solidarity. But Christian love of neighbor is
the affirmation of an identity among persons that lies beyond
all differences of community membership and local culture.
Communitarian solidarity, on the other hand, is based precisely on an affirmation and cultivation of such differences. It
then would seem that the communitarian solidarity necessary
for the survival of Christian churches stands in hopeless conflict with the highest ideals of the Christian love of neighbor.

Furthermore, Christian love of neighbor is libertarian in
a way that could promote, at the limit, the abandonment of
community membership entirely. Christian charity is the
bond of affection that unites persons in their pursuit of the
Christian good, the love of God. As we have seen, the love of
God releases human desire from its bondage to the logic of
narrative representation. The love of God consists of a transformation of human desire for desire such that desire
receives its perfect completion as the desire for the unnarratable, dateless present. This standpoint of the eternal present
provides the Christian with a radically new identity, an identity wholly stripped of all those personal properties that define
the main character of any particular personal life narrative.

The Christian love of God realizes the most extreme liberation of human self-understanding from the constraints of
narrative representation.

For the Christian, this unnarratable identity becomes the
"real," or preferred self. Christian love of neighbor is the
recognition and affirmation of either the actuality or poten-
tiality of such a "real" self in all other persons at all times and
in all places. But such an unnarrated self must always be juxta-
posed with a narratable identity. Human beings are living
things whose desire is subject to narrative representation. It is
as narratively representable selves that human being speak
and interact with one another. It is as narratively representable selves that human beings organize community life
and enjoy communitarian solidarity. But the Christian love of
neighbor seems to require a turning away from narratively
representable selfhood and association. The Christian love of
neighbor seems to follow a logic that leads toward a radical
separation of the City of God from the City of Man. It would
seem to promote an otherworldliness utterly inhospitable to
involvement in temporal affairs and participation in the life of
any particularistic community. Thus, like civic friendship,
Christian love of neighbor seems to stand in a very uneasy
relationship to communitarian solidarity, potentially generating its own unique forms of disaffection from particularistic
desire and alienation from particularistic community life.

The chance that these forms of disaffection and alienation
might be actualized among Christians, however, is greatly
reduced by the nature of the collective narrative that unites
the Christian community. The collective narrative of the
Christian community, the narrative into which every Christian
incorporates his or her personal life narrative, is grounded in
the narratives contained in the Bible. These narratives are
accorded extraordinary status. This extraordinary status attributed to them gives the collective narrative of the Christian
community its power to hold together Christian love of neighbor and communitarian solidarity in a mutually supportive
and creative tension. For Christians who are also citizens, this
synthesis of charity and communitarian friendship made possible by biblical narrative could provide, in the context of a

postmodern civic culture, a model for an analogous synthesis of civic friendship and communitarian solidarity. A clear articulation of this analogy by an explicitly civic Christian theology could perhaps have the effect of limiting, for Christians and those citizens influenced by Christianity, the risks of nihilism and alienation endemic to libertarian and egalitarian civic friendship. Given the fact that the great majority of citizens in North Atlantic liberal democracies are at least nominal Christians, such a civic theology could make a significant contribution to the creation of a viable postmodern civic culture. It would provide a resource for the motivation of civic virtue that could perhaps be developed in no other way. Let me briefly sketch here, in conclusion, the outlines of a postmodern civic theology that might accomplish this.

The capacity of the Christian community to unite Christian charity and communitarian solidarity into a creative synthesis hinges on the extraordinary status Christianity accords to biblical narrative. In the vocabulary of theology and faith, biblical narratives constitute revealed or divinely inspired truth. The import of this description is to affirm that the narratives contained in the Bible are not subject to the standards applied to stories told by human beings. In order to understand the rhetorical function of this extraordinary status accorded to biblical narrative by Christians, we must briefly consider once again the variety of rhetorical functions served by narratives in general.

As we have noted, stories told by human beings may be divided into two different kinds: closed-criterion narratives (i.e., stories whose narrative closure is fixed and predetermined) and open-criterion narratives (i.e., stories whose narrative closure is not fixed, stories whose narrative order is therefore always subject to revision). In any narrative, the order and significance of the events described are determined by their relationship to the end of the story. The end of the story, the narrative closure, serves as the criterion for determining narrative order and significance. Stories told by human beings most typically are closed-criterion narratives. During a trial, for example, stories are told as part of the presentation of evidence. The criterion of relevance that determines the narrative order and significance assigned to events in these stories is the question, "Guilty or innocent?" On other occasions and with respect to other criteria of relevance, many different stories could be and always are constructed out of the very "same" events described in witness narratives. This, of course, does not mean that the narrative of a crime finally constructed by a jury, when it arrives at its verdict, is somehow fabricated or false. As long as there is consensus regarding the narrative criterion to be applied in constructing a story, there can be consensus about the order and narrative significance of the events described by the story. Storytelling has many different rhetorical functions. Human beings tell stories to entertain, to inform, to explain, to warn, to give advice, to command, and so on. Whenever a story performs its rhetorical function successfully for a given audience, it is because the story was constructed artfully and in accordance with a narrative criterion acceptable to its audience.

Literary or fictional narratives constitute one special class of closed-criterion narratives. An understanding of the way in which fictional narratives differ from "historical" narratives is important for an understanding of the extraordinary status accorded to biblical narrative in Christianity. Fictional or literary narratives differ from "historical" narratives in that the events related by fictional narratives are invented. When a person constructs a story about events that actually occurred (i.e., that the person did not deliberately invent or imagine), he or she imposes a narrative order on those events that is only one possible narrative order among others. It is always possible to construct other stories about or to impose a different narrative order on those events for different purposes and different audiences. Thus, historical events such as the Battle of Waterloo or the assassination of Lincoln can be woven into any number of different stories and given any number of different narrative interpretations. However, in the case of fictional or literary narratives, it makes no sense to incorporate the events described into different stories, to impose a new narrative order on them. The narrative order and significance of the events described in a fictional or literary narrative are fixed once and for all because they are a matter of decision for its author. The author determines the narrative closure to which all the events described refer. Once the end of the story is known to its audience, the events it relates are understood with finality in their narrative order and significance.

Keeping this difference between fictional/literary and historical narratives clearly in view, we must recall one further point before returning to the question of the extraordinary status of biblical narrative. Human life narratives, both personal and collective, differ from both historical and literary narratives. Human life narratives describe events that have actually occurred. In that respect, they are like any historical narrative. Many different stories can be constructed out of the events occurring during a particular person's life. But human life narratives differ from historical narratives by virtue of their special rhetorical function. As we have seen, human life narratives serve to provide meaning and direction to human desire. To construct a life narrative is to construct a life. A person relates the story of his or her life to others (including self, as other) in order to render intelligible and to assess the current status of desire with respect to its satisfaction. By virtue of having this function, human life narratives belong to the class of open-criterion narratives. In their function of providing meaning and direction to human desire, human life narratives are never finished. The order and significance of human life events always depend upon the future (i.e., depend upon events that have not yet occurred), and therefore are subject to nearly infinite reassessment and reinterpretation in terms of different possible narrative closures. Where the end of the story is always not yet finally determined, the narrative order and significance of events are also always not yet finally determined.

When persons do construct their own life narratives as if they were closed-criterion narratives, imposing a fixed narrative order and meaning on their lives, they often do this because their life narrative has become bound up with some malady of desire. To construct a human life narrative as if it were a closed-criterion narrative—as if the end of the story were fixed and the narrative significance of particular events were determined with finality—is to construct a human life as if it were a work of fiction. The fictionalizing of human life narratives is always motivated in some way. For example, when persons have done or experienced something that would, if incorporated into their acknowledged life narrative, disrupt or threaten the narrative significance of their lives as a whole, then those events are either excluded from the narrative (i.e., "repressed") or arbitrarily given a significance that consists in a denial of the significance that they threaten to have. The function of psychoanalysis, understood as a "talking cure," is the de-fictionalization of life narrative meaning. Only because such fictionalization is bound up with a malady of desire can the de-fictionalization of life narrative meaning constitute a cure for that malady. To de-fictionalize a personal life narrative is to incorporate into that life narrative events excluded or denied because they were too disruptive of narrative coherence and significance. Such a cure always amounts to a restoration of the proper rhetorical function to human life narratives, the function of rendering intelligible and assessing the current status of desire with regard to its satisfaction. Persons who are cured of maladies of desire in this way are once again free to take up the construction of their own life narratives as open-criterion narratives, as narratives that are indefinitely revisable.

In view of these distinctions, we can perhaps now understand properly the rhetorical significance of the extraordinary status assigned by Christian faith to biblical narratives. To say that the narratives contained in the Bible are "revealed," "divinely inspired," or "literally meaningful or true"[31] is to attribute to biblical narrative characteristics of all three types of narratives we have discussed. First, it is to take biblical narratives as historical narratives in that they relate events that actually occurred (i.e., events about which it makes sense to offer alternative stories). Second, it is also to take biblical narrative as a species of fictional or literary narrative, in that bibli-

---

[31] "Literally meaningful," that is, in the sense of "literal" as defined by Hans Frei in his book, *The Eclipse of Biblical Narrative* (New Haven: Yale University Press, 1974), pp. 1–16.

cal narratives determine with finality the intrinsic narrative order and significance of the events they describe. The final and authoritative determination of the intrinsic narrative order and significance of events is possible only if the end of the story is infallibly known. This is possible in fictional/literary narratives because the end of the story is a matter of decision for the author. To attribute to biblical narratives, as historical narratives, this property of literary/fictional narratives is to attribute to the authors of these narratives an extraordinary status. Biblical narratives define the narrative significance of the events they describe in terms of a narrative framework that encompasses the totality of historical events. Biblical narratives describe the beginning of time and speak of the end of time. To assert that biblical narratives have this literary characteristic of determining with finality the intrinsic narrative order and significance of the particular range of events they cover, therefore, is to assert that those narratives were written by authors possessing a privileged understanding of the relevant narrative closure—in the case of biblical narratives, a privileged understanding of the end of time, the last things. Since only a divine author could possess such a privileged understanding, biblical narratives are thereby attributed to an authorship beyond that of the human beings who clothed the narratives in words.

Finally, biblical narratives also have the character of life narratives—they together constitute the basis for the collective life narrative of the Christian community. Just as the civic community is united by a collective life narrative whose theme is the pursuit of civic freedom and civic justice, so also the Christian community is united by a collective life narrative whose beginnings and narrative foundations are offered in the Bible. If the collective life narrative of the civic community is the story of liberty, then the collective life narrative of the Christian community, whose basis lies in biblical narrative, is the story of salvation, the story of the attainment and full possession of the Christian good. Like all collective life narratives, the rhetorical function of the Christian collective life narrative is to give meaning and direction to a collective pursuit of the good. But the Christian collective life narrative, by virtue

of possessing characteristics of both historical and literary narratives, differs significantly from the collective life narratives
of other communities. The collective life narrative of the civic
community tells a story of the quest for political liberty. It
begins with certain events—political reforms or revolution,
for example—and tells a story of continuing struggle for civic
freedom and civic justice that anticipates victory, but includes
also the possibility of failure. On the other hand, the Christian collective life narrative encompasses the whole of historical time, and tells a story of the pursuit of a good whose final
and perfect attainment can never be in doubt, because the
divine author of the story has already decided upon its narrative closure—the salvation of all those who accept this story in
faith.

It is the blending of these three narrative properties that
constitutes the extraordinary status accorded to biblical narrative by the Christian community. To say that the narratives of
the Bible are divinely inspired, or constitute revealed truth, is
to say that those narratives define with finality the narrative
order and significance of the historical events they describe
because they are "authored" by one who knows, and who has
decided upon, the end of the story—the end of the story of
salvation. God, as the ultimate author of scriptural narrative,
knows the end of the story because God, in the biblical tradition, is defined as the ruler of history, the ultimate author
who determines the narrative significance of all actually
occurring events from the beginning of time until the end.
God, as the ruler of history, as the inventor of the final narrative significance of all historical events, foresees and fore-
knows the end of the story. In foreseeing the end, God provides narrative order and meaning to all historical events. The
narrative order God provides constitutes the providential
order—the story that describes the totality of historical events
in their intrinsic narrative significance as a story whose narrative closure is the salvation of all particularistic desire.

Of course, even though the providential order encompasses all narratively representable events, this does not mean that
Christians can claim to possess a privileged knowledge of the
meaning of historical events beyond those described in the

Bible. The narratives contained in the Bible offer Christians their only authoritative access to the narrative order willed by God—the Divine Plan, the "real story." The narratives of the Bible reveal, open a window upon, the story that is written into the very fabric of things. Beyond the events described in biblical narratives, however, the details of the Divine Plan— the final narrative significance of historical events—must remain forever hidden from those who live through them. The affirmation of the "revealed" or "divinely inspired" character of the biblical narratives, therefore, constitutes an affirmation that such a Divine Plan exists, that all events do in fact have a preordained and final narrative significance, even though Christians can have no final or authoritative knowledge of it.

Perhaps now, with these points in view, it is possible to understand how this concept of the providential order of history can ground a collective life narrative that enables the Christian community to reconcile the love of God, the desire for the eternal present, with an affirmation of particularistic desire and communitarian solidarity. The collective life narrative that unites Christians encompasses historical events in their entirety (i.e., encompasses the entire sphere of narrative representation). Christians who, in faith, accept the narratives of the Bible as a revelation of the Divine Plan affirm also that the Divine Plan encompasses their own lives as well. Even though Christians do not and cannot have any privileged insight into the final narrative significance of events occurring in their own lives, they can nevertheless affirm that there is indeed a Divine Plan working itself out in their own lives, and that they are constructing a personal life narrative that has already been written into the universal story of salvation by the very author of that story.

By incorporating their own personal life narratives into this collective life narrative of the Christian community, Christians are given cultural support for a two-fold affirmation of the temporal order and of particularistic desire. First, since every event that occurs belongs to the story of salvation willed by its author, no event can disrupt the final narrative coherence of human life, and thereby threaten to strip human life

of its narrative significance. Natural catastrophes, unemployment, illness, death—events that can threaten to disrupt and
even destroy the narrative coherence of human life unsup-
ported by the Christian collective life narrative—can be
affirmed in their narrative significance by being written into
the collective story of human salvation. In the vocabulary of
faith, regardless of what events occur to threaten the desire
for narrative significance, nothing occurs without God willing
it as part of an overall Divine Plan for salvation, a Divine Plan
that guarantees the narrative significance of all human life
events. Second, since the providential order embraces all historical events, even the most apparently insignificant, every
event of a Christian's life can be viewed as a manifestation of
the Divine Plan. This means that the Christian can conform to
the Divine Plan, and thus affirm the narrative significance of
events, whatever may be his or her particular life circumstances. In the vocabulary of faith, God's narrative will for particular persons is to be detected in the particular events and
choices that are decisive for their lives.

This two-fold affirmation of narrative significance and particularistic desire, when it is effective in a particular life, can
mediate and reconcile the conflict between Christian love of
neighbor and Christian communitarian solidarity. As we
noted earlier, the Christian love of God and neighbor can create a certain kind of disaffection from particularistic community life, and from the goals sought by particularistic desire
itself. Christian love of neighbor is an affirmation of an identity with the neighbor that lies beyond all differences of culture
and personal traits. Christian love of God is a desire for the
eternal present that stands essentially beyond all possibilities
of narration. In both of these ways, Christian love of God and
neighbor tends to pull those persons governed by it away from
the particular narratable circumstances of their lives. It can
create an "otherworldliness" that seems to entail a generalized rejection of the sphere of narratively representable
events, the realm of temporal affairs. But the collective life
narrative of the Christian community, the concept of history
as a providential order whose narrative significance is determined by God alone, operates as a countervailing force in

Christian life to prevent all disaffection from the narrative order and from the goals of particularistic desire.

When Christians read their own personal life narratives into the narrative framework of the providential order of history, the temporal order and particularistic desire are saved in a special sense. Particularistic desire is saved most fundamentally by the transformation of desire, by which human desire for desire becomes the desire for the eternal present. But particularistic desire is saved, in this secondary sense by its narrative incorporation into the order of providence. God, as the author of the story of salvation, determines the narrative order and significance of events by reference to an end of the story—the end of time—that is already known. Faith in God's providence, faith in God's knowledge of the narrative closure of all history, mirrors within the realm of temporal affairs the closing of the circle of desire achieved through the unnarratable love of the eternal present. In this way, by the affirmation of God's providential role in history, historical events themselves gain their meaning by reference to this eternal present. Particularistic desire is permitted to flourish in full confidence that no human aspiration is foreign to the love of God, and that the love of God is most fully realized in the providentially directed service of human aspiration.

Christians whose self-understanding has been shaped by this concept of the providential order of history could conceivably draw a parallel between this Christian concept of history and the liberal democratic collective life narrative. As we have noted, the representation of history as the story of liberty also introduces a tension into the relationship between civic friendship and communitarian solidarity. The demands of citizenship, too, can create an alienation and disaffection from the pursuit of particularistic concepts of the good. However, the collective life narrative of the liberal democratic community offers no specific remedy for this. Left to the resources of the story of liberty alone, citizens seem faced with a choice between a commitment to libertarian and egalitarian civic values, and commitment to the hierarchical values of communitarian solidarity. The civic affirmation of the equality of all particularistic desire seems to undermine the narrative intelligibility of desire itself. The civic affirmation of difference and otherness seems to call into question the validity of human goals and aspirations. The demand that citizens cultivate both civic friendship and communitarian solidarity thus makes liberal democratic civic culture continuously vulnerable to the threats of alienation and nihilism.

It may be possible for Christians who are also citizens to neutralize these threats, at least among Christians, and thus to close this gap between civic and communitarian virtue by an appeal to elements of the Christian collective life narrative. In such an appeal, an explicit parallel would be drawn between the Christian love of neighbor and civic friendship. The libertarian and egalitarian nature of the Christian love of neighbor would be articulated in its analogy to the libertarian and egalitarian nature of civic friendship. The practice of civic friendship by Christians would then be viewed as not only consistent with, but even demanded by Christian charity. In the same way, this parallel would inform the practice of civic friendship, keeping clearly in focus those attributes of civic friendship that liken it to the Christian love of neighbor. Once this analogy has been recognized, the cultural resources offered by the Christian collective life narrative could then support, at least for Christians, an overcoming of the tensions between civic friendship and communitarian solidarity in the same way that they support an overcoming of the tensions between Christian charity and communitarian solidarity.

The Christian collective life narrative supports both the unnarratable love of God and neighbor, and the commitment to the narrative significance of participation in the life of particularistic cultural communities. It accomplishes this synthesis by its affirmation of the temporal order, the order of narrative representation, as the providential order—an order in which the narrative significance of events is determined finally by the will of God. As we have seen, Christian faith requires an abandonment of the standpoint of particularistic desire for the sake of the salvation of particularistic desire. The Christian affirmation of the temporal order as the providential order, in effect, transforms the Christian abandonment of the standpoint of particularistic desire into a commitment to and affirmation of all human aspiration. In faith and guided by the love of God, the desire for the eternal present, Christians submit to God's providential or narrative will, for them, by serving human aspiration in the particularistic communities and in the particular historical circumstances where God has placed them. In this way, the most perfect liberation of desire from the logic of narrative representation becomes identified with the most perfect service of narratable human aspiration.

For Christians, this concept of the providential order could also provide the cultural basis for a synthesis of civic and communitarian virtue. The pursuit of the civic good also requires a certain abandonment of the standpoint of particularistic desire for the sake of the liberation of particularistic desire. As we have seen, it is this requirement that introduces tension into the relationship between civic friendship and communitarian solidarity. For Christians guided by a recognition of the parallels between Christian love of neighbor and civic friendship, however, these tensions between civic friendship and communitarian solidarity can come to be viewed simply as a special case of the tensions produced by the intersection of the eternal and the temporal orders of human desire. Christians as Christians understand their eternal destiny to be bound up with the providentially assigned historical circumstances of their lives. Christians as citizens can understand, in the same way, that the practice of civic virtue and civic friendship is to be identified not merely with active participation in the political sphere, but also with active participation in the life of particularistic cultural communities. Christians as Christians understand that the love of God, the desire for the eternal present, is to be achieved most perfectly not through a withdrawal from temporal affairs, but rather through an abandonment to the providential will of God realized in service to others at a particular time and place. Christians as citizens can understand, in the same way, that love of civic freedom and civic justice can be fully exercised not only in the political sphere, but also through the progressive "civilization"—that is, the progressive realization of the civic values of liberty and equality—within particularistic hierarchical and exclusive cultural communities.

A Christian community shaped by this analogy between the Christian good and the civic good, between the Christian love of neighbor and civic friendship, would provide immense support for the cultivation of civic virtue in the emerging postmodern era. Given the numbers and the influence of Christian communities, it is in fact difficult to imagine a viable and effective postmodern civic culture without this support. In order to shape an explicitly civic form of Christianity, a new civic theology is required—a theology dedicated to the persuasive articulation of the parallels between the love of civic justice and the love of God. But a Christian community shaped by such a theology could also serve as the model for all other cultural communities party to the overlapping consensus required to support liberal political institutions.

All the particularistic cultural communities that comprise particular liberal democracies stand under a similar civic obligation. Each such community must identify, within its own cultural traditions, resources that encourage its members to cultivate capacities for civic freedom and civic justice. Communities without such a commitment will effectively exclude their members from participation in liberal democratic political life. Every such community that refuses or fails in this commitment will, with all certainty, contribute to the failure of the institutions of liberty bequeathed to us by the Enlightenment.

INDEX

265